THE
CURTAIN
MAKER
OF BEIRUT

THE
CURTAIN
MAKER
OF BEIRUT

Conversations with the Lebanese

Teresa Thornhill

BERKSHIRE ACADEMIC PRESS

THE CURTAIN MAKER OF BEIRUT:
CONVERSATIONS WITH THE LEBANESE

Published by
Berkshire Academic Press Limited
The Barn
Milestone Cottage
Highclere
Berkshire
RG20 9QA
UK
www.berkshireacademicpress.co.uk

First Edition

Hardback ISBN-13: 978-1-90778-401-9
Paperback ISBN-13: 978-1-90778-406-4

British Library Cataloguing-in-Publication Data
A catalogue record for this book is available from
the British Library.

Cover design by Danica Rosso
Cover photograph reproduced courtesy of Tracey Mansell

Printed in China through Printworks Int. Ltd.

For Tim and Isaac, with love

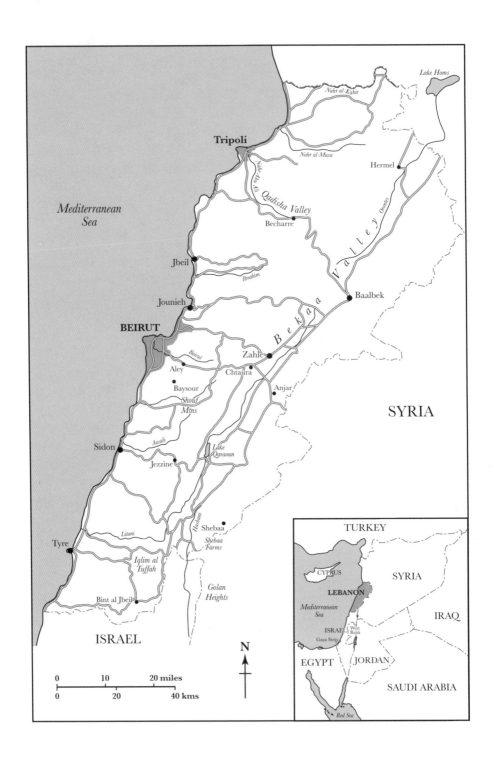

Mediterranean
Sea

Lake Homs

Nahr al-Kabir

Tripoli

Nahr al-Musa

Hermel

Nahr Abu Ali

Qadisha Valley

Becharre

Jbeil

Ibrahim

Baalbek

Jounieh

BEIRUT

Beirut

Zahle

Aley

Chtaura

Baysour

Anjar

Shouf
Mtns

SYRIA

Awali

Lake
Qaraoun

Sidon

Jezzine

Hasbani

Shebaa

Litani

Shebaa
Farms

Tyre

Iqlim al
Tuffah

Golan
Heights

Bint al Jbeil

ISRAEL

N

0   10   20 miles

0   20   40 kms

TURKEY

CYPRUS

SYRIA

LEBANON

Mediterranean
Sea

ISRAEL   West
Bank

IRAQ

Gaza Strip

EGYPT   JORDAN

SAUDI ARABIA

Red Sea

CONTENTS

✧

ACKNOWLEDGEMENTS

I would like to thank the following people for their invaluable assistance and encouragement while I was writing this book.

Bahia; Ahmed Beydoun; Tim Blanc; Frances Bradshaw; Alison Brown; Lindsay Clarke; Gabriel Reiser Craven; Hassan Daoud; Rob Evans; Ghina; Stephanie Hale; Nehad al Hamwi; Georg Herrmann; Nancy Hocking; Dima al Husseini; Rim Joundi; Nikki Kenna; Kanan Makiya; Najwa; Sarah Rodgerson; Hazim Saggiyeh; Sheila Thornhill; Walid; Medea Mahdavi Walker; Philip Walker; Helen Woodcock; and many other Lebanese and Palestinians who prefer not to be named.

AUTHOR'S NOTE

I have changed the names of most of the Lebanese and Palestinians with whom I spoke on my visits to Lebanon. I have only used the real names of those who are well known or who expressly gave their consent to my doing so.

I have used the simplest transliteration available.

FOREWORD

This book is based on visits to Lebanon between September 1999 and April 2006 and addresses the question of how the Lebanese (and the Palestinians who live among them) were then managing to coexist in the wake of their long and appallingly violent civil war, which began in 1975 and ended, roughly speaking, in 1990. It is also a record of my personal relationship with Lebanon and the Lebanese, which coincided with my first pregnancy and my son's early years.

In July 2006, Hizbullah captured two Israeli soldiers in a major cross-border raid and shot dead a further five. Israel's retaliation with a sea blockade, massive aerial bombardment and a ground offensive developed into a war which lasted 34 days and left 1,100 Lebanese and forty-three Israelis dead. I summarise these events in Chapter 29.

I did not return to Lebanon in the aftermath of the July war because I felt that the moment had passed for questioning people about their feelings towards those who had hurt them sixteen or more years earlier during the civil war. But now, in 2010, it is clear that the July war did not bring to a sharply defined end the post civil war period. Rather, the inter-sectarian rivalries and fears which formed the backdrop to the conversations which I had between 1999 and 2006 have deepened, and continue to dominate the daily lives of many Lebanese.

I summarise the political developments of the last four years in the epilogue, and reflect on how they were partially prefigured in comments made to me by some of the men and women I spoke with in 2006.

Four years is a long time in politics, but an infinitesimally short time in the history of a people and their culture. Thus most of the issues which came out in the conversations on which this book is based are just as relevant to understanding Lebanon in 2010 as they were to understanding the country prior to the July war.

The book stands as a series of portraits of a number of Lebanese from different sects and a handful of Palestinian refugees with whom I was lucky enough to come into contact. Woven in with our conversations and encounters is my attempt to explain, for those who have little or no knowledge of the Middle East, how the state of Lebanon came into being and why it was that it imploded in 1975. The book is, more than anything, an account of the fraught relationship between on the one hand the Lebanese (Christian, Sunni, Shi'a and Druze) and on the other hand the Palestinians, who, for the last sixty years, have been obliged to live among them. This relationship is ongoing, and will very likely have to be endured by both sides for many years to come.

TT
July 2010

PART ONE

1

THE SIT-IN FOR THE DISAPPEARED

Beirut, 31 March 2006

✧

I was looking for a tent, the headquarters of a year-long sit-in by relatives of the disappeared.

Where I stood, a hundred yards from the glass and steel tower block which housed the UN, a row of concrete bollards demarcated the boundary of a small piazza. There were benches, gravel pathways and young trees bearing shafts of dark pink blossom. In a parking bay on the far side, a group of soldiers in helmets and green fatigues stood beside a stationary tank, fingering the catches of their machine guns, while the never-ending Beirut traffic sped above their heads on a section of flyover.

A certain stillness graced the piazza. At the end of the central pathway, my eyes alighted on a pair of display boards crammed with portrait photographs. Behind them stood a brown canvas tent with vertical walls, a pitched roof and a small Lebanese flag fluttering over its doorway. I walked to the first board and crouched down to examine the photographs, some of which were enlarged copies of identity cards, with names and dates of birth set out in Arabic lettering. The rest were carefully posed portraits.

But it was hard to look without wincing. Here were the faces of young men who were barely out of childhood. Big eyes gazed tenderly at the photographer, over fresh, unblemished cheeks, perfect noses and full, soft lips. These were the sorts of photographs that a mother would frame and keep on her mantelpiece until she died, to remind her of how her beloved child had looked at age sixteen.

My son was only six, but I could understand the impulse.

The young men's clothing and hairstyles belonged to a bygone era. Many had been photographed in collar and tie, their thick black hair parted at the side and Brill-creamed into place, leaving only the odd curl to stray across the forehead. The earliest of the Syrian 'kidnappings', as the Lebanese called them, had occurred in 1976, when the Syrian army

[3]

first entered Lebanon, early in the civil war. Thirty years later, more than a thousand people remained unaccounted for.

I was still squatting on the ground when a man appeared at the door of the tent. He was casually dressed and looked about fifty.

'*Ittfaddali,*' he said when I looked up, 'come in.'

Inside, two grey-haired women sat on a narrow bed, drinking coffee from plastic cups. They nodded as I walked in, and gestured to me to sit on the bed opposite them, which was covered with a red blanket.

'Tourist?'

'Not exactly. I'm a writer... I heard about your protest, and thought I'd come and visit you.' A small, old-fashioned fridge stood just inside the door. A little camping stove was perched on the top, and beside it a long-handled *briq* for making coffee.

'Welcome, welcome. You speak Arabic? Okay, good.' The man gazed at me. 'We have been here nearly one year now, and we're not going to leave until we're told the truth about what happened to our brothers and our sons.'

On 11 April 2005, in the heady days of the anti-Syrian 'Cedar Revolution' and only one day after the final withdrawal from Lebanon of the Syrian army, a man called Ghazi A'ad had put out a call for families who believed their missing relatives to have been taken by the Syrians to participate in a demonstration. A large number had come forward and the sit-in had been established, with the permission of the UN.

'Do all the protesters have a relative missing?' I glanced from the man to the grey-haired women.

The woman seated closest to me cleared her throat. 'Everyone has had somebody taken.' She wore a long grey cardigan over a black, knee-length skirt and although her features were firmly composed, she exuded a sense of utter despair. An enlarged copy of the ID card of a teenage boy was pinned to her button hole. 'We are very many now.' She picked up a large album which had been lying on the bed beside her and handed it to me. I leafed through more portrait photographs and copy ID cards. 'Six hundred and forty families have given us the details of their missing, but there are more people out there who are too afraid to come forward.'

'Is it dangerous?'

She sucked her teeth dismissively, as did the man standing by the door. 'People *think* something bad will happen to them if they come here, that's all.' She sighed.

'Do you come every day?'

'Not every day, but frequently. I am from Zahle, it's a long journey for me.' Zahle was a Christian town on the edge of the Bekaa valley. 'But there are always people here. Two members of the protest sleep in the tent every night. We have a rota.'

I looked at her, trying to muster my courage. 'Would you tell me the story of what happened to…'

'My son.' She returned my gaze, her expression almost blank. 'He was taken by the Syrians in 1978.'

'How old was he then?'

'Sixteen. He was a schoolboy.' She paused, fingering the ID card pinned to her buttonhole.

I felt my composure threaten to dissolve as I took in the double shock of the boy's age and the enormous length of time which had elapsed since his detention began. The shadows beneath the woman's eyes and the greyness of her cheeks told me as much as I could bear to know about the torment she had suffered for almost half her lifetime.

'What was his name?' I asked softly. Twenty-eight years. If the son were still alive, by now he would be forty-four.

'Michel.' Briefly, the woman made eye contact.

'And your name?'

'I'd prefer not to give my name.'

'Okay.' There was no need for her to explain. 'What happened exactly? How was he taken?'

Michel's mother coughed, pulling a handkerchief from the pocket of her cardigan. 'I was at a funeral at my friend's house in a village near Zahle and my son was meant to be coming to collect me. He set off from our house, but he never arrived.' Her voice was dry and husky. 'Some children came and found me, saying that *mukhaberaat* (secret police) had picked up Michel in the street outside my friend's house. My brother saw the arrest, too. He asked the Syrians why they were taking Michel. They said they needed Michel to help them with some enquiries they were making, and that they would bring him back.' She coughed again. 'As soon as I learned what had happened, I went to the *mukhaberaat* office in Zahle and asked the officer in charge, Abu Ali, if I could see my son. He denied he had him. I didn't believe him, so I went to my neighbour for help. My neighbour knew Abu Ali personally, and we went back to see him together. But Abu Ali still denied he had Michel.'

She paused. 'It was a lie, of course. Michel told me later that he had heard my voice. He had shouted "Mum, Mum!" but I hadn't heard him because I was arguing with Abu Ali.

'When I got nowhere, I went to the governor of Zahle and asked him to help me. He phoned the *mukhaberaat* and asked them to free Michel, but they said they couldn't do anything. From Zahle the Syrians took Michel to the prison in the neighbouring town of Chtaura, then to another prison on the Syrian border. Eventually, Abu Ali admitted to me that they had Michel and told me where he had been taken. I went to Chtaura to get permission to see him. I had to pay a lot of money in bribes and eventually I got it. But when I reached the prison on the border, they said "Okay, you can see your son, but not now. Come back in a week." I asked them to give Michel the clean clothes I had brought for him and to give me his dirty clothes, because I wanted to be sure it really was him.

'A week later I went back to the border and this time I was allowed to see my son.' The frown marks on Michel's mother's forehead deepened as she spoke. 'He was in a terrible condition. His feet were very swollen. They had beaten him repeatedly on his soles.' She started to cough again. 'My son knelt on the floor and kept kissing my feet and pleading with me. He was saying "Mum, please help me, get me out of here, please."' As she paused, I felt my eyes fill with tears. 'It turned out they were accusing him of being a member of one of the small militias which were fighting against Syria at the time. It was absurd because he was a schoolboy and his father had worked with the Syrians and had never been anti-Syrian.' Her voice rose in anger. 'Someone had stitched Michel up.' She fell silent for a moment. 'From then on, for the next year and a half, I saw him every other Friday, at the prison on the border. After the first time I saw him, his condition slowly improved. I used to take him food and clean clothes and eventually he started to look better.

'When I visited, we used to sit really close to each other and talk. One time, he showed me a necklace which Mary's son had given him.' Michel's mother nodded at the woman sitting beside her. 'We think our sons were held together in the same prison, although we can't be sure.'

She cleared her throat and sighed. 'Then one day I arrived to visit Michel and they told me he had been moved to Syria. When I asked the reason, they said "For interrogation". I asked how long it would take. They said "We don't know. One year, two years…" I started to panic. I cried and shouted, but they took no notice of me.

'For the next few months I made trips to Syria. I travelled from place to place, visiting different prisons and trying to get permission to see Michel, but I got nowhere. Eventually, I began to question whether Michel had genuinely been taken to Syria at all. One day, a man who had been in the prison on the border at the same time as Michel came to see me. He said that on the day Michel was moved from that prison, he had been able to look out of a window and watch the car in which Michel was travelling. He said the car had set off towards Syria, but had then changed direction and driven towards Chtaura. When I was told that, I didn't know what to think.

'I stayed with that uncertainty for many years. Then, about eight years ago, a family from the south came to see me. They told me that their son was with my son, in the Palestine Department, a prison in Damascus. They said I should take some clean clothes for Michel and go and visit him. So I went to Damascus and found the Palestine Department. The man in charge looked at his list of prisoners and told me that Michel wasn't there. I went to another prison in Damascus. Here, the man in charge told me to wait while he went to check whether or not they were holding Michel. When he came back he said "Yes, your son is with us. He is safe and well and he sends you his greetings." I asked if I could see him, but the man said "Not today. You will be able to see him soon."' She fell silent, shifting her position on the edge of the bed. 'Every time I went back it was the same, and to this day they've never let me see him.'

Michel's mother spoke as if she were his only close relative. 'What about your husband?' I enquired, hoping I was not treading on delicate ground. 'Did he help you to look for Michel?'

Michel's mother looked at me sharply. 'He's dead,' she replied, without offering further explanation.

'Do you have other children?'

'One other son. He died, too.'

The man in the doorway was greeting a woman with long brown hair who had just arrived. She wore jeans and a T-shirt and held a packet of coffee in her hand. Michel's mother turned towards her and waved.

'This is Leyla,' she explained as the woman prepared to brew up on the camping stove. 'Her brother was kidnapped by the Syrians.' I nodded and smiled. Leyla's movements were swift and energetic and her presence lightened the atmosphere in a matter of seconds. She looked about thirty.

I turned back to Michel's mum. 'Did you ever try to get legal representation for your son?'

'I didn't try when he disappeared, because the war was on and it would have been pointless. I tried about three years ago. But all the lawyers I approached refused to go to Syria. They said "Sorry, we don't take this sort of case."'

'What about the Lebanese government? Have you tried approaching them?'

'Of course.' She gazed at her hands, which rested in her lap. 'Lots of us have tried asking the government for help. We have all tried everything possible to get our children back. But the government says "Okay, okay we will help you," and does nothing.'

'Who did you go to?'

'I went to everyone. I even spoke to Elias Hrawi, when he was president, but he did nothing. That was several years ago now.'

'Did you go to Hariri?' Rafiq Hariri had led the post-war reconstruction of Lebanon during his two terms as prime minister between 1992 and 2004. His assassination on 14 February 2005 had set in chain the events which lead to the Cedar Revolution and the Syrian withdrawal.

'No.'

The man in the doorway butted in. 'Lots of people have offered to help us, you wouldn't believe it. They say "Give me twenty thousand lira, and I'll get your son out in a week." Or "Give me ten thousand lira and I'll get you some information..." But in reality, it's always a con.'

'Have you asked the UN?'

Michel's mother clicked her tongue. 'Right now, we are asking the Lebanese government to help us. If they refuse, we will ask the UN. If *they* refuse we will go outside the country, for foreign help.' She paused, her features tight with anger. 'I am sure my son is in the custody of the Syrians. I want him back, alive or dead. What right do they have to hold our children like this?' Her voice was choked. 'They should send them back to Lebanon. Let the Lebanese police deal with them, if they've done something wrong.'

Mary had sat in silence while Michel's mother was talking. Now she got up, walked to the door and returned with a bunch of bananas, which she handed round, insisting that I take two.

'Are you a journalist?' she asked. She was small, with short grey hair, dressed in black.

'No,' I replied, 'I'm writing a book about how the Lebanese live with their memories of the civil war.' I hesitated. 'Was your son taken by the Syrians, too?'

Without further prompting, Mary described how her son had disappeared on his way to work in East Beirut in 1986, when he was twenty-one. Like Michel's mother, she was convinced he remained in Syrian custody. Mary was an Armenian Christian from Bourj al Hammoud, a district of east Beirut.

I was mulling over Mary's story and taking bites of banana when a large figure blocked the doorway for a second, plunging the tent into near darkness. A moment later, a tall man in a brown suit stepped in, swinging a pair of wraparound dark glasses from one hand and doubling over to avoid bumping his head against the roof. He uttered a quiet greeting, stumbled past me and sat down at the far end of the bed.

'Mr Abu Harb would like to tell you his story, too,' said Michel's mother, jutting her chin at the man and raising her eyebrows. 'Tell her, Wisam,' she added, 'we have already spoken about our children.'

'Yes, please,' I added, 'I would like to hear it.' Mr Abu Harb had a big nose and pointed chin. He was dark-skinned and his smart suit suggested a more affluent background than those of the women. I thought he was in his mid fifties.

He looked at me for a few seconds then laced his fingers together and stared at his huge hands. His back was arched in an awkward position against the rear wall of the tent.

'I am a Druze,' he began, 'from the Shouf.' The Shouf was a range of mountains to the south east of Beirut. 'My brother was a member of the Lebanese police force. One day in 1983, when he was about twenty-seven, his little son became sick and he came to Beirut to buy medicine for him. He never returned.'

'And you believe it was the Syrians who took him?'

'Ten years ago, a Syrian who had been in Palmyra prison in Syria came to my house. He told me he had been held for a time in the same prison as my brother.'

Briefly, I made eye contact with Mr Abu Harb. 'Have you considered going there to look for your brother?'

The man shook his head. 'No, that would be very dangerous.' He looked down again at his hands. I wondered why it had been safe enough for Michel's mother to go to Syria but not for Mr Abu Harb. I decided not to ask; there might be all sorts of good reasons why he would be at risk in Syria, and possibly the mere fact of being male was one of them. 'For a time,' he went on, 'I gave money to some Syrian soldiers who said they could bring me information. I must have paid them nearly three thousand dollars. But it was a trick and they let me down.'

'What happened to your brother's wife?' I asked. 'Is she still alive?' The 'little son', I calculated, would be in his twenties by now.

'She's alive. She lives with us in the Shouf.'

'Does she come to the protest?'

'No, she doesn't come.'

I was feeling weary now, and overwhelmed by the pain of what I was listening to. I thanked Mary for the bananas and the juice and glanced round at the assembled group.

'Thank you all for telling me your stories,' I said. 'I hope you are successful in persuading the government to help you – or if not the government, then the UN.'

'You're welcome, very welcome,' murmured Michel's mother, Mary, Leyla, Mr Abu Harb and the man in the doorway. Their smiles were well-meaning and kind. But I sensed that I was one of a long stream of foreigners and journalists to whom they had spoken in the last twelve months. They were under no illusions that anything which anybody wrote would have the power to bring back their loved ones.

Outside, the sun was warm on my face. I didn't feel ready to face the maelstrom of the traffic, so I took a stroll around the piazza. I hoped that by feasting my eyes on the fresh pink blossom I might ease the dark, heavy feeling which gripped my being. This was my fourth visit to Lebanon in six years, but today was the first time I'd come face to face with the terrible pain which damned the lives of many of its inhabitants.

I had known that this was where I was heading, but right now it was almost more than I could bear.

On my first visit in 1999, my travelling companion was Deirdre, a Scottish friend with whom I had worked in a Palestinian human rights organisation in East Jerusalem in 1990. We had studied Arabic side by side and travelled through Jordan and Syria during vacations. In those days Lebanon, just a hundred kilometres to our north, had lain closed to western visitors, writhing in the final throes of civil war. As a forbidden place it had exerted a powerful attraction for both of us. Besides, every Arab we spoke with claimed that Lebanon was the most beautiful of all the Arab countries.

By 1999, Lebanon's new peace was well-established and Deirdre and I were living in Britain, but our desire to see Lebanon had not diminished. Personally, I was fascinated by the idea of an Arab country recovering from war where wealthy Christians danced in nightclubs to French pop songs while some of their Moslem compatriots lived by *Sharia* law.

Deirdre didn't want to go to Beirut, so we spent most of our trip exploring a rural area in the north of Mount Lebanon. As we walked in the sunshine and sat beside streams, I wondered what I would focus on if in the future I wrote about Lebanon. The thing I most wanted to understand, I decided, was how the Lebanese were managing to co-exist in the wake of their long, appallingly violent sectarian civil war, which had ended in 1990. Lebanon was unique among Arab countries in the complexity of its sectarian make-up: the population of three and a half million included eighteen distinct religious sects, encompassing Christians, Moslems and Jews. I wanted to know how members of formerly-warring sects felt about each other now, nine years after the war had ended. And I wanted to know how individuals lived with their memories of kidnapping, terror and loss.

There were other questions which intrigued me, too, such as how the Lebanese as a people felt about the Syrians, who had occupied the north and east of their country since 1976 and dominated almost all of it since 1990; and how they felt about the Israelis, who had devastated west Beirut in 1982 and even now continued to occupy the southern border areas. Another, closely intertwined issue was that of relations between the Lebanese and the Palestinian refugees who lived among them: many Lebanese considered the Palestinian presence to have been the main cause of the war.

[11]

Chewing over these questions with Deirdre, I became fired up with excitement. But the rural north, where we were, lay far from Beirut and the south, the sites of most of the war-time violence. In the heady September sunshine, lulled by the whirring of crickets, it was all too easy to forget that to answer such questions I would need to spend time in Beirut and the south, and there confront the ordeal which the Lebanese had been through.

In 1993 I had tasted comparable suffering in Iraqi Kurdistan. In the aftermath of the Gulf War and the 1991 Kurdish uprising against Saddam Hussein, I had spent seven weeks sitting in the homes of Kurdish women, listening to stories of babies who had died whilst fleeing across the mountains into Turkey; of women raped in Saddam's prisons; of disappeared husbands whose bodies were subsequently found on rubbish dumps and of villagers massacred in the Anfal campaign of rural genocide.

The sense of terrible darkness I had experienced in Iraqi Kurdistan was coming back to me now, as I paced slowly round the flowering trees, focussing my eyes on the deep, rich pink. What was I doing, I asked myself, choosing once more to face into this darkness, this deathliness? Was it really what I wanted? And was I strong enough to endure it? So much had changed in my life since the spring and autumn I had spent in Kurdistan. I was thirteen years older, my life had moved on, and, most important of all, I was now a mother. Whereas in the past I had felt a compulsion to face up to the pain of the world, these days I tried to shield myself from horror.

When I came back to the tent to take a last look at the photographs, I noticed a rough-looking man sitting on a bench beside the display boards. He was dressed like a construction worker, in a dirty T-shirt and battered cotton trousers. Reddish brown hair curled onto the back of his neck and his belly protruded over the waistband of his trousers. He greeted me as if he knew me, and asked if I wanted to hear his story. He had been imprisoned by the Syrians, he said, in 1989.

I didn't feel ready to hear any more distressing stories, but the man clearly wanted to talk. 'Yes, please,' I replied. 'I was here earlier and some of the others spoke to me.'

'I know,' he replied. 'You're a writer, aren't you?'

'That's right.' I sat down on the bench a few feet from him.

'My name is Nizar Mortada. If you write about me, use my real name, okay?'

I nodded. The man's feet bulged through the sides of his ancient trainers, stretching the laces tight.

'I'm a Shi'a from Ba'albek,' he went on, 'but in 1989, when the war between Michel Aoun and the Lebanese army began, I was working in Beirut. D'you know about the war with Aoun?'

In 1989 the populist Christian General Michel Aoun had led a prolonged battle against the Syrians in Beirut, making the dubious claim that he had been elected as Lebanese president. In the final weeks, as the Syrians gained the upper hand, in what would prove to be the last major battle of the civil war, Aoun had taken refuge in the presidential palace in Ba'abda, before fleeing to France.

'I wasn't involved in the fighting. I was only sixteen that year,' Nizar went on. 'I was living in Bourj al Hamoud, which was under the control of the Lebanese army. At the end of 1989 my brother was martyred in the south, in a place called Iqlim al Tufaah. He was fighting with the Lebanese army against the Israelis.'

'My brother's funeral was held in Chtaura, in the Bekaa, where my family live. When I arrived in Chtaura, the Syrian army picked me up at a checkpoint, but they let me go after not very long. At the next checkpoint they stopped me again. I got out of the *servees* to walk to my family's home in the village and I saw a *mukhaberaat* car.

'On the way to the house I stopped to visit a friend. He told me to run away, because the *mukhaberaat* had gone to my family's house, asking for me. So I stayed at my friend's and didn't go home that night.' Nizar Mortada cleared his throat and spat on the ground. 'In the morning I went to see my family. After I had been there for an hour or so, my father arrived from work. He acted normally towards me, but he asked if I had had anything to do with the Lebanese army or the Phalange militia. I told him I had not.'

Something bothered me about Nizar Mortada's face, but I didn't want to stare at him to work out what it was. He had thick, heavy eyebrows and a bony ridge in the middle of his nose. As he spoke the right side of his upper lip lifted slightly, revealing the top row of his teeth.

'I was planning to return to Beirut the same day, but my uncle told me not to. I had previously had a falling out with my uncle and when he asked me to stay I felt that something funny was going on. I tried to leave the house, but two friends of my uncle came and held onto me. Eventually I escaped and ran out of the house, but the Syrian *mukhaberaat* saw me and chased me. I jumped into a river and started swimming, but they pulled me out and dragged me into a car. I was handcuffed and blindfolded. When I asked where they were taking me, they said they would be five minutes with me, and then I could go back to my family.

'Of course it was a lie. They took me to Ghayan and put me in a tiny cell which measured one and a half metres by one and a half, with a low ceiling and no window. After 15 minutes, my uncle turned up. The *mukhaberaat* told him to come back the following day to collect me.

'But the following day they started to interrogate me. They asked me what I did in Beirut, and weren't satisfied when I said I had a job there. They accused me of working with the Lebanese army and dealing in drugs, which I denied. Then they took me to a special room and tortured me with electricity. They did this every day until I went into a coma. They would give me half an hour to recover and then they would take me for another form of torture. The officer I remember most was called Abdullah.

'After a while they wrote a confession for me to sign, although I had said nothing. For three days they didn't feed me. At one point they took me to Ghazi Kanaan's prison in Dowra, in Beirut, but only for two hours.' Ghazi Kanaan was a senior figure in the Syrian *mukhaberaat*. 'Then they took me to Anjar prison near Chtaura.' Nizar paused. 'Everybody knows that most people who were taken to Anjar died there.

'In Anjar they hit me on the back of my neck. They removed all my clothes except my underpants and kept on beating me. Then they put me in a cell with prisoners from other countries. At night they used to take me out and torture me. I was becoming totally exhausted by now.' Nizar threw his hands apart in a gesture of disgust. 'They hung me from my wrists over a hole in the ground which was full of rubbish and broken glass, but I never once shouted out in pain.'

By now I was feeling sick, but Nizar Mortada spoke in a tone of resignation.

'Eventually they moved me to a different prison, in another part of Anjar. They continued to interrogate me about being in the Lebanese army and dealing in drugs and I continued to deny it. I was blindfolded while they were questioning me. One day someone hit me with his fist on the side of my face. Then they hit me at the bottom of my abdomen, with such force that I was thrown against the wall. But I could no longer feel anything. I was taken to another cell and told "confess everything and we'll let you go." At that point they put some string round my penis and pulled it tight. I screamed and they stopped. They just wanted to hear me scream.

'Three days later they took me to Syria. They put me in what was called the "Palestine Department", where all the non-Syrian prisoners were held. It was underground. I was there for three months and the torture continued.

'From the Palestine Department they took me to Maza prison, and there the torture stopped. I was there for two years. I met these lads in Maza.' Nizar stood up for a moment, pointing to the photographs of three young men on the display board.

I got up too and peered at the photographs. 'What sort of state were they in?'

Nizar resumed his seat on the bench and took out his packet of cigarettes. 'They were okay at the time.' He placed a cigarette between his lips and cupped his hands around a match. 'After some time I was taken to appear before the military court.'

'Did you have a lawyer?' I butted in. To my surprise, Nizar Mortada nodded.

'There was one lawyer for the whole prison. The judge asked the lawyer if the charges against me were true and the lawyer said "no". I took down my trousers to show the judge how I had been tortured in Anjar, but it didn't make any difference: I was given a fifteen-year sentence, although on appeal it was reduced to seven years. I was sent back to prison.'

'Did you serve the seven years?'

'No. About a year later, one of my uncles offered to pay a bribe to the Syrians to get me out, and I was released. That was in 1993.'

Nizar drew on his cigarette, staring straight in front of him, his forearms resting on his thighs.

'My family were very surprised to see me,' he mused. 'Very surprised.'

We sat in silence for a few minutes. A sharp breeze had got up and was rustling the leaves on the tree behind the bench. I felt very tired, but there was a question which I wanted to ask.

'Can you tell me this: were any women taken by the Syrians?'

'Of course.' Nizar dropped his cigarette butt and ground it into the paving stone with the heel of his shoe. 'Mostly they took men, but a few women were taken.' He gestured at the nearest display board.

I got up and squatted in front of it. I had to look quite carefully to pick out three photographs of women from the rows of men. In the first two photographs the quality of the image was poor, but the third showed a strikingly beautiful young woman with pale skin and a dense black buffon. I felt my body temperature dropping as I gazed into the woman's large, confident eyes. Beneath her face was written the name 'Florence Michelle Raad' and some text in French, indicating that she was a journalist and had disappeared in 1985. Anyone having information as to her fate or whereabouts was invited to telephone two Beirut numbers. I took out my notebook and wrote them down.

2

A Walk in the Qadisha Valley

Northern Lebanon, September 1999

✧

I sit on a ledge of rock beside a fast-flowing stream, on the cusp of darkness and light, watching the place where the tree shadows end. The sound of rushing water fills my head. Above the torrent, clusters of leaves shine lemon yellow and sap green in the pure light.

Deirdre's haversack lies a few feet away: she is exploring by herself and will come back for me soon. We are down on the floor of the Qadisha gorge, somewhere between the Maronite Christian monasteries of Mar Elisha and Deer as Salib. Behind the trees, a dark pink cliff rises a thousand metres into the sky.

I reach for Deirdre's bag and pull out the bottle of water she has carried from our hotel in Becharre. For me it's too hot to walk much further and my belly is aching down in the pit, alarming me. I lean back, resting against warm stone. Inches away, a grey-green lizard stops, quivers, listens. The water races on. I hear footsteps from the left; but no-one comes.

At half past twelve Deirdre re-appears.

'I've found a better place for you to sit,' she says, 'Just a bit further on.' She holds out her hand and pulls me to my feet.

We sling our bags over our shoulders and climb back up to the wide track that runs along this side of the valley. For the first few hundred metres it is over-hung by trees and we walk steadily, our sticks tapping softly on the dry earth. Then the track climbs up and swings round, leaving the river-bed far below. The trees thin out, the earth turns to sand, young shrubs and thistles grow on the verges and the air vibrates with the humming of crickets. The full heat of the sun confronts us.

'Not far now,' Deirdre promises. 'You'll like it when we get there. And I'll go on for a while, see if I can find Qanoubian.' She walks beside me without a hat, her fair curls lifting and dropping on the back of her neck. Her arms are turning a gingery brown.

I pull the brim of my hat over my eyes and walk slowly. In the distance a couple of old cars are parked across the track. On the far side of the valley, perched above the river, I see the square stone forms of ancient buildings. As we pass the cars, we hear voices. The track dips down and there, ahead of us, is a large Coca-Cola sign fixed to the wall of a little house. Beside it, I read the words 'Restaurant *Abu Josef*'. A group of children watch three men who stoop over shovels, digging a trench at the side of the house. A woman sits at a table in the shade, preparing food. The men straighten up as we appear.

'*Itfaddalu!*' they cry, 'Welcome!', pointing to the flat roof of the house which is crowded with tables and chairs under a cloth awning. I wave to Deirdre and stagger up the outside steps.

I choose a table in the shade, enjoying the slight breeze that rises from the river. The leaves of a grape vine trail from the metal frame that supports the awning, making patterns of light and dark on the concrete parapet. The other tables are deserted apart from a couple who are getting up to go. The man has an expensive-looking camera and I guess they are French. We greet each other and I add, stating the obvious, '*Il fait chaud, hein?*' Pilgrims, I wonder, or just casual tourists?

'*Bof, pas tellement,*' the man brushes away my remark. This heat is nothing to a Frenchman. He strides to the edge of the roof, screws up his eyes and focusses the camera. 'This is the Holy Valley,' he announces with solemnity, 'the refuge of the Maronite saints, who lived encircled by Islam.' His expression implies that no fate could have been worse. The man has a thick beard and is dressed in baggy shorts. '*On y va, Helene?*' he says to his companion.

I walk to the edge of the roof, wondering if the man has confused the past with the present. The Qadisha valley is celebrated in local lore as the historic 'place of refuge' of the Maronite holy men, but the refuge they sought was from their fellow Christians, not from Moslems. The Maronites are the descendants of a small Christian sect originally from Arabia, whose doctrines were declared heretical by the Orthodox Byzantine church in 680 AD. In the tenth century, after persecution in the Orontes valley to the north, the Maronites migrated south to Mount Lebanon, preferring to live under Moslem rule. Their holy men settled in the Qadisha valley, which in those days was cut off by snow for half the year and in summer accessible from the surrounding mountains only by precipitous paths cut into walls of rock. Two centuries later, in 1180, the Maronites became Catholics, and from the sixteenth century on they developed close ties with France.

Below the restaurant, the gorge opens out. Abandoned terraces follow the contours of the rock on either side of the valley, making rhythms of green and brown. Half a dozen grey stone houses stand above the river, shaded by fruit trees. A figure in a long black habit moves on a balcony... or am I seeing things? These houses are likely to be long deserted.

I hear movement behind me. A girl of about nine has come to ask what I want to drink. She has thick dark hair which falls over her shoulders, pale skin and eyes of a colour between black and green.

'There's Coca-Cola' she says in French, 'or Fanta.' She hovers beside the tall, glass-fronted fridge that stands in one corner.

'Mm,' I reply, 'I'll have a Coca-Cola.'

While I remove my walking boots the girl brings a bottle with a straw and sits down beside me. I ask her how far it is to Qanoubian and she points up the valley, in the direction taken by Deirdre.

'It's not far,' she says, smiling, 'I'll show you, if you want.'

But I shake my head. 'No thanks, I need to rest for a while.' The girl gets up and fetches a little leaflet in French with a map of the valley. All the monasteries, chapels and grottoes are marked. 'D'you live here?' I ask.

'No, no, we live in Blawza,' she points to the cliff tops which tower above us on the right side of the gorge, 'but in summer we come here every day. My dad's building two toilets for the restaurant.' She looks at me. 'D'you know, in the past, lots and lots of people lived in this valley.'

'Where've they all gone?'

'To Canada and Australia and... lots of different places.'

'Are they going to come back?'

'No, they're not coming back. We don't even know exactly where they are, most of them.' She stares at me, as if trying to formulate a question. 'Have you been to Lebanon before?'

'No, this is my first time. I've been to the Middle East before though, I've been to Palestine and Syria and Iraq...'

'And Australia?'

I smile. 'Australia's a long, long way away.'

The girl rests her forearms on the brown plastic table-cloth and swings her feet under the table. After a few moments she says, 'My mum's cooking downstairs... D'you want something to eat?'

'What have you got?'

'*Hummous, mouttabal*, meatballs, salad, *pommes frites...*'

'A plate of *hummous* would be nice.'

'Just *hummous*?' The girl's eyes grow larger.

I smile. 'I'll have *hummous*, then I'll see.'

She runs downstairs and returns after a couple of minutes with a little dish of *hummous* and a basket of bread. 'My mum's made *mujeddera*' she announces. 'She says you can have some if you like.' I smile in delight. *Mujeddera* is one of my favourite Levantine dishes. 'Go on then,' I say, 'just a small dish.'

The girl runs downstairs again and returns with a plate of lentils and rice stewed in cumin. 'Sometimes I make it myself,' she says with pride.

I eat the *mujeddera* and push the plate of *hummous* towards my companion, but she refuses it.

'Where's your friend gone?' she asks.

'To see the monastery at Qanoubian.'

'Has she got a telephone?'

'What, with her? No.'

'We have three telephones,' the girl tells me in a serious voice. 'One mobile, one land line downstairs and one in Blawza.'

'Have you!' I was surprised, earlier, to see telegraph wires in the valley.

'Why didn't you go with your friend to the monastery?'

'I was too tired.' Should I tell her? I wonder. 'I'm pregnant. I can't walk very far at the moment, I have to rest a lot.'

The little girl nods. 'When you finish your food you can lie down on the bed there.' She points to a rickety bed in the corner, half sheltered by the awning and half in the sun.

When she stacks up the plates and carries them down the stairs, I pad over to the edge of the roof in my socks. Behind the restaurant the men have stopped digging, leaving their spades propped against the side of the trench. The toilets they are building will be squalid huts plagued by flies, but badly needed, all the same. If it weren't so hot I would wander off in search of a well-hidden spot among the abandoned fruit trees. But the sun is at its zenith. I step back beneath the awning, roll a jersey from my bag into a pillow and lie down on the bed. My head and shoulders are in the shade, while sunlight plays over my legs. Tendrils of grape vine shift in the air above me, making patterns on my stomach. I wonder if the baby is enjoying the warmth.

Who he or she is, I don't yet know. I feel something akin to shyness as I lay a hand upon my bump. Shyness and anxiety. For it remains to be seen whether the baby will forgive me this last jamboree, this final fling of childless woman freedom which I am seizing on the eve of motherhood.

Two months earlier, when I asked my GP if I would be crazy to visit Lebanon in the sixteenth week of pregnancy, she replied blandly 'Just be careful what you eat. No salad, no unpasteurised soft white cheese.' Then a funny look came into her eyes. 'Of course, if something goes wrong, you won't have the same medical care you would have here.'

I walked home slowly, imagining the worst.

But a day later I called Deirdre to see if she wanted to come with me.

'Lebanon?' said Deirdre in her soft Scottish accent. 'Sure, I'll come. But not to Beirut.' Deirdre hated cities. 'Let's go walking in the mountains.'

'I won't be able to walk as far as you.'

'No matter. If we go in September it should be good weather. Bring a drawing book, you can sit under a tree while I go on a bit.'

I longed to see Beirut, but I could wait: if Lebanon was safe, as by all accounts it was, perhaps I'd go back when the baby was old enough to travel. Meanwhile, some fresh air and Arabic conversation would do me good. 'Fine,' I said, 'let's go and see the north.'

I drift in and out of sleep, mindful of the risk of sun-stroke but longing to give way to my body's weariness. A breath of air touches my cheek and I half open my eyes to find that white clouds are floating in the space between the canopy and the parapet. Closing them again, I turn on my side. If the weather turned cooler, what a blessing that would be. A box spring digs into my shoulder.

After half an hour I push myself slowly upright and swing my legs over the side of the bed. The cramping in my belly has abated and a thirst for hot, sweet tea drives me. I press my fingers into the corners of my eyes and force my feet into my walking boots.

At the foot of the outside steps I hear the clanking of pots. Rounding the corner of the building, through an open window I see a woman standing at a table, her hands buried in a bowl containing a moist, brown mixture. The smell of raw onions reaches me. The woman is plump and pretty with her daughter's dark hair and pale skin.

'Hello!' I say in Arabic, 'Your *mujeddera* was delicious.'

She looks pleased. 'Glad you enjoyed it.' She presses a dollop of the brown mixture against the sides of a small bowl, tosses a wedge of dripping into the centre and turns out the bowl-shaped cake onto a metal tray. I watch, trying to decide whether it's sweet or savoury.

'What's that you're making?'

'Bulgar cakes.' She presses another dollop of mixture into the bowl.

'Does it have meat in?'

'Of course. Meat, bulgar, garlic, onion. You've never tried it?' The woman looks at me with an air of disbelief. She wears her blouse open at the neck, draped loosely over her large bosom.

'I was wondering,' I say, 'could I have a cup of tea?'

My friend sits on a stool at the back of the kitchen. 'Sara!' the woman shouts. 'Put water on to boil. Have a seat, please.' She waves me to an outside table, beneath another trellised vine.

When Sara brings the tea I hear a man's voice in the kitchen. Looking up I see him standing beside the woman, telling her a joke, as he washes his hands in the sink. His arms are tanned dark gold.

'Your dad?' I ask Sara.

'My uncle.'

The man appears round the side of the house and walks towards us, holding out his hand.

'Your friend still not back yet?' he asks as he greets me.

'She went to see the monastery, I'll go and look for her in a while.'

'It's better now,' he nods. 'Getting cooler.' His trousers are caked with soil and beads of sweat stand out on his neck. The sleeves of his shirt are rolled above his elbows and his shirt is half unbuttoned. A brush of wiry hair springs up from his forehead.

He is surprised that I speak Arabic and asks me where I learned it. Hesitantly, I tell him that I once spent a year in Palestine. Many Maronites dislike the Palestinians, but the man appears unconcerned. 'First time in Lebanon? You saw Qadisha, Becharre? All this area is beautiful.'

'It's fantastic.'

He smiles, but when I asked him what life's like now that the war is over, his forehead contracts into a mass of furrows.

'Things are very difficult. The economy's in a big mess. You see, during the war there was money. Especially in this area. We're close to the Bekaa valley.' The man opens his eyes wide. 'Every inch of the Bekaa was used to cultivate hashish. And they brought it out across these mountains.' He gestures towards the head of the valley. 'In those days, nobody went without. Today, some people are even saying they want to return to the days of war, because of the money we had then.'

'Hashish is illegal now, isn't it?'

'You won't find a single field of hashish down there. Have you been to the Bekaa?'

'Not yet.' I wonder whether the man means that I won't find hashish or that it isn't there. The penalty for growing hashish today is life imprisonment with hard labour. But I've read that some desperate peasants are resuming its cultivation in fields far from the roads. In the high, arid valley, little else will grow. 'But I thought lots of money flowed into Lebanon after the war,' I go on. 'Into Beirut, anyway?' In the early nineties the government raised millions of dollars from Lebanese ex-patriates to reconstruct the centre of Beirut.

The man lights a cigarette and looks at me across the table. 'A few years back, there was a lot of money. Two years ago, I was working in Beirut for Solidere, the government construction company. It was good for a while; but then the money ran out!' He raises his big hands from the table top in despair. 'Every building gang that used to have ten workers, now has four or five.' He shakes his head. 'The big money's gone.'

I stir sugar into my tea. 'D'you still live in Beirut?'

'In Jounieh, just up the coast.' Jounieh was a fishing village at the start of the war in 1975, but soon became a stronghold of the Christian right and the port through which they received weapons from the Israelis. The man brightens. 'Jounieh is beautiful! You must go there. Here everything is old,' he gestures dismissively at the valley around us. 'But in Jounieh it's all new. All nightclubs and casinos and hotels... really, you'll love the place. I'll give you my address.' He takes out a piece of paper and asks me for a pen. *Tony Chedid*, he writes in Latin letters on a slant, followed by a phone number. He looks up, slightly embarassed. 'When you telephone,' he says, 'You'll get my Madame. If you tell me your name I'll explain that you'll be phoning.'

I give Tony my name and ask if he has children.

'Two boys. And you?'

I pat my stomach. 'First one on the way.'

'Oh,' he raises his eyebrows. 'It's not obvious, to look at you. Just a couple of months?'

'Four.' I wish for the hundredth time that my bump was bigger.

'Where's your husband?'

'At home. He was too busy at work to come with me.' This is a half truth, but it will do. Paul did not demur when I told him I was planning to travel with Deirdre.

'Your friend's coming back for you?'

I take a swig of tea. 'In a minute I'll wander up the path and look for her.'

The cloud has cleared, but the air is cooler as I set out along the path to Qanoubian. Perhaps Deirdre has twisted her ankle, or fallen asleep in the sun. On Tony Chedid's directions, I follow a sandy track until I come to a wooden signpost wedged into the ground, pointing to a smaller path which leads upwards into the scrub. Soon I see a square stone building in front of me with pale blue wooden shutters. A flight of steps leads to a raised courtyard at the back of the building. On the roof stands a stumpy wooden cross. I stop and listen, wondering what I'll do if Deirdre isn't here. The monastery has the air of being deserted, and my ears bring me no sounds. Even the crickets have gone quiet. Far below me in the gorge, the river whispers.

I feel uneasy. Perhaps the Maronite saints of old left a spirit of hostility to strangers in the place. I am from the Christian west, as a child I even briefly attended a church school, but I am not a practising Christian.

I walk slowly up the steps, emerging in the courtyard. On the far side, the facade of a chapel projects from the rock face. Several feet above the ground, a lizard clings amongst the lichen, its tail curled, its body a-quiver.

To my left, a cloister runs along the side of the square building. Underfoot, the flagstones are uneven. Weeds push up between the cracks.

'Hiya!' Deirdre's voice sings out from high above me. She is waving from the monastery roof. I watch while she saunters down another flight of steps. 'Have you been asleep?' she asks. 'Your cheeks are rosy. Come

[24]

and see inside the chapel.' I follow her across the courtyard, glad to have found her. 'There were some people here earlier,' she remarks, 'a French couple. They said the place has been re-opened recently. Nuns live here in the summer, playing host to young Maronites from abroad who want to find their ancestral roots. There's a kitchen over there, and some cells.' She waves towards the cloister. 'And there used to be a tunnel for the Patriarch to escape in times of danger.'

Inside the chapel, a weak electric light illuminates a fresco that fills one wall from floor to ceiling. The Virgin Mary is being crowned by three wise men. The figures are bordered on either side by a column of blond, cherubic angels with black, outstretched wings. A mediaeval-looking sun hangs above one column, a moon above the other.

Deirdre turns to me. 'They mummified the body of one of the patriarchs who lived here.' Her face bears a look midway between fascination and abhorrence. 'He's in a glass case in a vault next to the chapel.'

I wrinkle up my nose. 'I don't want to see him.'

Deirdre smiles.

It is five o'clock and time to begin the hour's walk back to Mar Elisha. We climb down the stone staircase and re-trace our steps to the restaurant *Abu Josef*. Sara's family and their helpers are sitting at a long tressle table against the house wall, eating a meal. They wave, call out greetings and invite us to join them, but we thank them and decline.

We march steadily down the track that runs above the river. The temperature is dropping and the sun has shifted to the far wall of the valley. The sound of the river grows louder, birds call to one another and in the freshness of the evening I am able to quicken my pace. The track leads through woods beside the river, until we emerge close to Mar Elisha. Our thoughts turn towards Becharre, where we are staying. Throwing back our heads we see, above the thousand metre wall of rock that seals the valley, a half-built apartment block against the fading sky.

Behind us, a car engine grinds into life. Turning, we see lights through the trees. We walk on, comforted by the feeling that others, too, are going home.

The car, an old Mercedes, halts beside us.

'*Ittfaddalu*! Get in!' The back door opens and I see Tony Chedid smiling at me through the gloaming. 'We're going through Becharre, we'll give you a ride.' He nods at Deirdre. 'Bonsoir!'

I stoop down and peer into the car. The upholstery is ripped and two windows are missing. Sara's mother sits in the front beside her husband, a weather-beaten man in a *keffiyah*. Sara perches on her mother's lap, jammed up against the gear-stick. In the back a little boy presses his face against the window. Tony Chedid climbs out.

I squash up beside the little boy and Deirdre gets in after me, gathering our haversacks on her lap. Tony climbs in beside Deirdre and slams the door. We murmur our gratitude, but our weary hosts do not reply. The man in the *keffiyah* sighs, changes gear and urges the over-laden car forwards.

In five minutes we are climbing steadily on the tarmac road, gaining height with every switch-back. I turn my head and gaze back down the valley. The sky is a shadey grey-blue, crowded with the dark forms of bushes, trees and rocks. A crag glows orange-pink in the last light, then turns to dirty purple. The day is done.

3

'NOT ARABIC, NOT FRENCH, BUT LEBANESE'

Becharre, northern Lebanon, September 1999

✧

I wake in Becharre to the sound of men working in the yard beside the hotel. Above the droning of a generator, their shouts are interspersed with the crunching sound of heavy objects being tossed, caught and stacked. I imagine a construction site, but when I get out of bed and walk to the window, I see a small, open-backed lorry, into which men are loading crates of large, red apples.

The sky is cloudless, the air warm. I stand on the balcony and look around. To my right, the land drops away steeply into the Qadisha gorge, the view obscured by a mass of leafy trees. To my left, the buildings of Becharre are spread out across the cliff top, dominated by a large, new church which blocks the sky-line. The building has the air of a fortress rather than a place of worship. My mind goes back to the Frenchman of the day before and his comment about the Maronite saints of old living 'encircled by Islam'. If the comment wasn't apt about the past, it would certainly be apt as a reference to how the modern Maronites felt about their Moslem compatriots at the outbreak of the civil war. The church suggests they feel this way still.

I stare in disbelief at the building's sheer size. Its pale pink stone is freshly cut and, as I watch, a small figure on a scaffold clads the twin spires with smooth red tiles.

Money is clearly in plentiful supply. Did fifteen years of civil war change nothing, I ask myself? How is it that in 1999 the Maronites are erecting a new symbol of power and domination, designed to be visible for miles around? Unless, perhaps, the church is an attempt to mitigate a Maronite sense of humiliation.

Beside the church, small groups of men hover in a square. Behind, the land begins to rise again, a lattice of back-streets in which old stone houses with iron balconies and bright flowers in pots stand shoulder to shoulder with breeze-block shops. Between gaps in the buildings I glimpse a pick-up truck bumping along a narrow street at the top of the town towards another, smaller church.

It's a pretty place, if you focus on the older buildings, but I am shocked by the noise. Standing here on the balcony I can hear traffic droning on the road which sweeps through the town, rounds the head of the gorge and follows its southern flank to Tripoli and the coast. The noise seems to bounce off the walls of the new apartment blocks that have been flung up on either side.

I dress and go downstairs, leaving Deirdre to sleep. I am past the feeling sick stage of pregnancy and my main symptom now is constant, barely satiable, hunger. In the lobby I find the hotel manager sitting behind the reception desk, drinking coffee. He is about thirty, with a slim body that exudes physical fitness.

'Salaamu a leekum,' I say, using the traditional Arabic-Islamic greeting out of habit. The man's eyes narrow and I realise, with interest, that I have made a gaffe. 'Bonjour,' I add, with an apologetic smile.

'Bonjour,' he replies, then breaks into English. After we've chatted for a few minutes I ask him why the people of Becharre greet each other in French.

'This is from the time of the French. Even at home, we use a mixture of French and Arabic.' He speaks with a rapid, energetic delivery. 'Salaamu a leekum, this is what the Moslems say, not us. You know, if you ask us what language we speak, we will tell you, "Lebanese". Not Arabic, not French, but "Lebanese".'

'I guess people learn French in school?'

'These days English is more important. It's the world language, isn't it? I myself went to a French school but I took my degree at the American University of Beirut.' The man watches me with his head on one side. 'What d'you think of Lebanon?'

'I've only been here a week.'

'You must realise that Lebanon's very different from other Arab countries.' He gazes at me steadily, as if it's important to him that I take this in. 'Much more advanced. Even the Moslems of Lebanon are more educated than the Moslems you'll find in other Arab countries, more open-minded.' I look at him and wonder what to say. I've met educated and open-minded Moslems in all the Arab countries I've been to. 'If you go to Jordan, Syria or Egypt,' the man continues, 'you'll notice the difference.'

I nod slowly. 'What are things like in Becharre since the war ended?'

The man tosses his head. 'Better, everything is better. There are still lots of problems, but we're making progress.' He lowers his voice. 'You know, the worst problems we are facing today come from outside, caused by the foreigners.' He looks at me hard and I tell him softly that I know what he means. He is referring to the Syrians.

Syrian troops have been in parts of Lebanon now for twenty-three years, since June 1976. During the first round of the civil war, the fighting was between the militias of the Maronites on the one hand and the combined forces of the (mainly Moslem) Lebanese National Movement and Palestine Liberation Organisation on the other. Both 'sides' appealed to Damascus for assistance, and President Hafez al-Assad did not hesitate to seize the opportunity to wade into the affairs of his smaller neighbour. An Arab summit in October 1976 authorised the Syrian troops to remain as the mainstay of an Arab Defence Force, and from then on they occupied the north and east of the country throughout the war.

Syria forged alliances at different times with virtually every internal party to the conflict. For Assad was a master at playing off one party against another, forming alliances where it suited him and breaking them when they no longer served his goals. He made ruthless use of his *mukhaberaat* to kidnap and assassinate political and militia leaders when they tried to steer too independent a course, and to silence intellectuals who criticized him.

Out in the street there are no pavements and I squeeze between parked cars and the walls of buildings. Vehicles roll towards me, driven by men who alternately lean on their horns and stop to shout greetings to acquaintances coming the other way. When the parked vehicles end, I tread inches from the path of a pick-up. The driver, cock-sure in a baseball cap, stops to chat with a youth on the far side of the road. Gangling and slender, the lad stands in the doorway of a grocer's shop. '*Cafe Najjar*' is written on a sign above the window, with a drawing of a cup of coffee from which steam spirals in a neat quiff. Conversation ended, the driver rams his foot on the accelerator and drives straight at me. I leap sideways and press my back to the wall, as the pick-up swerves out into the middle of the road.

'Bastard,' I mutter, instinctively covering my belly with my hand. I am wedged beside a glass cabinet in which the skin-less carcass of an animal hangs from a hook. I cover my nose with my hand and walk around it, avoiding the eyes of an elderly couple who watch me from the adjoining butcher's shop. Pregnancy has sharpened my sense of smell to a degree that is sometimes intolerable. Ten paces further on I step with relief into the safety of the *Mini-Market Chbat*. Two dark-haired girls hover behind the counter while a man unloads packets from a cardboard box.

'*Bonjour*,' the girls sing out, soothing me with their smiles. To them, I sense, I am special because I am European. I take a basket and cruise along the shelves. I have no pressing need to buy, but am driven by curiousity as to what the Maronite housewife feeds her family on. Tins, jars, packets and bottles are stacked to the ceiling. I see nothing that is fresh, nothing that is not processed. Even the bread comes in mean, wafer-thin rounds packed into clear plastic bags – the eastern equivalent of Mother's Pride.

I take a small bottle of water from the fridge and place it on the counter.

'*Merci*,' the girls smile again as the one at the till rings up my money. Their jeans and T- shirts hug their trim figures. Bemused, I step back into the street. Elsewhere in the Arab world, such clothes would brand them as hussies, but here in Becharre, it seem, the dress code comes from France. I feel out of place in my loose, figure-concealing blouse and baggy trousers.

Ten paces further on I pick up the aroma of *menaish bi zaater*, a freshly-baked bread coated with olive oil and thyme which once I used to buy for breakfast in the the old city of Jerusalem. I step through a pair of wooden doors into the dark concrete cavern of a bakery, where a man wearing gloves thrusts a long-handled metal spatula into the mouth of a huge gas oven. A neat row of blue and yellow flames illuminates the dark rounds of bread, inflating in the heat.

'*Bonjour*.' The man's eyes rest on me for a second before he resumes a conversation in Arabic with the woman who works beside him. She is rolling balls of dough into neat, flat rounds.

'*Bonjour*,' I reply. I order two *menaish* and sit down at a plastic table. A boy comes in, goes to the fridge and takes out a bottle of Fanta.

'My mum wants six with cheese,' he says to the baker 'and two with *zaater*. She'll be here in a minute.' The baker grunts, pulls his spatula out of the oven and flips two sizzling *menaish* onto the counter.

'Here you are, *madame*,' he says to me. 'Do you want them cut in slices?' He lays them on sheets of old newsprint and I carry them to the table and watch the street through the open doorway. A Volkswagen beetle has pulled up outside and the boy with the Fanta is talking to the driver. Except it isn't really a Volkswagen, it's a chassis with four wheels, an engine, one seat and a steering wheel, all open to the sky. The driver is a man in his twenties with a pointed, stubbly chin. He wears his base-ball cap with the brim facing backwards and keeps the engine running while he talks. His sharp knees project through the denim of his jeans like pieces of machinery. Suddenly the boy turns away and the driver revs his engine and rattles off down the street, causing the bakery to fill with exhaust fumes. I stare after him. I've never seen Arabs who look this way before.

I pay and walk out, this time searching for a cup of tea. I am halfway out of town before I find a cafe and the sun is hot on my head. To my right, the verandahs of old houses project over the gorge, shady and inviting. The road is wide, bordered on the left by panel beaters' workshops, where naked flames flash in the hands of weary-faced men. A cow stands in the doorway of an upholsterer's shop, the first live animal I've seen. An old woman dressed in black waves to me as I pass. I reach a petrol station, next to which stands a large, modern coffee bar with plate glass windows. *Pizza, Sandwich* is written on the glass in large red letters. It doesn't look appealing, but it's all there is.

Inside, the cafe is cool, clean and spacious. White plastic tables and chairs are screwed to the floor, shiny and new. At the back, floor to ceiling mirrors reflect the hillside opposite, making the space seem even larger. I cross the crazy-paving linoleum and hover at the counter, where a new espresso machine stands idle. Nobody comes. In a little office at the far end of the room, a middle-aged man stands at a desk, shouting into a telephone. A taller, younger man sits beside him on an easy chair. Now a girl of twenty walks towards me, clutching a toddler against her stomach with a dummy protruding from his mouth. The girl isn't smiling.

'Yes?' she shouts when she's a dozen feet from me.

'D'you do tea?' I shout back, doing my best to match her scowl. I feel like an intruder.

Without a nod she walks past me, toddler dangling, and steps behind the counter. Her red T-shirt is new, her trousers sleek against her hips. The child waves its arms in the air like a drowning swimmer. I watch as, with one hand, the girl assembles a tea cup, a saucer and a

Lipton's tea bag. She flicks the tap on the espresso machine, fills the cup half full and shoves it towards me.

'Sugar?' I enquire.

'On the table.'

I sit with my legs outstretched, letting the tea slowly wake me up. My gaze shifts from the sun-flooded hillside outside to the relative darkness of the cafe. The middle-aged man stands with his back to the room, smoking. The girl sits with the toddler on her lap, staring at nothing. The younger man has gone. The girl's expression surprises me, modern and urban in its coldness. Looking round, I catch sight of myself in the floor-to-ceiling mirror, back straight against the plastic chair, pregnant belly almost flat, legs long. What an alien I am in this country, I think, as if it almost explains the girl's rudeness. So thin, so tall, I simply don't fit in.

I slip my hand under my shirt and rest my palm on my belly. Perhaps today, for the first time, I'll feel the baby move. I try to picture the little creature Paul and I glimpsed on a monitor during a scan the previous week, all head and not much body, sucking its tiny thumb with gusto. Perhaps a little focussed attention will elicit a kick or a wriggle. But nothing happens. I feel a sudden pang of missing Paul.

One tea isn't enough and when the girl gets up I ask her for another. While she's at the espresso machine, I form a plan.

'Isn't it hot!' I exclaim, smiling, when she brings me the tea. 'Not for you, for me!' I wave towards the open doors. 'You're used to this heat, but I'm not.' A glimmer of recognition passes across the girl's face. 'Beautiful place,' I add, 'Becharre.'

Now she smiles, a short, brisk smile. 'It's good.' She turns her back and steps into the sunshine.

On our last day, a Saturday, we get up early and hitch a ride to Ehden, a small town seventeen kilometres from Becharre where we've heard there is a nature reserve. A man in a large green saloon car gives us a lift. Deirdre sits beside him in the front and I sit in the back, enjoying the smell of the leather seats. He's about fifty, heavily built but diffident in manner. He replies softly in English to Deirdre's remarks in Arabic, but most of what he says makes little sense. She abandons Arabic for English, but still the man speaks gibberish.

Halfway to Ehden he stops the car to show us the view. We cross the road and stand looking down at the wide sweep of terraces where the Qadisha valley opens out. Thirty kilometres away, the city of Tripoli sprawls in a band of dirty white flecks. Behind it, the pale blue sea blends into the sky.

As we're getting back into the car I notice an encampment of old canvas tents by the side of the road.

'Who lives in those?' I ask the man.

'Syrians,' he replies. Even while their government holds Lebanon tightly in its grip, poverty has brought half a million Syrians to Lebanon in search of work.

'Unemployed?'

'Yes, and so they live like that.' The man half turns towards me as he speaks, his eyes revealing a mixture of embarrassment and pity.

We spend the day walking and talking in the nature reserve a couple of miles north of Ehden. In the late afternoon we're back on the outskirts of town, trying for a lift. The second car to pass us stops. It's a Fiat; neither new nor clean, driven by a man of twenty something. When I ask if he's going to Becharre, he says simply, 'Get in.' As I sink into the seat beside him, I see that the floor of the car is scattered with cigarette ash. The man has a small head on a short, stumpy body.

'I am *bolees*,' he announces in Arabic, using an Arabised version of the English word. As he does so he picks a plastic ID card off the floor and thrusts it into my hand. 'You see? I am a *rajul amn* – security man.' He points to the words written on the card, while I study the photograph. Two small black eyes stare out of the round face.

'Yes,' I reply, seeing that some response is expected. The man's hair is shorn to within a few milimetres of his skull.

'*Bolees, bolees*, you know what this is?'

'Yes.' I look at him blankly. 'You're a *shurta*' – I used the Arabic equivalent of 'copper'.

'No, no, I'm a security man! I work for Interpol!' Swinging onto the wrong side of the road to overtake a lorry, the man reaches for something heavy at his feet and waves it at me. It's a pistol.

[33]

'You have a weapon,' I say calmly, 'you're a security man.' I don't like the way he's thrusting the pistol into the space between us, but I'm pretty sure he's only trying to impress.

'Interpol! You know what Interpol is?'

'Yes I do.' And Interpol men don't drive filthy, beat-up Fiats. A moment later we slow for a military check-point. I've learned by now to recognise the uniforms of the Syrians, but I pretend otherwise. 'Is this check-point operated by the Lebanese army?' I ask as we pull away.

The man practically spits. 'No!' he shrieks. 'These are Syrians! The sons of bitches who occupy our beloved country!' He rams his foot down on the accelerator and sends us shooting up the road, his voice tailing off in a string of expletives.

In 1990, the civil war finally came to an end under the terms of an agreement negotiated in Ta'if in Saudi Arabia in 1989. This required Syria to withdraw its troops from Lebanon within two years. Syria's anticipated future role in Lebanon was dressed in the language of 'brotherhood' and 'co-operation' between the two countries, but everyone knew that these words were euphemisms for Syrian domination. Many in Lebanon were unhappy with the entrenchment of Syria's role, but in 1990 this was the price for bringing the fighting to an end. In the event, Syria kept its troops in Lebanon until April 2005, retaining a tight hold over Lebanese politics throughout the post-war period.

Startled by the Interpol man's fury, I glance at Deirdre on the back seat, whose face conveys a mixture of amusement and concern. We've left Ehden behind and are speeding round hairpin bends when the man speaks again.

'How long have you been in Lebanon?'

'Just a week.'

'It's beautiful?'

'Very.'

'Wonderful landscape,' he gestures at the valley dropping away to our right, bathed now in evening sunshine. 'Perfect weather, and you won't find better people anywhere in the world.'

'Yes,' I aquiesce, hoping to humour him, 'the people we've met have been very nice.' I stare at the road ahead.

'And Becharre's the best of Lebanon,' he adds. 'I'm from Becharre.' I smile indulgently and he goes on to ask where I learned Arabic.

I hesitate. It might not be wise to mention Palestine to a Maronite so fired up with love for his country. 'In Jordan.'

'You've been there?' The man's eyes are full of suspicion.

'I've been all over the Middle East. Iraq, Egypt, Syria...'

'Syria!' This time the man actually spits. 'What d'you go there for?'

'A holiday.'

I am aware of Deirdre putting her hand over her face as the man hunches himself into a ball over the steering wheel and accelerates into the path of a pick-up truck. Only when it becomes obvious that it isn't going to slow down does he pull back, cursing loudly.

'Which is better,' he growls, without taking his eyes off the road, 'Lebanon or Syria?'

Deirdre is jabbing her knee into my back. 'They're completely different,' I reply. 'Syria's mostly desert.' After a moment I add, 'Have you been to Syria?'

'No way!' he spits again. 'It's the last place I'd ever go! The Syrians are a bunch of filthy, scummy dogs!'

Wondering if I've pushed the man too far I withdraw a little, shifting my eyes to the village we're passing through, where the concrete frames of new apartment buildings jut on stilts over the gorge. Above them, the pale blue sky is tinged with pink.

'You girls married?' the man snarls.

'Of course!' we chorus, brandishing our 'wedding' rings. Deirdre's is a spare silver one she switched over from her right hand on the plane. I bought mine earlier in the year in preparation for a trip to Jordan with Paul. 'Our husbands are in Britain,' I explain.

We're nearing the check-point at the entrance to Becharre. The man winds down his window and slows to a near halt as we draw level with the soldiers. He salutes and wishes them good evening. As he pulls away he smiles to himself. 'This one is *our* check-point,' he announces. 'Manned by our beloved Lebanese army.'

4

THE ASSEMBLING OF A NATION

England, 1999–2001

Lebanon stayed with me throughout my pregnancy. As I drove from work to ante-natal appointments in the November drizzle, I remembered the sun-baked paths of the Qadisha valley and imagined walking there again in a couple of years' time with Paul, our child-to-be perched on his shoulders. Paul would love the springy turf beneath his boots, the walls of rock, the clear light, and walking was the thing we did most happily together.

And so, while the baby grew inside my belly, Lebanon gestated in my imagination.

I was clear now that if I wrote about Lebanon, my focus would be on how members of its formerly-warring sects were managing to co-exist in the wake of the war. From Qadisha my thoughts shifted to Beirut, for I would need to spend time there. In self-contained communities like Becharre, the Maronites had been relatively cushioned from the conflict, whereas in Beirut, people from warring sects had lived in close proximity to one another.

The war had ended in 1990 without a clear victory by one community over the others, though with Maronite power considerably diminished. In the first nine years of peace the government had made no serious attempt to bring about reconciliation – there had been no truth commission as in South Africa, no Balkan-style war crimes tribunal. Apartment blocks, roads and bridges had been re-built, but the social and psychological wounds of the war had been left to heal – or fester – by themselves. What, I wondered, had people done with their painful memories? How did they *feel* about one another?

After my son was born, all thoughts of travel left me. I spent several months welded to the sofa, gazing at his smooth round head buried in my breast, my heart full of awe, my mind a blur. I had waited so long to become a mother, I felt so desperately tired and I loved him beyond words.

For much of Dan's first year, I remained in this state of contented exhaustion. But eventually he started sleeping more and feeding less and my mind began to sharpen up. When he was ten months old we spent a week in West Wales, before Christmas, and I stole away to read for an hour each day, leaving Dan to push his baby walker round the living room under Paul's fond eye. The book I chose was Kemal Salibi's *A House of Many Mansions: the History of Lebanon Reconsidered.* I read at most ten pages at a sitting, but the shorter the passage the more I savoured it.

Over the next few months Lebanon's history became my private world, a fascinating realm into which I could retreat when I wearied of grilling fish fingers, changing nappies and hanging out the washing. I read everything I could find until gradually I formed a picture of Lebanon's various sects and the pressures both internal and external which had led to the civil war.

Lebanon as we know it was created in the aftermath of the First World War, out of a portion of the Ottoman province of Greater Syria. It took its name from Mount Lebanon, which since the tenth and eleventh centuries had served as a place of refuge for both the Maronite Christians and the Druze. The Druze are a sub-sect of Shi'a Islam, who closed the door to new converts early in their history. Communal bonds are very strong among the Druze, and religious practices are kept secret from outsiders.

From the mid-sixteenth century to 1840, though nominally part of the Ottoman Empire, the Mountain was more or less independent and life was organised on feudal lines under a series of mainly Christian dynasties. The population was four-fifths Christian and one-fifth Moslem and relations between the two faiths were reasonably harmonious. By the nineteenth century, silk production was at the heart of the Mountain's economy.

From 1840, however, communal relations deteriorated and in 1860 serious violence broke out, culminating in the killing of 11,000 Christians by armed Druze bands.

In order to deter full-scale European intervention to protect the Christians, the Ottomans agreed in 1861 that the Mountain be declared a governorate with special political status and European protection. This arrangement succeeded in restoring calm, and the ensuing period to 1915 is often referred to as 'the long peace', during which the population of the Mountain prospered. French firms established silk thread factories in a number of villages and the Maronites sent their children to schools run by missionaries, where they underwent a western education. At the outbreak of World War One, the Maronites both formed an absolute majority of the population and constituted the largest single sect living on the Mountain.

In 1920, following the collapse of the Ottoman Empire, the European war victors agreed that the northern parts of Greater Syria, including Mount Lebanon and what was to become modern Syria, would be held by the French as a mandate under the League of Nations.

When the French weighed up how to organise their new territories, two considerations were uppermost in their minds. Firstly, they wished to contain the burgeoning Arab nationalist movement centred in Damascus; and secondly, the Lebanese Maronites, with whom they had long-standing ties, were the only community on whom they could rely. The Maronites had been lobbying since 1900 for the expansion of their mountain territory to what they claimed were its natural and historic boundaries, by the addition of the coastal cities of Beirut, Tripoli, Sidon and Tyre and the eastern valley of the Bekaa. The Maronite leaders' demand for a distinct state of 'Greater Lebanon' was linked to their perception of themselves as culturally, educationally and economically more advanced than the largely Moslem population of the Syrian interior.

In the clarity of their political agenda, the Maronites were indeed ahead of the other Christian and Moslem Arabs of the area. However, when the French-mandated state of 'Grand Liban' was declared in August 1920, shortly after the creation of French-mandated Syria in July of that year, many of its new citizens were deeply unhappy with their lot. Very few of the inhabitants of the towns and villages that had been annexed to the Mountain were Maronites. More than half were Sunni Moslems, more than a quarter were Shi'a and most of the rest were non-Maronite Christians.

The Sunnis, as adherents of what, in world terms, is the dominant and largest branch of Islam, had always had a strong sense of being part of the wider Arab world. Their merchant class, based in Beirut and Tripoli, had already profited to some extent from the silk trade and had access to education. Politically they tended to be supporters of Arab nationalism and looked to Damascus and the Syrian interior as their natural heartland; certainly they had no wish to find themselves cut adrift in a European-oriented statelet under French control.

The non-Maronite Christians fell into two groups: Catholics in communion with Rome, who included members of Syrian, Greek and Armenian churches; and members of the Orthodox or Eastern Churches. The latter have always seen themselves very much as Arabs and many had similar feelings about the new state to the Sunni Moslems, with whom they tended to associate themselves politically.

In 1920 the Shi'a population of Mount Lebanon was small, mostly residing on the peripheries of the new state in the Bekaa valley in the east and in the towns and villages of the south, close to Palestine. The majority of the Shi'a were peasants living in poverty under feudal lords, with little or no access to education. Shi'ism is the minority branch of Islam and traditionally Shi'a in the Arab world have found themselves excluded from political power, living a life of subdued opposition. The Lebanese Shi'a felt little more sense of solidarity with the Sunnis than they did with the Druze or the Christians. The new state meant nothing to them.

To the Maronites, in 1920, the feelings of their new compatriots were of little import. Many Maronites saw themselves as the 'true' Lebanese, the descendants of the Phoenicians who had dwelled in city states on the Levantine coastal plain many millenia before. They thought they represented an island of 'civilised Christendom' in a sea of 'Moslem barbarism'. That the sea had grown larger through the creation of Grand Liban was in their view the unfortunate price they had had to pay for the acquisition of extra territory, and one which made it imperative that they retain the upper hand politically. For, although the Maronites were still the largest single community, they no longer formed an outright majority. A census held in 1932 would show that the Maronites represented 29% of the population, the Sunnis 22% and the Shi'a 20%. Christians outnumbered Moslems overall, but only by a relatively slender majority.

Lebanon became independent from France in 1943. The unwritten National Pact of that year laid down that, in all spheres of public life, politics, the civil service and the armed forces, power was to be distributed among the various sects according to their presumed numbers in the population. The posts of the presidency and commander-in-chief of the armed forces went to the Maronites, while the Sunnis took the premiership and the Shi'a the post of speaker of the chamber of deputies. The Christian-Moslem balance in the chamber of deputies was maintained by the imposition of a fixed ratio of six Christians to every five Moslems.

It is ironic that, from independence until the early 1970s, the country was often cited by western political scientists as a model of stability, notwithstanding the brief civil war of June–July 1958 when newly-radicalised Sunnis came into conflict with the Maronite presidency. (The conflict was quickly suppressed by the landing of US troops.) Between the early 1950s and the late 1960s, the trade and financial sectors came to dominate the economy at the expense of industry and agriculture and Beirut became a major financial and service centre for the Eastern Mediterranean. At the same time it became a holiday destination for wealthy Arabs from the oil-producing states.

The businessmen engaged in trade and finance had a deep interest in the maintenance of the Lebanese state as a weak one which would continue to adopt a laissez-faire policy towards them, with low taxation and minimal tariff control. Meanwhile, at the other end of the social scale, those who had traditionally been employed in agriculture were forced to abandon the land, from which they could no longer make a living, and become wage labourers in the cities or join the ranks of the unemployed. At the same time Beirut, with its liberal atmosphere and relative press freedom, came to be known among the middle classes as 'the Paris of the Middle East' – a haven for artists, writers and intellectuals from more repressive parts of the Arab world.

In 1948, following the creation of the state of Israel, 150,000 Palestinian refugees were allowed into Lebanon, where they settled in camps around the main cities. By 1956 the population of the country had almost doubled since 1932, bringing it to around one and a half million. The demographic balance had tipped in favour of the Moslems, so that the Christians now made up only about forty-three percent of the population.

The concentration of wealth in the hands of the Christians caused mounting discontent among Moslems. Their resentment was exacerbated by the inherent unfairness of the confessional political system and the failure of the state to provide adequate social services or education. Disillusioned with its own leadership, the Moslem working class came under the influence of Egypt's Arab nationalist president Gamal Abdul Nasser. Then, in 1967, the Arab defeat in the Six Days' War with Israel accelerated the process of radicalisation of both the Moslem intelligentsia and the rural and urban poor. Meanwhile, Palestinian commandos began to enter and operate from Lebanon.

By the 1960s, the presence of the Palestinians made many Maronites extremely uneasy. Since most Palestinians were Moslem, their presence threatened to alter the demographic balance on which Maronite privilege was supposedly based. Most Lebanese Moslems, on the other hand, sympathised with the Palestinians and supported their cause. A major new cleavage was opening within Lebanon's already very divided society. Ten years later it would lead to civil war.

In the spring of 2001 Dan learned to walk and we spent many happy hours together toddling round the park examining flowers, small stones and discarded sweet wrappers. Words were coming now, some learned, some invented, such as 'daw-daw' for bird and 'law-law' for aeroplane. I wrote them all down, enthralled at my son's creative genius. And at night, as I breastfed him to get him off to sleep, I began to plan a return trip to Lebanon.

As I didn't intend to work much for the next couple of years, it seemed a good opportunity to travel. I imagined Dan tottering around a Lebanese mountain village in the sunshine, enjoying the attention the Lebanese were sure to lavish on him. This time, Paul wanted to come. He loved travelling and was keen to spend more time with Dan.

We would go next spring, we decided, after Dan turned two, when the weather would be pleasant but not too hot. We'd make a recce of three or four weeks and, if things went well, return the following year for longer. Friends told us Dan would be fine, provided we stayed in clean accommodation and gave him a routine. Best to do your travelling now, they said, once he starts school you won't be able to. I pictured us in a rented apartment on the coast or in the Mountain. Paul and Dan would spend their days pottering in olive groves or on the beach, while I made forays into Beirut. I need never be gone more than a few hours, I figured: Lebanon was so small that you could get from one end of the country to the other in less than half a day.

But there were moments when I thought we were mad even to contemplate taking Dan to the Middle East. What if he got sick? And was the country *really* safe these days? Or might the violence of the war years erupt again without warning? Everyone I asked assured me it was safe, but they could be mistaken.

One night after his feed, Dan slid off the breast with a little grunt of satisfaction. He slept in my arms while I sat on in the dark, trying to re-draw my future at home. I would go back to my old work as a child abuse lawyer, working three days a week until he started school. I'd forget the Middle East, my Arabic, the journeys of my childless years. It would mean giving up a whole piece of myself, but perhaps that was what motherhood required of me. Time stretched ahead and I saw myself in court, garbed in black, wrestling with cases in which every party was a loser.

As my spirits sank, Dan grew heavy in my arms. I lifted him into his cot, arranged the blankets and kissed him on the forehead. Then, as I stood up, my soul rebelled. No, I thought, the war's over and Lebanon's safe enough. We're going.

On September 11th 2001, two hijacked planes were flown into the World Trade Center in New York and US president George W. Bush launched his 'War on Terror'. Paul and I spent the autumn following the news, touched by the suffering of the families of the dead but appalled by the rhetoric of revenge flowing out of Washington. We watched in dismay as Tony Blair announced he would stand shoulder to shoulder with the Americans, even if this meant an assault on Afghanistan. Twice we joined anti-war marches through central London with Dan on Paul's shoulders. When the Taliban fell we were happy for the Afghans, but still worried about the precedent the war had set. International law had been made a mockery of by the world's one remaining super-power. The future looked very bleak indeed.

I began to enquire among Lebanese friends whether the autumn's events might prejudice our safety in Lebanon. Moslems were angry with Britain and America for attacking Afghanistan, and western visitors to the Arab world could be made to pay the price. But everyone I spoke with said no, not in Lebanon, the country was safe for westerners these days. The destruction of the twin towers had engendered little excitement in a country that had recently known war. And the attack on Afghanistan was perceived as far away: with their own economy in crisis, most Lebanese were preoccupied with making a living.

Of more concern, by the spring of 2002, was the conflict consuming the West Bank and Gaza, where the second Palestinian *intifada* was in its eighteenth month. With Lebanon's Palestinian population now numbering four hundred thousand, Ariel Sharon's attempts to crush the uprising would be very much a live issue there.

5

'CATCHING THE DAW-DAWS OUT OF THE SKY'

Beirut, March 2002

At Gate 53 of Heathrow Airport, Dan threw himself on the floor and began to crawl around the feet of the airline security staff. Up to that point he had walked along quite happily, holding Paul's hand. I crouched down and asked him to stand up, but he protested that he was being a cat and continued to scurry on all fours around the stand where the ground staff were waiting to check our boarding passes. I glanced at them anxiously. It was the first time I had flown since September 11th and I didn't think they would appreciate a toddler making light of their security procedures. To my surprise, they were smiling.

'Come on, Dan,' I said, gathering him up in my arms as Paul produced our passports. 'Why d'you have to be a cat right now?'

By way of response Dan shook his head so that his blond curls bobbed up and down, chanting 'I'm a cat, I'm a cat!' while Paul added my haversack to the four items of hand luggage he had already slung about his person. Weighed down like this, we staggered into the departure lounge. Once we were seated Paul and I started to laugh.

On the plane Dan stood on my thighs and made eyes at the young Lebanese woman in the seat behind us. When he tired of this he stretched his hands towards the ceiling, telling me he was catching the *daw-daws* out of the sky. At midnight he was still wide awake, succumbing to sleep only after I had recited every nursery rhyme I knew and a few more I invented on the spur of the moment. I ached with fatigue but it was too late to relax: through the window of the plane the lights of Beirut were winking below us.

It was four a.m. by the time we lay down in our hotel room. We slept late and woke in the morning to clear blue skies and a serene silence in the streets. I got out of bed and stood on the balcony with Dan in my arms, wondering why it was so quiet, until I remembered that today was Sunday. My eyes traced the hoops and dots of the Arabic lettering on the shop sign opposite until I pronounced the words *Maktabet Najma*, 'Star Stationers'. Miraculous, I thought, how the language comes back after long disuse. I had not looked at my Arabic grammar in two and a half years.

'What dat, mummy?' Dan was pointing at the fringed leaves of a small palm in a pot on the balcony facing us.

'That's a tree, Dan, a special tree you haven't seen at home.' I took a step closer to the edge of the balcony, blinking in the unaccustomed light as I noted the sharp drop onto the pavement. We were in a narrow side street lined by apartment blocks of five or six storeys and the sun was warm on my skin. In front of the stationers, a tiny old woman dressed in black was being helped out of a car. I craned my neck to see the far end of the street, where a couple of girls stood chatting at the door of a supermarket and a black man in overalls swept the steps of another hotel. I yawned, stepped back into the room and set Dan down on the carpet.

In the first round of the civil war from 1975–1976, the Maronite militias confronted the Lebanese National Movement (LNM) and the Palestine Liberation Organisation (PLO). Under the leadership of the Druze Kamal Jumblatt, the LNM demanded the abolition of the confessional political system and its replacement by a secular, democratic state. The LNM was closely allied with the PLO.

Much of the fighting took the form of massacres, in which Christians set upon Moslems and Moslems set upon Christians. Beirut cleaved in two along religious lines, the East becoming exclusively Christian and the West almost exclusively Moslem. By June 1976, thirty thousand had been killed and a third of the population forced from their homes.

Heavy fighting took place in 1975–1976 in Beirut's central business district between the parliament building and the Place des Martyrs. From there to the south of the city, a battle-flattened no-man's land opened between the two sectors, known in English as the 'Green Line'. For the next fifteen years, Beirutis only crossed from one sector to the other if they really had to, running the risk of being kidnapped or shot dead at militia-controlled check points.

Today, although the inhabitants of East Beirut remained largely Christian and those of West Beirut largely Moslem, you could travel from one side of the city to the other without facing any danger.

Our hotel was in Hamra, the heart of West Beirut. Hamra was a rare district where Moslems and Christians had traditionally lived, worked and studied side by side. Although during the war most of the Christians had left, some were now returning. Hamra had taken a severe battering during the Israeli siege of West Beirut in 1982, but the area was wealthy and most of the damaged apartment blocks had been re-built. The atmosphere was open and tolerant, the population cosmopolitan.

We ate breakfast and spent the middle part of the day playing trains, moving our bags around the room and searching for things we knew we'd packed but couldn't find. Finally, in the late afternoon, too tired to feel enthusiastic but tempted by the sunshine, we sauntered out into the street.

We were only half a dozen blocks from the American University of Beirut, better known as AUB. One of the most prestigious universities in the Arab world, AUB had always attracted academics from Europe and the USA. Several such staff members had fallen prey to kidnappers and assassins during the civil war, including an American president of the university, Malcolm Kerr, who was murdered in his office on the campus in 1984.

Hiba, a Lebanese friend who lived near me in Britain, had told me that AUB had fabulous gardens and was one of the few places in the city where you could escape from the chug of diesel engines and the tooting of horns.

We walked the length of Rue Omar Ibn Abdul Aziz, wheeling the buggy around the craters in the pavement and peering in the windows of the shops, most of which were closed. A mobile phone shop advertised the latest models from Nokia and Motarola. A small boutique sold women's underwear, as provocative as anything on sale in Europe; next door an optician displayed designer sunglasses. The shop which intrigued me the most was a slimming parlour at the far end of the street. Stencilled on the window in orange paint were the silhouettes of two naked women, one 'before' (written in English), all flab and bulge, the other 'after', slim and svelte. Behind the stencil stood a large white screen, so that you could only guess at what went on within.

Outside the slimming parlour, a young woman in a headscarf sat cross-legged on the pavement with a child in her arms. The girl was Dan's age, but listless and thin with pockmarks on her face. Her eyes were closed and I thought she had gone limp with fever, the condition I dreaded when he got ill. The woman, perhaps seeing Dan and sensing my unease, fixed me with pleading eyes and beseeched me in a whisper to give her some money. On the far side of Abdul Aziz stood the metal gates to the American University Hospital, where Hiba had advised me to take Dan in case of emergency. I delved in my pocket and gave the woman all my change. But when I passed by again the following day, the child was playing on the pavement and I realised that she had simply been asleep.

At the top of Abdul Aziz we turned left into Rue Bliss, named after Daniel Bliss, the American Protestant missionary who founded AUB in 1866. Bookshops and stationers stood wedged between *falafel* bars, bakeries, ice cream parlours and travel agents. Most of the people crowding the pavements looked like students and I overheard conversations in Arabic, French and American-accented English.

Crossing the road we pushed the buggy through the side entrance to the campus. Remembering something Hiba had said, I nodded at the guards and headed for the trees. Western visitors were rarely challenged, for the guards assumed they must be on the staff.

We walked slowly, watching the students who sat talking and smoking on benches and walls in twos and threes, the women lithe in tight jeans, the men smooth-skinned and young. For a few moments the fragrance of pine needles and the neat, tarmac paths with their little signs in English ('College Hall', 'AUB Bookstore') gave me the odd sensation that I had been transported to New England. But the golden stone facade of College Hall was artificially smooth, giving away at first glance that the building was a replica. The original had been destroyed by a car bomb in 1991. And when we turned away from the faculty buildings, New England vanished without trace. The path zig-zagged down the hillside towards the sea through a loosely planted jungle of palms, cypresses and wild pines. Here and there the waxy, sap green leaves of a ficus tree burgeoned in an arc above its smooth white trunk. At the bottom of the hill the blue waters of the Mediterranean seemed to tilt up at an angle and blend into the sky, while, to the right and left, solitary apartment blocks rose up through the trees to frame the view, the pale ochre of their concrete walls warming the green of the foliage and the blue of the waves. It was like walking into one of those early paintings by Picasso, where the sea is seen through an open window.

In fifteen minutes we reached the bottom of the hill and emerged through a gate onto the Corniche, where two lanes of cars streamed steadily in both directions. The light was beginning to lose its intensity. A quarter of a mile away along the Corniche, the fifteen-storey Inter-continental Hotel formed an island in the traffic. To the hotel's left the road swung out towards the docks and to the right it veered towards 'downtown', the re-constructed city centre. Behind us, stacked up the hillside overlooking the sea, stood caramel and bronze high-rise hotels and luxury apartment blocks. Some had their names emblazoned in giant letters: the Bayview, the Cadmos, the Hotel Palm Beach. Between these palaces, in the soft spring light one barely noticed the stains and shell holes in the walls of the older buildings.

We crossed the road on a zebra crossing, braving a line of slow-moving vehicles, and stood on the sea wall in a throng of families and youth. A young man with a fishing rod stubbed out a cigarette and smiled at us.

'Russian?' he asked Paul, who had the buggy. Behind him, waves slapped against the concrete.

'No, from Britain.' Paul smiled back.

'Britain! Welcome.' He stooped down and peered at Dan, who was sucking his thumb, half asleep, half awake. 'Nice looking boy! How old is he?'

'Just two.'

The young man raised his eyebrows. 'But he's big! Looks more like three!'

I smiled now, absurdly pleased, as if Dan's size reflected on my mothering.

'Been here long?' the young man asked.

'Just arrived this morning.'

He raised his eyebrows in surprise. 'Welcome.'

✧

[49]

We took life easy for the next few days, pottering about Hamra in the mornings, walking in the AUB gardens and taking siestas in the afternoons. Paul and I thought it best to acclimatise slowly, taking in the sounds and smells of the city and letting Dan adjust to his new surroundings.

One morning I walked with Dan to the Supermarket Idriss, to buy croissants for breakfast. We went down in the lift, stopping in the lobby to say good morning to the hotel manager. Then we set off along the wide pavement hand-in-hand. Dan was hesitant at first, unsure what to make of the slow-moving vehicles, the incessant hooting and the tall buildings which, to him, must have seemed to touch the sky. I felt the palm of his hand soft and warm against mine and walked slowly, wishing I could explain to him why we had uprooted ourselves and come to this unfamiliar place. I looked to the right and left, ready to snatch him up at a second's notice should a car lumber onto the kerb. After the first block the pavement shrank to a couple of feet, its surface broken by potholes and piles of rubble.

When we got back to the hotel, the door of our room stood propped open with a plastic bucket and a mop. Paul sat on the sofa changing the battery of his camera while a young African woman cleaned the basin in the bathroom. She wore a dark red scarf over her hair.

'Hello,' I said in Arabic, 'how are you?'

The woman glanced at me shyly. '*Alhamdulillah.*' She was beautiful in a cotton skirt and blouse which left her arms bare. She smiled at Dan, who was clinging to my legs. Tossing her head, she picked up her rag and turned back to the basin. But a moment later, she looked at me again. 'Where are you from?'

When I told her, she nodded. 'And you?' Her accent was very different from the local one.

'Sudan.'

'How long have you been in Lebanon?'

'Six years.' The woman stopped scrubbing and straightened her back.

'How d'you find it?'

'Expensive.' She scowled.

'Isn't it?' I replied. 'Do you have children?' I had noticed several young African women cleaning the hotel that morning.

Her face lit up. 'A boy and a girl.'

'With you in Beirut?'

'No, no.' She sighed and wagged her finger. 'With my mother in Sudan.'

'So far away!' I glanced at Dan. 'That must be hard.'

'Yes.' She looked me in the eye. 'It's very hard.'

'D'you go back from time to time?'

'Every two years. I can't go more.' She rubbed her thumb against the tips of her fingers, indicating a big wad of notes. 'The ticket costs a lot of money.'

6

'EVERYTHING IS LOVELY NOW'

Beirut, March 2002

✧

'The official ethos is that we should forget the war. Everything is lovely now, Lebanon is beautiful, life is beautiful.' Rim Joundi tilted back her head and raised her thick, dark eyebrows. She was small with high cheek bones, kohl-rimmed eyes and dark red hair cut in a bob. 'But yes, amongst ourselves we talk about it. Of course.' She lifted a smouldering cigarette from the ashtray and inhaled deeply, sitting back in the cafe chair and gazing at me. I thought I saw mistrust in her large eyes, as if she was wondering what my motives might be for the questions I was asking.

On the far side of the table, the writer Hassan Daoud stirred sugar into his coffee. I had come to meet him at the Cafe Modca on the introduction of a friend, while Paul and Dan explored the museum at AUB. Daoud was a Shi'a from the south, the author of five novels and editor of a cultural supplement of one of Lebanon's leading newspapers. We had been sitting under the cafe awning talking when his friend Rim walked by.

'Rim is a fine painter,' Hassan remarked when she stopped speaking. 'You should try to see her work.'

'I'd love to,' I replied. Behind me, on Rue Hamra, three lanes of cars crawled along in the sunshine, but I was learning to ignore the tooting of their horns.

'You see,' Rim began again, 'the problems that led to the war haven't gone away, but we are not supposed to look at them. The official line is, everything is fine. In fact, things are not fine. People are *more* fanatical now than they were before! And there are so many unanswered questions. Such as,' she looked at me intently, 'why was there a war? And why did it end when it did? And *when* did it end?' She delivered her words very fast, holding her cigarette down by the side of her chair, so that the smoke blew away from us. 'In the end it was small things

[53]

that made me realise the war was over. I'll give you an example. For years and years, every day, a little way from my house, I passed this wall. It was an ordinary concrete wall, in front of an apartment block, just two or three metres high. During the war, the wall was always covered with faces. Every time somebody was killed, or disappeared, the family would put a poster with the photograph and the name. The political parties did it, too. If someone was martyred, they put up a poster. So this wall was always covered with faces. And every day I passed by.

'Later, I used this wall in my paintings. I did a series in which there were masks and faces and sometimes you couldn't tell which was a mask and which a face.' She paused, as if calling the paintings to mind. 'What was I saying? So one day, it was a few years ago but I can't tell you precisely when, one day I passed this wall in the *servees*. The traffic wasn't moving so I had time to look out, and I saw that all the posters had gone and the wall had been painted! Now, for me, that was a sign that the war really *was* over.' Rim ground the stub of her cigarette into the ashtray.

'What did you feel?'

'I felt a kind of rage. Because that wall had meant so much to me. It was like a record of all the people who had died. I felt as if someone had come along and tried to make us forget them.'

Although the street was full of sunlight, the air was cold.

'You know,' said Hassan, 'there are three groups of people who really cannot forget the war. The first is the families of the kidnapped: most of them still don't know what happened to their relatives. And the government says nothing and refuses to investigate. Even the political parties say nothing. The only one to speak on the subject was Walid Jumblatt.' Jumblatt was the son and political heir of Kamal Jumblatt. 'Jumblatt said: "We killed them."' Hassan grimaced. 'At least it was an acknowledgement. The second group is the people who were badly injured, the people who lost a leg or an arm or their sight. You don't see them on the streets: they are all hidden away behind closed doors, in their homes. And the third group is the relatives of the people who were killed.'

'Roughly how many would that come to?' I asked.

'It varies so much from area to area. In Beirut, pretty much everyone was touched by the war in a personal way. And in the south. But if you go to the north, there are Christian areas where people were barely affected at all.'

The waiter brought more coffee and a small glass of water for each of us. Rim took out a packet of cigarettes and lit up again.

Hassan leant back in his chair. 'What Rim says is very true. People have become more fanatical as a result of the war. Each sect is more obsessed than before with asserting its identity.'

I decided to ask a question that had been puzzling me. I knew that every Lebanese had their religious affiliation inscribed on their identity card, but how, in the course of everyday life, did people tell to which sect a stranger belonged?

'People don't ask directly, but there are ways of finding out. Sometimes by the accent, and if that doesn't tell you, always by the place they come from, the town or village. People will ask and ask until they can place you.' He smiled. 'Once, a few years back, I was in Boston in the United States. I had just arrived by train from New York and it was late at night, so I took a taxi. The driver asked me where I was from, and I said "From Lebanon."

'"Ah!" said the driver, "Very good, I am Lebanese too. Where in Lebanon are you from?"

'"The south," I replied.

'"Whereabouts in the south?"

'I deliberately named a town which is mixed Christian and Moslem.'

'"Oh yes," said the driver, "but from which village, precisely?"

'And so he went on, all because he simply had to know if I was a Shi'a or a Christian.'

Rim was smiling now. 'For children, this is very confusing. I have a son, he is nine years old. One day he came home from school and said, "Mum, what are we?" He meant what is our religion, which sect do we belong to?

'"We are nothing," I said. Which is true, I am from a Shi'a family but I am not religious. Then he asked me about God and I said "there is no God". The next day I went to a bookshop and I bought him a Larousse encyclopaedia, so that he could read about the origins of the world from a scientific perspective. A couple of weeks later, his teacher called me into the school. She said he had upset the other children and made a little girl cry by announcing that there is no god!' Rim began to laugh. 'My son was telling the children that the world began when three molecules came together...'

Hassan chuckled. 'During the war, my son came home one day and said to me, "Dad, I don't understand, are we Shi'a or *Shu'i*?"' *Shu'i* is the Arabic word for Communist.

'How old is your son?' I asked when Hassan stopped laughing.

'Now he's 24 years old. He's studying at university.'

'And were you in Beirut right through the war?'

'Most of my friends left, but I stayed the whole time.' Hassan gazed at me steadily. 'I wanted to leave, but my wife would not.'

'She didn't want to?'

'She's a Beiruti. All her family were here and she didn't feel she could.'

'It must have been awful to be here with young children.'

Hassan breathed in sharply. 'It was really terrible. In 1982, when the Israelis besieged West Beirut, that was the worst. My son was four, my daughter two. Every night when the planes came over we were running down to the basement with the other families in our building. The lights would go out, the women would start to cry, then the children. Even now I think they are still affected by what they went through.'

At the time of the Israeli invasion in June 1982, most of Lebanon was partitioned in two. A 'Red line' separated the Syrian zone of influence in the north from an Israeli one in the south. The latter had been established following a smaller Israeli invasion in 1978.

Israel's main agenda in Lebanon was to crush the PLO and help the coalition of Maronite militias known as the Lebanese Forces (LF) to establish their domination over the entire country, thereby creating a western-leaning, friendly state as their northern neighbour. Close links were forged by the Israelis with Bashir Gemmayel, the young Maronite leader then in command of the LF, and a plan was formed whereby the latter would try to link up with the Israelis' proxy force, the South Lebanese Army, in the south. The LF's Moslem opponents in Beirut and the south would be surrounded and the remaining Moslem populations would be left isolated and leaderless.

In June 1982, under cover of a devastating aerial bombardment of the coastal cities, in which thousands of civilians were crushed to death in collapsing apartment blocks, Israeli troops entered Lebanon from the south and the sea. Within a week they had encircled West Beirut, then the stronghold of the PLO, in response to which the Syrians withdrew to the Bekaa. After a siege of the city lasting three months, and the deaths of some twenty thousand Lebanese and Palestinians, mostly civilians, an agreement was reached whereby the PLO fighters would be evacuated from Lebanon under safe conduct provided by the USA and Europe.

In August 1982, Bashir Gemmayel was elected president under Israeli protection. The joint Israeli-Maronite plan might have succeeded, but for his assassination, 18 days later.

A couple of days after meeting Hassan Daoud I was woken at four a.m. by a storm. Flashes of lightning lit up the ceiling of the hotel room, followed after only two or three seconds by loud claps of thunder that made the French windows rattle. I lay still, hoping the storm would pass quickly. But instead the claps grew louder and Dan woke with a wail. He had never experienced a thunderstorm before. I sat up in bed and pulled him onto my lap, rocking him from side to side.

'Want dat to go away!' he cried, looking at me in alarm and pointing at the window.

'It's only thunder, my love,' I replied, trying to sound as if I liked it. Another flash of light, followed by another crash and Dan started to cry. Paul was stirring beside us. I got out of bed, held Dan so that his heart was pressed against mine and walked slowly to the far end of the room. I had carried him like this since he was a little baby and it always seemed to calm him down. When he stopped crying I sat down on the floor, cradled him on my lap and put him on the breast.

The storm was starting to recede and a pale light filtered through the curtains. I settled on the threadbare carpet as Dan grew heavier against my legs, counting the lengthening seconds between the flashes and crashes and thanking the gods that it was only a thunder storm.

7

AN ANCIENT CITY FOR THE FUTURE

Beirut, March 2002

✧

'Have you seen downtown yet?' the hotel manager, a squat man with a square face, peered at me over his bi-focals.

'I'm going this morning.' "Downtown" was the business district between the old parliament building and the Place des Martyrs where in the 1950s, 1960s and early 1970s Lebanon's merchants and financial magnates had conducted their affairs. The Lebanese have always had a talent for making money and in the pre-war climate of low taxation and minimal state interference, big fortunes were amassed by a small elite of Christian and Sunni entrepreneurs.

'Good, you will enjoy it.' His face broke into a slow, kindly smile as he leaned towards me. 'Downtown is very beautiful,' he confided in a low voice, laden with pride. 'They did a good job, I think you'll find.'

I smiled, placed the key on the desk and waved goodbye. "They" seemed to refer to Rafiq Hariri and his construction consortium Solidere. Besides being a politician, Hariri had been a billionaire businessman with a background in the construction industry in Saudi Arabia, where he made his fortune as a young man. His appointment as Lebanese prime minister in 1992 had been supported by the Syrians in the hope that he would take control of the country's ailing economy and attract foreign aid. Later, some of his critics would say that he had rebuilt Lebanon's physical infrastructure while neglecting the social needs of its traumatised people.

Hariri had set himself the task of re-establishing Lebanon in its pre-war role of financial and service centre for the Middle East. In the early 1990s, peace with Israel had seemed a real possibility and Hariri had wanted Lebanon to be ready to compete in the new regional markets that peace would open up. A key element in his strategy was the reconstruction of Beirut's war-damaged business district.

Under Hariri's guidance, in 1992 the Lebanese parliament had formed the Lebanese Company for the Development and Reconstruction of Beirut Central District, which soon became known by its French acronym, Solidere. Solidere acquired by compulsory purchase most of the land and surviving buildings in the old commercial and financial district, located between the Place des Martyrs and the Place d'Etoile, and the adjoining area of the ancient *souqs*. Work began to reclaim some extra land from the sea and architects were hired.

Hariri made vigorous efforts to persuade Lebanese expatriates to invest in the project, sending representatives of Solidere to tour western capitals with promotional slide shows and scale models of the Master Plan for Beirut. I had attended one of these, by chance, in 1997 in London. Beirut's entire downtown area was to be bulldozed and the last vestiges of its wartime history destroyed, making way for the construction of high specification office space for multi-national companies, and shopping, homes and entertainment for the rich. I was struck by Solidere's slick, business-like presentation, in the course of which the civil war – the reason, after all, why reconstruction was required – did not receive a passing mention.

After a fast drive through the mid-morning traffic I asked the *servees* driver to drop me near the Place d'Etoile. He pulled up on a corner by a building site.

'Down there,' he said, gesturing to our right. 'I can't drive in, see the soldiers.'

I nodded and got out. Five soldiers dressed in grey camouflage fatigues stood beside a barrier that blocked the road. I peered through the tarpaulin that shrouded the building site, catching a glimpse of a digger at work in a pit below the level of the pavement. To one side the remains of a Roman column shone creamy white in the sun. I turned round and glanced again at the soldiers before strolling past the barrier.

Six side streets converged at the circular Place d'Etoile. They were flanked by terraces of newly-built, four-storey buildings faced in stone, at the base of which ran a colonnade of arches. Behind the colonnades, shop fronts with plate-glass windows lined the streets, while the apartments above might have been intended to serve as offices or homes. It was pleasant enough, yet strangely devoid of life.

I trailed slowly around the silent streets, trying to figure out why the place felt dead. Wrought iron street lamps were set into the pavement at regular intervals and in between, in tiny squares of soil, grew sapling ficus trees. But the trees, so attractive in Hamra, looked ridiculous, and for a moment I wondered if they were artificial. I stopped to examine one. Its bright, waxy foliage had been trimmed to form the shape of an upside down pudding basin. Poor tree, I thought with irritation. It had lost all its character and lolled at an angle, supported by a stake.

Through the arch of a colonnade I read the words *Snack Bar* in English in purple neon, followed by *Baguettes*. The nextdoor shop offered *Souvenirs*. Further down the street, chrome tables and chairs were set out on the pavement, empty save for a lone man reading a newspaper. I crossed the street. SHOP TO RENT, read a printed notice on a plate-glass window. I stepped backwards, wondering if the offices above were empty, too, struggling to make sense of the light reflected in their window panes. Few businesses could afford the rents asked by Solidere. Peace with Israel had not materialised; and Lebanon was in the throes of economic crisis.

At the end of the street I turned left into a cul de sac, where a Pizza Hut had arranged its chairs and tables right across the road. A pair of European women chatted over coffee; a be-suited Arab man was speaking on a mobile phone. In the distance, a bulldozer growled its way backwards and forwards over rough ground. Feeling jaded, I sat down and ordered tea.

The waiter addressed me in American English. He brought a pot of hot water and flicked open a mahogany box containing neatly stacked rows of Twinings tea bags. There was everything from 'Orange tea with rose petals' to 'Lemon tea with nettleweed'. I searched in vain for simple tea, settling for 'Lady Grey'. Brewed in the now tepid water it tasted disgusting.

I pulled a map out of my bag and a Solidere pamphlet. Why did Solidere call its project one of 'reconstruction', I wondered, when what they had done was to wipe the slate clean and build everything anew? And why had they chosen to demolish buildings that could have been salvaged? Beirut's old *souqs* had been located a few hundred yards from where I sat and at the end of the war some of the shops had remained standing. But instead of restoring those and adding to them, Solidere had sent in the bulldozers and razed everything to the ground, leaving a vast hole that was now to become an underground carpark. The planners, according to the leaflet, intended that the new downtown should 'recreate' the atmosphere of the old Beirut *souqs*. But the atmosphere of the pre-war *souqs* had derived from the unique medley of merchants who had made their livelihoods there, making it a meeting ground for Lebanon's religious sects. The Sunni coffeeseller's shop had stood next door to the Greek Orthodox moneychanger's, the Maronite shoe-maker and the Shi'a grocer. Did Solidere seriously imagine this atmosphere could be re-created by renting shop space to McDonalds, the Body Shop, Starbucks and Burger King?

As if to counterbalance its destructiveness towards the relatively recent past, Solidere had made some concessions to Beirut's earlier history. A handful of mosques and churches were undergoing renovation and archaeologists had been briefly allowed to dig at some of the many sites which were thought to contain Phoenician, Greek and Roman remains, before these were once again covered over. Relics of ancient history, it seemed, were acceptable; reminders of the civil war were not. Perhaps this was the coded message in Solidere's slogan, *An Ancient City for the Future*: 'let's forget what happened in the middle'.

Resting my elbows on the round metal table, I stared at the blank windows on the far side of the street. I had arrived too late, it appeared, to see the Beirut I had wanted to see: the interesting bits lay buried beneath this globalised business park.

I stood up and walked to the low wall that sealed the cul de sac. On the far side the ground dropped twenty feet to a small garden in which fragments of carved stone and broken Roman columns stood amongst weeds and wild flowers. Beyond, a crane towered over a building site. In the distance, traffic surged around a grey strip of soil the size of a football pitch.

I found the waiter and paid for my tea.

'What's that?' I asked, pointing at the garden.

'Ancient ruins, they're going to make a garden around them.'

I had read about this. It was to be called 'The Garden of Forgiveness' in an oblique reference to the war.

I walked away, but it was too soon to go back to the hotel in Hamra; and I felt too frustrated. Perhaps, I thought, if I strolled towards the former Green line, I would find something more interesting. Was it voyeurism, I wondered, that made me want to see some physical evidence of the war? Certainly its furious violence had fascinated me. But that wasn't my only motivation. Solidere's desire to erase all physical traces of the conflict produced a feeling of acute unease. If the Lebanese couldn't bear to look the devastation in the eye, how were they going to learn from what had happened? And if they didn't learn, might not history repeat itself?

When I reached the football pitch-sized square, I recognised the Place des Martyrs. Originally named after the leaders of a rebellion against the Ottomans during World War I, the Place had once been the hub of Beirut's commercial life. I had seen old photographs of it in which pedestrians and buses circulated around a bright garden of flowers and palm trees. By the end of the war, the only thing to remain standing in the dustbowl to which the square had been reduced was the famous Martyrs' statue, badly disfigured by shrapnel. But Solidere was having the statue restored to its original condition, and it was nowhere to be seen.

On the far side of the Place rose the Parisian-style apartment blocks of Achraffiyeh, in East Beirut; on my side lay a wasteland. Turning my back to the traffic, I peered through a hoarding at a deserted building site and a hole in the ground. I felt marooned. But a couple of hundred yards ahead, at the eastern end of the square, the buildings began again, on the West Beirut side of the old Green line. As I walked along, my eyes fastened on the nearest structure that remained standing, a bulging concrete body on tall stilts, the height of a small office block and without a single window. The sight of it both frightened and intrigued me. I went up to a man who was sweeping the road and asked him what it was.

'That?' he said, pointing to the building, 'that was the old Cinema du Rivoli.' He stared at me for a moment, as if pleased to have been asked.

Leaving the square behind, I stopped a few minutes later at the foot of an apartment building which rose five storeys tall at the corner of a street. The surface of its dirty brown facade resembled a foam mattress dumped on a rubbish tip and left in the rain: from the pavement to the roof, it was pockmarked with holes left by bullets and shells. I stared closely at the surface. If I went up to the wall and pressed my fingers into it, the rancid foam would surely not resist. On every balcony children's clothes were hanging out to dry. Broken chairs faced the sun; a potted palm thrust dusty branches towards the sky. I felt excited now. This was the Beirut which the developers had wanted to obliterate, and here was a part of it still standing.

Sensing someone watching me, I turned and picked my way through the piles of sand and garbage that marked the edge of the street, passing the remains of a church which had lost its roof and most of its walls. The sun was hot on the top of my head, the air saturated with exhaust fumes. At the end of the block a woman in a headscarf and *gelabeyya* waited for a *servees*. I turned the corner and crossed to the far side of the road, where shade extended a few feet from the walls of the buildings. A man with no legs rode by on a tricycle; I couldn't see how he was making it move. A shoe-shine boy with a gleaming brass box walked in the road beside him.

I passed a cluster of school boys buying *menaish* from an open-fronted bakery. Next door, in the cool, ill-lit depths of a barber's salon, a young man wrapped in aprons sat in a plastic swivel chair fixed to the floor. He perched with his upper body tipped forwards, the hair on the back of his head neatly cropped in a V shape, while an older man dusted loose strands from his neck with a soft, flat brush.

In the nextdoor lot stood the stained yellow carcass of another badly damaged apartment block. Where the windows should have been, dark cavities gaped like missing eyes. I walked on slowly, wondering what it was like to live in a street where so much violence had taken place.

I was hungry now and starting to feel tired. On the far side of the street, men ate *foules* and *hommous* in a little cafe. The words *Matam Hassan* were painted on the window in red and yellow. I crossed and loitered by the window of the shoe shop next door. I wanted to eat, but felt too conspicuous. I knew I would be served, but my presence would cause discomfort. Women do not eat in this kind of cafe in the Middle East, particularly if they are alone. Better to hail a *servees* and ride back to Hamra, where Paul and Dan would be back from their morning outing. I turned towards the street, where a procession of cars ground towards me. As my hand fluttered up, an old green Mercedes with red number plates swooped into the kerb. A lone passenger sat in the back.

'Going to Hamra?' I asked the driver.

'*Ittfaddali*,' he replied, 'get in.' He was skinny and wrinkled and I liked his face.

I slid into the front passenger seat, enjoying the feeling that its leather had been polished by a hundred thousand bottoms. Cracks fanned out from a tiny hole on the driver's side of the windscreen.

'What's the name of this district?'

'Mazra.' The driver waved at a gutted building. 'That's Mazra church over there.'

'Did Mazra get hit a lot in the war?' It was a silly question, but I was curious to see how the subject would go down.

'Not as much as down there.' He pointed over to the right, in the direction of the pitted-foam apartment block. 'A tram used to run on this street,' he added enthusiastically. 'Look, there in the road, you can still see where the steel tracks lay.' I couldn't, but I nodded anyway. I'd seen old photos of trams in Beirut. 'When was that?'

'Ages ago.'

Did he mean before the war?

'Before, but not that long before. Trams used to run all around the city.'

The traffic was barely moving. I wound down my window, bared my elbow to the sun and settled in for a chat. But the man in the back seat was stirring.

'Whirr you from?' he breathed in English. I pretended I hadn't heard. 'There are hardly any tourists,' I remarked to the driver.

'Before, there were lots. And in three years' time, they'll be back.' He sat relaxed at the steering wheel, inching forwards, wizened and humorous. 'All the Lebanese have gone too!' he went on. 'There are twenty million outside, in America, Africa, Australia. Here everyone is Syrian, Egyptian or from Bangladesh, Sri Lanka, India!' He chuckled and looked at me. 'Only two million Lebanese in the whole country!'

It was true that hundreds of thousands of Lebanese had left the country during the war; and that, from the late nineteenth century on, Lebanese from the poorer communities had emigrated in large numbers out of economic necessity. But I doubted that the driver's figure of twenty million emigres bore much relation to reality.

'Whirr you from?' The breathy whisper again from the back seat. Again I made no response. After a few seconds the young man leant forward and asked me, in Arabic, how long I'd been here.

'Six days.'

'Your Arabic is good!' The young man had pudding cheeks. He told me he worked in Hamra repairing cameras.

'I've been a driver for forty years!' the driver interrupted him. 'I used to have a lorry. For thirty years I drove up and down the coast, between Beirut and the Israeli border! And when I wasn't driving I worked as a fisherman!' He reached in the pocket on the inside of his door and handed me a wad of dirty snapshots. 'Look at the size of the fish I used to catch!' His eyes sparkled with delight. In the first photo a younger, stronger man with golden skin stood in the sea in boxer shorts, holding a large, slippery fish by the tail. 'That's me!' he cried in delight. 'Look at the size of the fish!'

'Enormous!' I exclaimed with admiration, flicking through the other pictures. The traffic was moving now and we sped around the Place des Martyrs, catching a glimpse of the pale blue sea before we turned off towards Hamra. 'But I thought the sea water was filthy?' I had read a chilling account of the marine pollution caused by the war.

'*Now*, it's filthy, of course, but that was *then*! In those days it was clean!' We were cruising along a medium-sized boulevard and the driver darted in towards the kerb to tout for business from a young woman who stood watching the traffic. '*Ittfaddali* Samira, Mounira, Emira!' he chanted gaily, more to me and the man in the back than to the girl.

But the girl shook her head and waved us away.

In another minute we had slowed to a walking pace, hemmed in on all sides by juddering cars and taxis as we ground along Rue Hamra. I spotted the awning of Cafe Modca, paid the driver and got out.

8

'WE'RE NOT ARABS, WE'RE PHOENICIANS!'

Jbeil, March 2002

Paul was getting restless. Beirut was too westernised for his liking, at least in the areas we had visited. He had spent the morning on his own wandering around Achraffiyeh, on the Christian side of the former green line. 'It's very like Paris,' he said when he returned. 'Tall narrow houses with balconies and shutters, little bistros, half the people speaking French.'

'Nice?' I enquired.

'Quite attractive in its way, but not what I was expecting...'

This was what I had feared. Paul would have liked the Qadisha valley, but not Beirut, with its heavy traffic and manic urban pace. I wasn't sure I *liked* it either, but it fascinated me.

'How about we go and stay in Jbeil?' I suggested with a sinking heart. Already I felt I was making slow progress with my project of trying to fathom how the Lebanese lived with their memories of the war. If we left Beirut I would be further from the people I needed to talk with. But I had known that being in Lebanon as a family might be difficult, and Paul's needs had to be taken into account.

A few days earlier we had met a woman called Raja, the sister of a friend of Paul's in London, whose family came from Jbeil. Jbeil lay up the coast to the north of Beirut and was, according to Raja, the perfect place for a young child.

'It will be ideal for Paul and Dan,' she had said as we drank tea on her roof terrace in Hamra, 'it's a quiet little place with ancient ruins and beautiful beaches. And Teresa can get into Beirut in half an hour, if she wants to see people. I'll ask my niece Sara to drive you up there.'

Jbeil – or Byblos as it is known in the west – was one of the oldest inhabited places on earth. It had been a city state under the Phoenicians in the third millenium BC, the port from which Lebanon's cedars were

exported to other Mediterranean cities. Today the town was mainly
Christian, with a small but old-established Moslem minority.

Sara collected us from our hotel the following morning at eleven.
She was young and pretty and made short work of loading our bags
into the back of her Peugeot. In half an hour we had crossed Beirut and
were speeding up the coast. The town of Jounieh sprawled below us to
our left, a connurbation of hotels and dirty white apartment buildings
packed tightly into the narrow strip of land between the highway and
the beach. I thought of Tony Chedid and his effusive description of
his hometown.

'This area is all brothels,' Sara waved at the area below us.
'Prostitutes and Russian belly dancers. And over there is the *Casino
du Liban.*'

More apartment buildings straggled up the mountainside that rose
abruptly to our right, on the top of which a large white statue of the
Virgin Mary stood out against the blue sky. The road itself was lined by
petrol stations and drive-in bakeries. Giant hoardings advertised Winston
cigarettes, Suzuki motorbikes and Pampers nappies. Heavy traffic cruised
three lanes deep in both directions, though there were no markings on
the road. I sat in the back of the car with Dan on my lap, wishing we
had insisted on strapping him into the car seat we had brought from
England. As he grew heavier against my arm and fell asleep, I watched the
drivers all around us change lanes without indicating, using their horns
if other vehicles failed to give way. In the top corner of the windscreen,
waves broke in bursts of white on a cobalt sea.

After a while the apartment buildings gave way to plastic polytunnels
on both sides of the road. We were on a flyover, looking down on a fresh
crop of squalid apartment blocks, when Sara announced that we had
reached Jbeil. I sat in unhappy silence, wondering how this could possibly
be the peaceful seaside town which Raja had told me about. Sara left
the highway by a slip road and we swept round a giant spaghetti curve
and descended into a wide street where cars were parked in front of
sleepy-looking shops.

'You'll find everything you need,' she cried gaily. 'There's a pharmacy
on the corner, meat, vegetables, a bakery.'

I glanced up and down the dusty row of flat-roofed concrete buildings
and tried to draw breath. It was like the main street of a small town in
the USA. Behind us, the flyover shook as the traffic roared across it.

'The best place to stay,' said Sara, 'is in the old town. I'm going to take you to my mum's cousin Elias, to see if you can rent the apartment above his restaurant.'

In seconds we had left the new town behind and were following a high stone wall down the hill towards the sea. Through an archway I glimpsed a cobbled street and at the end of it a pale stone church. Relief washed over me as the car swung round, onto the quay of a pretty fishing harbour.

Elias' restaurant was in a square stone building in the heart of the old town, opposite the entrance to Jbeil's archaeological site. The building had the character and feel of a warehouse more than a home, with a series of porthole windows set just under the eaves. The restaurant was named Abi Chemmou, after a king of ancient Byblos. To enter, you had to climb a large flight of stone steps, brushing past the tendrils of a trellised rose.

We found Elias seated at a table with a paintbrush and daler board, copying a photograph of a Phoenician pitcher from a book. Tubes of oil paint were laid out neatly in a row on the table. When he stood up to greet us, I saw a tall, good-looking man of about fifty with spiky grey hair cropped close to his skull. His eyes bore an expression of discreet amusement, as if he had been mulling over a good joke that someone had told him, or re-living in his mind an illicit encounter. When we asked to see the apartment, he led us up a spiral staircase that rose beside the reception desk at the front of the restaurant. At the top, a sturdy wooden door opened onto a large living space which ran the full length of the building. Elias called this the 'salon'. At one end, a row of porthole windows gave onto a restored mediaeval *souq* and a crusader castle. At the far end, more portholes looked across the gardens of the old town to the sea.

In the centre of the floor, a raised platform occupied an area roughly twenty foot square. It was reached by two steps and bordered on one side by a curious wrought iron railing, the spikes of which were tipped with gold paint.

'We use this for wedding receptions,' Elias gestured at the platform, as if no further explanation were required. 'In summer time,' he added, 'not now'. In the middle of the platform, two of the largest sofas I had ever seen and two equally vast matching armchairs were arranged around a glass coffee table, where ash trays decorated with bronze and silver shells sat on a gilt cloth. The curves of the upholstery bulged obscenely through their red, blue and gold striped covers. It was easy enough to imagine a lavishly made-up bride perching anxiously in her white dress on the edge of a sofa, posing for photographs.

To our eyes the salon was eccentric, to say the least; but pleasant and immaculately clean. Given Elias' assurance that we would not be disturbed by bridal photo shoots, it would suit our purposes quite well. He showed us the bedroom, bathroom and kitchen and we told him we would like to stay for a couple of weeks. After a little bit of friendly haggling, we agreed upon the price.

'What about the windows?' I asked. The catches were easily within Dan's reach.

'You're worried about the little one?' Elias looked serious. 'I'll wire them shut. No problem.'

Dan loved our new penthouse. That first afternoon he spent hours chuntering around the salon being a train, clenching his fists and rotating his arms like pistons. He was happiest when Paul walked behind him, making the same motion with his arms and uttering 'Ch-ch-ch-choo,' and 'Too-toot!' In the evening, Dan arranged a bolster to bridge the gap between the sofas. Once it was in place, he got down on the floor and crawled through the gap, giggling loudly when he succeeded, howling with rage when he dislodged the bolster.

Bedtime was tricky. When Dan was in his pyjamas I drew the curtains in the bedroom, turned out the light and sat him on my lap for a breast feed. But just as I thought he was drifting off to sleep, the call to prayer sounded from the old stone mosque fifty metres across the way.

'Dat?' said Dan, opening his eyes and pointing at the window.

'It's the *muezzin*,' said I, 'He's singing to tell people that it's time to come and pray.'

'Zee!'

'He's in his tower, over the way.'

'Zee!'

I thought Dan might find an invisible singer alarming, unless I let him satisfy his curiosity. So we climbed off the bed and went to the window, lifted the curtain and craned our necks at the porthole. Through the darkness we could just make out the domed roof of the mosque and the minaret with its loudspeaker.

'Look,' I said, 'that's the *muezzin's* tower, he sings from up there.' I side-stepped the fact that the call to prayer is tape-recorded these days, for that was too complicated to explain. The words sounded on the night air, crackle-free and beautiful, and I told myself it was just possible that here in the historic city of Jbeil the singing was done by a real, live *muezzin*.

'*All-a-hu akbar,*' the voice wailed, '*all-a-hu akbar*'. For me the dry, sorrowful wail of the *muezzin* evoked the Middle East more strongly than any other sound or smell or sight. Hundreds of times in the last thirteen years it had woken me in the night or stopped me in my tracks in the day; and every time I had felt 'I'm here, I'm where I want to be.' It touched me that now my little son was responding to it, too.

'Man in d'tower!' shouted Dan. 'Uppa guy!' (up in the sky). After a few moments I picked him up and tucked him into bed. But when the call to prayer finished, he sat up and shouted 'More!'

'He won't sing any more for a bit, Dan,' I said gently, 'he's going down into the mosque now to say his prayers.'

The next day Elias told me that no *muezzin* had climbed the tower for at least thirty years. Dan asked me several times about the singer. I promised to take him across to the mosque and show him the minaret from close up, but somehow I forgot. I felt a little sheepish about the fact that he would certainly be disappointed in his hope of seeing the singer standing at the loudspeaker.

Although the weather was sunny, a cold wind blew off the sea, sending a draught through the badly fitting portholes. One morning I found a gas heater in a corner of the salon, but the cylinder was empty. I went downstairs and found Elias sauntering about the flagstone floor of the restaurant in a heavy leather coat, looking closely at the small oil paintings that hung on the walls. Some showed the port with the blue sea beyond; others were antique motifs from the ruins. Each one was signed 'Elias Andre'.

'*Bonjour*,' Elias said quietly when he saw me, his throat full of gravel. 'How's it going up there?' He jerked his head towards the ceiling. His eyes bore the same amused air of the day before, only this time I saw a trace of sadness, too.

'It's lovely,' I replied, 'but we're cold!' I raised my shoulders to my ears and pretended to shiver.

'Well, yes,' he looked at me blankly, 'it's only March.' For a moment he seemed to come on the hard business man. Then he softened. 'Did you put on the gas fire?'

'The bottle's empty.'

'Okay, I'll get you a refill.' His face broke into a broad smile as he walked to the top of the stone steps. 'Ismael! Bring a new gas bottle.' A man put his head round the trellis from the bottom of the steps and nodded. While we waited I asked about the origins of the building.

'It's over two hundred years old,' Elias replied with enthusiasm. 'When I bought it, it was a one-storey house, belonging to the parliamentary deputy to Jbeil. That was in 1973. I pulled it down and re-built it. I had a team of forty labourers, twenty working during the day and twenty at night. And in nine months, it was done.' He looked pleased with himself.

'And the round windows?'

'They were my idea.'

'So you opened the restaurant shortly before the war?'

'In the autumn of 1974.' Elias rested an elbow on the bar and looked at me. Once more his brown eyes glinted with laughter, as if he were privy to a hilarious secret.

'Wasn't that a bad time?'

'On the contrary! The war was very good for business!' He lowered his voice. 'For the first seven years, till 1982, the restaurant was busy. All the Christians flocked here, from Beirut, the Shouf, the north... They came to take refuge because Jbeil was the one place where there wasn't any fighting.'

'Why not?'

Elias shrugged his shoulders. 'The people of Jbeil never let the war touch them. We always had peace, Christians and Moslems living side by side. Perhaps once or twice there was some little problem, but the leaders were quick to sort it out.' He half-closed his eyes and turned his head away, giving me the impression that he didn't want to be pressed on the subject.

The wind had dropped and the sun was warm on our heads as we walked along the quay, where most of the old stone buildings had been converted into restaurants. A modern hotel stood on the headland, with the words *Byblos sur Mer* in large neon letters projecting from the flat roof. By a little ruined fort at the entrance to the harbour, two men in shorts stood with fishing rods cast onto the waves, neither moving nor speaking. Below them, half a dozen wooden boats bobbed on the surface of the water. They looked like pleasure craft with plastic chairs set out along the sides and canvas canopies to give protection from the sun, but in the back lay the tangled mesh of fishing nets. As I stood wondering what was to prevent the wind from tossing the plastic chairs into the water, a black Range Rover glided past us, followed by a BMW. The strains of a French pop song wafted across the quay.

In the 1960s and early 1970s, Jbeil had been a fashionable tourist resort, its harbour frequented by the private yachts of international celebrities and Mediterranean jet setters. During the war years they had taken their trade elsewhere, but the bars and restaurants we found along the quay suggested the town was beginning to revive. The season had barely begun, and only a handful of people strolled in front of us. Most of the women were blond or brunette, stylishly dressed in scoop-necked T-shirts and tailored trousers.

Am I really in the Arab world? I kept thinking, *or in the south of France?* Never before had I known an Arab country where women bared their necks and shoulders. For a moment I thought I understood why war had been inevitable. For how could traditional Moslem Arabs coexist in such a tiny country with Christians who behaved like Europeans?

[73]

The names of the bars were written in English and French, with not a word of Arabic to be seen. *The Zanzibar, Le Café du Port, Pepe's Fishing Club*. Behind, the gardens, domes and arches of the old town filled the lower slopes of the hillside, with here and there a palm tree or a cypress. Paul stopped as we passed the gate to *Pepe's Fishing Club*.

'Want a beer?'

'Okay.' I was curious to see what lay within. We helped Dan up the stone steps and crossed a rocky garden of trellises and vines. Under a colonnade, a collection of framed photographs covered the outer wall of the club. In each one a man with a heavy jowl in a sea captain's cap stood beside a different French politician or celebrity: Pepe with General de Gaulle, Pepe with Brigitte Bardot, Pepe with Marlon Brando, Pepe with Chirac, until the collection degenerated into pictures of Pepe with an assortment of busty women in bikinis. Pepe, we discovered, was a former Lebanese Christian playboy born in Mexico. He had opened the Fishing Club in 1963 and by 1975 it had been one of the most fashionable bars in the Mediterranean.

After finishing our beer we decided to explore the beach. To get there we had to leave the harbour behind and walk up through the back streets of the new town. It began at the far end of the reconstructed *souq*, in a narrow road lined with shoe shops where the air smelled of dust and rotting garbage. People chatted in doorways, young men rode by on mopeds and women smiled at Dan as we passed. He sat in the backpack sucking his thumb, his face almost hidden by his floppy cloth sunhat.

The buildings of the new town were three- and four-storey concrete boxes, with shops on the ground floor and balconied apartments above. Some stood unfinished, with metal rods bristling into the sky, awaiting the addition of another storey. We walked slowly in the shadows, avoiding the main street, and in a couple of hundred yards found ourselves on an overgrown lane bordered by a banana grove. Scraps of paper and old drink cans lay among the weeds. But this was nothing compared to what we saw when we reached the beach. It was as if a strong wind had lifted up the contents of a rubbish dump and spread them evenly over the sand.

'What a mess!' Paul exclaimed. He stepped onto a weathered grey plank of driftwood. 'Some of this stuff is surgical waste! Look, down there, a syringe carton. And another one over there.' I followed his gaze. 'This is stuff that's been dumped at sea and floated in on the tide.'

A moment later he stepped off the plank and prodded something with his toe.

'What's that?'

'A dead chicken.' Beside his boot lay a plucked carcass, the webbed foot still attached to the leg. Next to it a large orange rotted in the sun. 'I guess the restaurants dump their leftovers here.' Paul scowled. 'So much for Dan playing on the beach!'

'I think he's fallen asleep,' I said, gently lifting the brim of Dan's sunhat. His cheek rested on the back of Paul's neck and his pale eyelids were pressed together. 'Let's walk a bit.' We picked our way through the rubbish until at last we reached the clean, wet sand at the edge of the waves. With our backs to Jbeil we looked out to sea, enjoying the wind in our hair and the salt air on our skin. After a few minutes we set off along the beach, staying close to the water's edge and leaving the town behind us. When we had walked a mile, I turned and looked back, hoping to see Jbeil in some kind of perspective. But from where I stood, the town appeared to have no boundaries. Apartment buildings littered the landscape in all directions, their vertical lines broken only by horizontal strips of polytunnel that glinted in the sun. The town had even spread across the coastal highway, trailing up into the rocky foothills of the Mountain. I gazed in anger at the ugly scene, wondering why, in a country where such a high value was placed on show and personal appearance, no-one seemed to care about the environment.

The problem was partly due to the construction frenzy that had gripped the country in the mid-1990s. There were few legal controls, and developers had thrown up buildings where they could without thinking of the consequences. But the ubiquitous litter was something else. I wondered if it might be an expression of a mutual disregard which the war-traumatised Lebanese felt towards each other.

The sky was turning dark blue at the windows when Raja put her head round the door of the salon. Her three-year-old daughter Salma stood at her feet, black corkscrew curls bushing out around her face.

'Hi!' Raja cried, 'we just arrived from Beirut. How're you doing?' It was the eve of Palm Sunday and they had come to spend the feast with Raja's mother.

'We're fine,' I replied, 'Very comfortable. But I've got lots of questions about Jbeil, can you stay for a cup of tea?'

'Okay, *habibti*, but only ten minutes, my mother is waiting for us.' She lifted Salma onto a sofa close to where Dan stood with a piece of jigsaw in his fist, regarding her with a look of suspicion.

As I set a pan of water to boil on the stove, Raja strolled around the room with a restless energy. She was elegant in a long, hip-hugging skirt, her russet hair well-shaped around her intelligent face, her slim hands expressive. She had treated me like a friend from the moment of meeting and I had liked her at once, as well as finding her intriguing because of the long journey she had travelled from her Maronite roots. Born to a working-class family native to Jbeil, Raja had moved to Beirut with her brother as a teenager to complete her education. It had been the early 1970s, when the Palestinians and Lebanese leftists were preparing to challenge Maronite privilege.

After taking up the cause of a Palestinian girl who had been refused admission to her high school, Raja had become a regular visitor to the refugee camps. Later she had trained as a nurse. She had spent the war years helping to establish health clinics in the camps and among the deprived Shi'a of Beirut's southern suburbs.

A beep sounded. Raja rushed to her bag and pulled out a small, green mobile.

'Allo?' she cried, lifting up her hair and holding the phone to her ear. The conversation lasted only seconds but no sooner had she put the phone away than it rang again. It had been this way when I met her in Beirut, with rarely five minutes between calls.

Raja smiled as she put the phone on the glass table beside Dan, who had gone back to his jigsaw. 'Sorry, Teresa, tell me what you want to know and I'll switch this thing off.'

'I want to understand why there wasn't any fighting here during the war – if that's true, of course?'

'Sure it's true. You see, the Christians of Jbeil are not fanatical, for the most part. Take my parents, for instance. My mother and father were believers, they went to church, but my father had a great respect for Islam. My father's best friend was the sheikh across the road, and the sheikh's daughter was *my* best friend. During Ramadan, my father wouldn't drink alcohol, out of sensitivity to the sheikh. And every morning he listened to a radio programme which began with the call to prayer, and recitation of Koranic verses. That was the first thing I heard when I woke up in the mornings.' She smiled, as if the memory were a happy one. 'So, although we were Christians, Islam was a normal part of our lives.'

I poured the tea. 'And was your family typical of the Jbeil Christians?'

'*Yani*, not every one was as open-minded as my father, but in general people here are not extremists.' She sighed. 'Jbeil wasn't always Maronite, by the way, did you know that? Two hundred years ago it was a Shi'a town.' She stirred sugar into her tea. 'For the most part, the Christians of Jbeil are simple, humble folk, trying to live their lives. They have a pleasant lifestyle by the sea, and centuries of trade have made them open-minded. But people like my parents were never very informed about politics. My mother grew up in the mountains and had no education; my father finished school at elementary level. They married and had eight children and they had to work hard to survive.

'My father drove a taxi, and he also had a truck for transporting sand. So he was always running from place to place.' Raja paused. 'When the war started my parents didn't know much about the Palestinians. They knew it was unfair that the Israelis had taken their land; that was all. Politics was something they left to other people.'

Although Raja had stepped completely out of line with her community, I knew she still had a strong bond with her parents. I asked her how they had felt about her work in the Palestinian camps.

'They were afraid for my safety, more than anything. But I tried not to tell them more than I had to, because I didn't want them to worry.'

'So what happened in Jbeil during the war?' I pictured crowds of people eating in the restaurant downstairs, enjoying their holiday from hell.

'By chance, Jbeil's MP was a man called Raymond Edde. He was a Christian, but a lay person, non-sectarian, one of the best. He was open-minded and I think his attitudes rubbed off on people.'

'Then is it true that there weren't really any problems?' Given what was going on in the rest of the country, I still found this incredible.

'There were some problems in the mountain villages, but the leaders got the situation under control very quickly.'

'Which leaders?'

'The MPs, the sheikhs, the community leaders. Because, deep down, they didn't feel like that.' Raja reached out a hand and stroked Dan's curls. Salma was playing on the floor with his farm animals. 'Even my Moslem friends took refuge here, when things were really heavy. We didn't have real problems. People never got into carrying guns.' She held her head on one side and smiled. 'We have a reputation for being chicken, in Jbeil, we're frightened. We hear one bomb in Beirut and we all rush back into our homes, leaving the streets empty...'

Salma was arranging the cows and the sheep in a line along the top of the sofa.

'You know,' Raja went on, 'the worst problem we have, is ignorance. Jbeil is like a village, with a low level of education. I'll tell you a story. You've seen the church of St John the Baptist,' she pointed towards the window, 'and the mosque just outside the restaurant here?'

I nodded.

'One day I was at a wedding at the church and the call to prayer began during the ceremony. A woman beside me growled, "They're singing it now because we're in the middle of the wedding, to provoke us!" She thought it was deliberate. I said, "No, no, the time is fixed by Islamic law, they don't have any choice." She didn't know this.'

I stared at Raja in disbelief.

'Wait, it gets worse than that!' Her eyebrows shot up. 'You may find this hard to believe, but some Christians don't even know that Islam has separate Shi'a and Sunni sects! But the problem is not just in Jbeil. All over Lebanon there's not enough education about Islam for the Christians, nor about Christianity for the Moslems. Before the war it was understandable, in a way. Rural people were busy with their lives, especially in the mountains, and they didn't travel to other parts of the country. And then the generation who should have received their education during the war years, did not. So we have a dangerous problem of ignorance, of lack of information. This is why we say that Hariri is re-building the stones of Lebanon, but not the human beings, when the thing we need most is to re-build the human beings.'

Salma was standing on the sofa with her arms around Raja's neck, her lips close to her mother's ear. 'Okay, *habibti*,' Raja wrapped her arms round Salma and stood up. 'We have to go. My mother's waiting for us and Salma's hungry.' When they got to the door she turned back. 'We're

[78]

going to church tomorrow morning. I don't suppose you want to come?' She wrinkled her lovely face into a grimace, conveying that she thought that we, as westerners, wouldn't choose to go to church. 'Look, I'll call by for you, just in case.'

I had seen the palm branches decorating the white stone niches of St John's when we walked past on our way home from the beach, and heard singing drifting through the open doorways. I wanted very much to attend a service, to hear the liturgy chanted in Syriac and see what the Maronites looked like en masse. But it was not to be. I threw up in the night and in the morning could not get out of bed. Searching for a remedy in the homeopathic travel kit, I decided that the phrase 'total physical prostration' best described my condition. Dan kept climbing up on the bed, tugging at the covers I had piled on to warm my chilled body, saying 'Mummy, get up!' but I could not. I lay still, listening to the crowds of people moving across the square below, and the strains of singing that the wind blew from the church.

Paul took Dan out, skipping the service but accepting Raja's invitation to join her family for lunch in her brother's seaside restaurant. They came back in the middle of the afternoon, Paul with his face and arms tinged golden by the sun. The town, he said, was full of little girls in white frilly dresses and women in smart hats and silky outfits. He and Dan had sat down with Raja and twenty of her kinsfolk to feast at a table laden with olives, *tabbouleh*, *moutabbal*, spinach pies and half a dozen different types of meat.

They had eaten their fill and Paul had joined in the conversation as best he could, until Dan got bored and tugged him away from the table. Paul had made his excuses and taken Dan to visit the fishermen on the sea wall.

It was drizzling as we climbed the long, flat steps to the castle on Maundy Thursday, but I had recovered my strength. Dan walked between us in his goretex boilersuit and wellies and Paul carried the empty backpack slung across his shoulder. The castle was a solid, square-cut fortress, built in the twelfth century by the French crusader Raymond de St Gilles, who went under the title 'Count of Tripoli'. Below us, the archaeological site occupied a windy promontory that jutted into the sea to one side of the harbour.

'Who lives in here?' Paul quizzed Dan as we reached the castle's iron-studded doorway.

'De raggon,' replied Dan (the dragon).

'That's right! A nice, friendly dragon.' Paul picked up Dan and swung him onto his shoulders as we stepped over the threshold into the central hall. A flight of steps descended into obscurity and a pair of slit windows gave onto the site, just wide enough for a child of Dan's age to slip through. But no dragon came to greet us and the gloomy hall was lacking in charm. We climbed some more stairs and emerged on the roof. To the south, the coastline stretched in a long white blur of apartment buildings all the way to Jounieh, while behind it Beirut had disappeared in fog. We turned our backs and gazed at the sea, where white breakers rolled towards the shore on grey blue waves.

An elegant Ottoman house stood alone on the cliff top, its shuttered windows shaded by palm trees, while in the surrounding meadow grass and yellow wildflowers flourished in the mild, salty air. Directly beneath us, neat gravel paths ran this way and that, connecting piles of stones with sunken foundations, ancient temples, well shafts and a fragment of Roman colonnade. Each exhibit was marked with an explanatory sign; for, unlike the beach and town, the site was maintained in immaculate condition.

When a small patch of blue opened in the clouds, we retraced our steps into the central hall and found a staircase leading down onto the meadow.

'Get down!' shouted Dan. 'Wanna walk!' Paul set him on his feet. For the next two hours, while the rain held off and the sun's weak rays bounced off the puddles, we meandered among the remains of half a dozen different epochs, discovering the floors of iron- and stone-age houses only metres from Phoenician tombs and ramparts, temples to Hellenic and Pharaonic gods, a Roman amphitheatre and a Persian fort.

As a trading city and religious centre, Byblos had fallen under the sway of all these civilisations in the seven millenia of its existence.

Cow parsley grew level with the lids of tombs and young olive trees nestled in the corners of temples. In the bracing air that blew off the sea, the vigour of the vegetation created a sense of abundance. I felt both the antiquity of the place, and that it was teeming with present life.

I spent some minutes at an oblong-shaped collection of standing obelisks, dedicated to Resheph, god of burning and destructive fire during the Amorite occupation of Byblos in the second millennium BC. Some of the votive offerings previously found at the temple were thought to have been connected with the rites of Adonis and Astarte. Astarte was the Greek goddess of spring and new life who was widely worshipped in Lebanon before the arrival of Christianity. Her cult had inspired Colin Thubron's walking tour through Lebanon in 1967, recounted in his poetic book, *The Hills of Adonis*. I had read the book during the latter weeks of my pregnancy and now I frequently thought of Thubron. He had roamed the country from south to north, ziz-zagging from the coast into the mountains and back again several times, in the spring that preceded the Six Days' Arab-Israeli war. At night he slept under olive trees or lodged with peasants. In those days, rural Lebanon remained unsullied by developers.

> The fishing villages are unspoilt along the Byblos coast, and there is an Ottoman doziness and permanence about their green-watered coves, idle with fishing boats.[1]

I was struggling to come to terms with the fact that Thubron's Lebanon had vanished under the combined onslaught of the civil war, the construction frenzy that had followed it and the callous individualism of modern Lebanese culture.

But when we climbed up to the amphitheatre which overlooked the sea, I felt I could still glimpse the world that he had known. Along the clifftop a line of stumpy palms waved their upturned branches in the clean, rain-washed air, beside wind-bowed pines and stripey cacti. At my feet the grass was scattered with scarlet poppies; yellow butterflies darted

---

1 Colin Thubron: *The Hills of Adonis.*

from shrub to shrub. I lifted Dan onto my hip and gazed at the sea, blue now under a clear sky.

That evening we decided to eat at a cafe in the new town which Paul had spotted on a trip to the bank. Because the menu was exclusively in Arabic, we supposed that the place might be Moslem-owned and less pretentious than the cafes on the quay, despite being called the Café Rock.

Dusk was falling and the pavements of the main street were crowded with people. We battled our way between moving cars and trucks, stopping to look in the window of a pastry shop before making our way to the cafe's brightly lit doorway. It was a spacious place with a spotless counter of stainless steel and glass behind which raw meat kebabs were displayed in neat rows. Slim, dark-haired waiters in black trousers and grey waistcoats moved among the white plastic tables. Hearing singing, Dan and I walked to the back of the cafe, where the picture on a giant TV screen quickly corrected our idea about the cafe's ownership. A women's choir was performing live in an Easter service from a church in Jounieh. Every few seconds the camera cut from the women's open mouths to an emaciated and bloody figurine of Christ on the cross.

We chose a table and I ordered in Arabic a medley of *hummous*, *tabbouleh*, *falafel* and chips from a fresh-faced boy of fifteen. He replied in Arabic and took our order with care.

But when I took Dan to the counter to choose his kebab, one of the older waiters waylaid me. He was tall with sharp cheekbones and greying hair.

'Oh!' he said in English. 'You speak Arabic!'

'Yes,' I replied, expecting the usual warm reaction. But the man screwed up his face.

'Arabic – rubbish!' he exclaimed.

'But you're Arabs!' I replied, with the brightest smile I could muster.

The man's eyes narrowed. 'No,' he snapped, 'We're not Arabs! We're Phoenicians!'

I looked at the waiter and thought of Raja's assertion that the Christians of Jbeil were not fanatical. I had read about Phoenicianism, the ideology which underpinned Maronite Christian supremacism. It had its roots in the mid-nineteenth century, when French and Lebanese Christian archaeologists began to explore Lebanon's past. In the 1920s and 1930s, Maronite ideologues used the archaeologists' work to "prove" an alleged link between ancient Phoenicia and the new state of Grand Liban. The 'true' Lebanese, they argued, were the direct descendants of a non-Arab Phoenician people and had inherited the latter's mercantile and intellectual talents. This highly dubious premise was used to bolster the view that the Christians should dominate the country politically at the expense of the Moslems, whose Arab identity was not in question.

When I returned to the table and lifted Dan onto the seat beside me, I glanced down at the man's feet. Beneath his neatly pressed trousers he wore black jack boots. I found myself wondering which militia he had fought in during the war.

9

'CHURCH BELLS SOUND MORE LOUDLY THAN BEFORE...'

Beirut, March 2002

✧

Life was restful in Jbeil, but I was feeling increasingly at a loss as to how to move my project forward. The people of Jbeil were pleasant enough, but I was not managing to have the kind of conversations with them which would enable me to answer the questions I had set myself. Every now and then I compared my experience thus far in Lebanon to my time in Iraqi Kurdistan. There, in 1993, people had literally queued up to tell me harrowing personal stories of what they had suffered under Saddam Hussein; whereas here, it was difficult to get beyond pleasantries. Part of the reason was the amount of time that had elapsed since the end of the civil war. Another was that, in Iraqi Kurdistan, I had had the assistance of a couple of women activists who had led me to people with interesting tales to tell, whereas in Lebanon my main contacts were with writers and intellectuals.

On Good Friday we woke to more grey skies and rain. I called a Lebanese historian, Ahmed Beydoun, whose name was on my list of contacts. Fortunately, he was free that afternoon. I left Dan and Paul playing trains in the salon and went into Beirut to meet him.

Mr Beydoun was a Shi'a from the south and, according to Hassan Daoud, one of the foremost writers in the Arab world. I must have been expecting to find him intimidating, for when he pushed open the door of the smart Hamra cafe where we had arranged to meet I felt a sense of relief. I saw a short man with a big head, cropped greying hair and a trim moustache. He wore a heavy wool cardigan over casual trousers and he smiled as he walked towards me with unassuming warmth.

After we had exchanged greetings and ordered tea I explained, in English, that I wanted to understand how the Lebanese lived with their memories of the war and how members of the different sects felt about each other.

'Those are good questions.' Ahmed Beydoun interlocked his large hands and rested them on the table. 'But first you should understand how the civil war changed Lebanese life. Can you follow if I speak in French?'

I wasn't at all sure that I could cope with historical analysis in French, but I agreed to try. For the next hour Mr Beydoun delivered his words with awe-inspiring clarity and precision, at the pace of a man giving a lecture to a large audience of students, but speaking so softly that no-one else in the cafe would have heard him. I grasped most, if not all, of what he said.

'The civil war,' Mr Beydoun began, 'exaggerated certain aspects of Lebanese social life which existed before the war and destroyed the counter balances which kept them in check. Before the war, for example, although there was a strong communal solidarity within each sect, there were also areas where people mixed with members of other sects. For example, in West Beirut, Moslems and Christians worked and lived together in the districts of Ras Beirut and Hamra; and in the Shouf mountain villages, Druze lived side by side with Maronite Christians.'

He stirred his tea and sighed. 'The effect of the war was to greatly exaggerate the cleavages between the communities. After the Mountain War in the Shouf between the Druze and Christians, for example, many Christians fled to the safety of East Beirut, and the mixed villages and districts were largely destroyed. So the communities became more separate and the opportunities for inter-communal communication were greatly reduced.

'This in turn had a negative effect on education. Prior to the war, poorer children of different sects had mixed in government schools, because the communities these served were mixed. Afterwards, with the segregation of communities, school children only mixed with children of the same sect.'

'Which made matters worse?'

'Precisely.'

I was beginning to realise that my question about how members of formerly warring sects were managing to live side by side was based on a false premise. These days, much more than before, the different sects lived separately, in their own areas.

'What happened in the south?' I asked. Traditionally, the southern rural population had been predominantly Shi'a with a substantial Christian minority. 'Were all the mixed villages destroyed?'

'Some villages were razed to the ground; in others the people fled, leaving the houses empty. In the south, two thirds of the population left their homes. *Two thirds.*' Mr Beydoun's gaze rested on my face, while he made sure that I had taken this in.

As a region the south had suffered more than any other part of Lebanon, and over a much longer period. For the south had borne the brunt of three decades of cross-border warfare, two Israeli invasions and many years of occupation. In March 1978, the Israelis had invaded as far as the Litani river, in response to a bomb attack by the PLO on a bus in Israel. During this incursion they killed approximately 2,000 Lebanese and Palestinians and sent another 250,000 into flight as refugees. Three months later they withdrew, after the passing of a number of UN resolutions and the installation of UNIFIL, a UN force with an international mandate to police the area. But before leaving, the Israelis created a buffer zone along the border, which they handed into the control of their proxy, the euphemistically named South Lebanon Army (SLA). Financed and equipped by Israel, the SLA was led by a Lebanese Christian, Major Sa'ad Haddad, and staffed by mainly Christian mercenaries recruited from villages in the border area.

Life remained extremely difficult for the southern population after the withdrawal, due to the continuation of Israeli cross-border raids and PLO retaliations. When the Israelis returned in June 1982, they sent a fresh column of southerners into flight towards Beirut. This time, the Israeli troops were to remain in occupation of much of the south until 1985. As well as imposing a military administration on the area, they did their best to disrupt the southern economy, destroying orchards and meadows and dumping large quantities of their own citrus fruit on the local market, at prices with which local producers could not compete. This, and brutal Israeli handling of the civilian population, deeply antagonised the Shi'a, who began to organise resistance operations under the auspices of their existing organisation, Amal, and their newly emerging organisation, Hizbullah.

When the troops partially withdrew from the south in the summer of 1985, they insisted on remaining in a 'security zone' along the southern border. This they continued to occupy until May 2000.

'Have the people who left their homes in the south in the '70s and '80s gone back?'

Mr Beydoun frowned. 'After the war the government put a lot of money into re-building villages in the south, but people were reluctant to return. You see, many of these villages were under Israeli occupation for twenty-two years. In that time, people had made their lives elsewhere, in Beirut, the USA, Canada, Australia... Some people returned, for example if they owned land in the south. But most went back only for a visit, to see what was once the village of their parents or grandparents and to claim their house, but not to live in it.'

I asked what Mr Beydoun thought about the war's impact on religion. Was it true, as several others had told me, that the war had made people more fanatical than they were before? His forehead creased into deep furrows.

'Before the war,' he replied, 'some communities were quite discreet in their religious practices. Now all that has changed and people go to church or mosque more as an act of communal solidarity than one of religion. Church bells sound more loudly than before,' he smiled at me sadly, 'with the help of electricity to amplify them. And the same is true of the call to prayer which blares from the loudspeakers.'

The Moslems had also begun to copy the Christians' taste for public rituals. In traditional Shi'ism, the believer does not pray in public at the mosque, but privately at home. Since the war, however, praying at the mosque had become a Shi'a duty. Another way in which the Shi'a had copied the Christians was in the creation of numerous new religious festivals. Before the war, they had only celebrated Ashura (the anniversary of the death of Hussein) and the feasts at the beginning and end of Ramadan. Now, they celebrated the births and deaths of all twelve of their Imams, with the result that there was a Shi'a festival to be celebrated most weeks throughout the year.

'But most people don't participate out of real religious feeling,' Mr Beydoun concluded with a look of distaste. 'Celebrating a festival has become a statement of your politics and identity. Outdoor religious processions have become like demonstrations. The call and response, between the *mullah* and the participants, are intended to make people believe that they are all the same.' He turned down the corners of his mouth in distaste.

When the waiter brought the bill, Mr Beydoun insisted on paying. 'Tell me,' he said as he took out his wallet, 'why does the British government slavishly support America in its foreign policy? What do they have to gain by this?'

'I think they have everything to lose,' I replied. 'And so do many people in Britain. But Tony Blair seems to enjoy playing the jet-lagged international diplomat. It's a good way to avoid domestic issues.'

10

ARAFAT UNDER SIEGE

Beirut, Jbeil and Tripoli, April 2002

After I thanked Ahmed Beydoun and said goodbye, I found a *servees* going to Dawra, the roundabout on the outskirts of East Beirut where the coastal buses began and ended their journeys. I got into the back beside a young woman and an old man. The driver, a large man of middle age, sat hunched behind the wheel, looking worried. Everyone in the car was listening intently to a news bulletin on the radio.

Yasir Arafat was under siege by the Israelis in his headquarters in Ramallah. The reporter described in an agitated voice how Israeli tanks had surrounded the compound and were pointing their gun turrets at its metal gates.

One by one the passengers got out, clicking their tongues in anger. I heard the driver cursing under his breath. Finally I asked him if I had understood correctly what was going on.

'They're at Arafat's door,' he cried, 'they want to kill him!'

I had lived in Ramallah in the summer of 1990 and I tried to imagine the scene. Critical though I was of Arafat as a leader, I was appalled by the prospect that he might be about to die at the hands of the Israelis.

'Sharon's a monster!' I exclaimed, wanting to let the driver know where my sympathies lay.

'Of course he is,' the driver replied. 'I should know, I'm Palestinian.'

Ariel Sharon is reviled by Palestinians as the man who bears ultimate responsibility for the massacre of Palestinian and Shi'a civilians at the Sabra and Shatila refugee camps in southern Beirut in September 1982. The killings were carried out by Maronite Christian militiamen of the Phalange militia, on the pretext of a search for the killers of president-elect Bashir Gemmayel. The massacre took place within sight and earshot of the occupying Israeli forces, who deliberately turned a blind eye to what was going on.[2]

'Where in Palestine are you from?' I enquired.

'From Nazareth. My family had fifty dunums of olive groves.' He slowed at traffic lights and glanced at me. 'Where are you from?'

'Britain.'

The driver shook his head. 'The deeds to my family's land are in your country: the British took them with them when they left.'

'Yes,' I nodded. This wasn't the first time a Palestinian had sought to remind me of Britain's contribution to the historic mess in which his people found themselves.

'Your family left in '48?' I ventured after a pause. The man didn't look old enough to have lived in Palestine himself. He was probably born in a camp in Lebanon.

'That's right, in '48.'

I was debating whether to tell the man that I had once lived in Ramallah when the lights changed and we surged towards the Dawra intersection. After I got out I was glad that I hadn't: I was ashamed of the fact that I had been free to live there, when he had never even seen his homeland.

Dawra was an ugly place dominated by a rickety black flyover. Cheap cafes lined the roundabout and buses circled slowly, their drivers shouting *Jounieh! Jounieh!* Taxi drivers stood by empty cars, talking and smoking in small, bad-tempered groups.

I was the only passenger waiting for a *servees* to Jbeil. I chatted with a short, red-faced Armenian driver in a black leather jacket who offered me coffee and promised that other travellers would appear shortly. He rubbed his hands together and looked up at me with an ingratiating leer, while talking about the Armenian community in Beirut and pointing

---

2   The Kahan Commission, the Israeli government's own commission of inquiry into the events at Sabra and Shatila, later found that Ariel Sharon bore 'personal responsibility' for what happened there.

out one of their churches. After half an hour he suggested that if I was in a hurry, and since it was a public holiday, I could pay for the whole taxi less any fares we might pick up along the way. Anxious not to be away from Dan for too long, I agreed.

A mile down the road we stopped for a young man who was going to Jounieh. He sat in the front and exchanged pleasantries with the driver, while the radio continued to describe events in the West Bank. When the man got out, I asked the driver what he thought about Arafat's plight.

'A hundred and fifty tanks have gone in!' His voice was full of glee. 'They've got him surrounded.' The speeedometer touched 120. 'The Arab world is full of Moslems,' he went on in a tone of disgust. 'They should all be killed! Kuwait, the Gulf, all the Arab countries are crawling with Moslems.' When I made no response, he lapsed momentarily into silence. Then he swivelled round in his seat, leaving one hand resting lightly on the steering wheel. 'The lad who just got out,' he jerked his head backwards, 'he was a Moslem.' He raised his upper lip and wrinkled his nose. 'Their skin smells bad!' He pulled at the slack skin on the inside of his forearm, to make sure I had understood. 'Skin! Bad smell! D'you understand me?'

It started to rain heavily as we reached Jbeil. I got out in the main street and ran through the cobbled *souq* and up the steps of Abi Chemmou. Elias stood in the lobby, his leather coat draped around his shoulders, watching the TV above the bar.

'*Bonsoir*,' he said, glancing at me. His eyes betrayed no emotion as they flicked back to the screen, where an Israeli tank blasted the wall of a Palestinian house.

'Have they said how many tanks the Israelis have sent in?' I was having trouble believing the Armenian's figure of 150.

Elias shrugged his shoulders and smiled nonchalantly. 'A lot. They're giving the Palestinians a good thrashing.'

I walked slowly up the spiral staircase, watching the rain drip off my jacket onto the wooden treads. Elias' attitude didn't really surprise me. Like many Maronites, he probably believed that the Palestinians' military activities in Lebanon had been the root cause of the civil war.

And although it didn't follow that the Palestinians in the West Bank deserved the beating they were getting today, there was some accuracy in the Maronite view. While the Palestinian presence in itself hadn't caused the war, the activities and conduct of the PLO had undoubtedly contributed to the destruction of the country.

On Easter Monday, weary of the unending rain, we hired a car and drove to Tripoli, half an hour up the coast. Tripoli was Lebanon's second city. It had a largely Sunni Moslem population and several Palestinian refugee camps.

After visiting the citadel and an eighteenth-century mosque, we spent a couple of hours wading the flooded alleys of the *souq*, where rain cascaded off corrugated iron roofs and boys swept water out of shoe shops with plastic brooms. Paul and I wore waterproofs and walking boots and Dan rode in the backpack on Paul's shoulders, sheltered by a little plastic canopy.

Unlike in Jbeil, where all the shops were shut, Tripoli's *souq* was having a normal working day; but business was quiet and by three o'clock many merchants had pulled down their shutters. Dan was nodding off to sleep when Paul stopped in the doorway of a tinbeater's workshop. Handcarved wooden spoons hung on strings beside metal soap moulds and aluminium oil cans with long, slender spouts.

Paul pulled the stopper out of an oil can and tried the handle. 'Dan would like one of those! He could use it as a watering can.'

Inside the shop, a man dressed in black sat under an electric bulb, alternately beating a piece of tin and heating it with a blow lamp. He was lean and bony with close cropped hair and a pointed chin. A softer-faced teenager stood in front of him. They spoke in low voices, glancing from time to time at the screen of a small television that flickered on a shelf a few feet away.

'*Salaamu a leekum*,' I said as I stepped towards the man in black, holding out some money to pay for the oil can.

'*A leekum issalaam!*' replied the tinbeater. As he fitted the can into a flimsy plastic bag, my eyes focussed for the first time on the pictures on the screen. Two Israeli tanks were rolling down Chicken Street in Ramallah, past the house where I had lived during the summer of 1990.

'*Itfaddali*,' said the tinbeater, nodding his head at the television and inviting me into the shop.

'Thanks,' I whispered, sinking onto the wooden stool which he offered me without taking my eyes off the screen. The tanks had stopped halfway down the hill and a crowd of children and youths stood in the road, pounding them with stones. Thick smoke clouded the air.

Paul took the oil can out of my hands. 'I'm going next door,' he said, 'I'll come back in a few minutes.'

'D'you want a coffee?' asked the tinbeater. As I looked up to murmur my assent, he held a rag over the mouth of a bottle and tipped it upside down. My nose filled with the smell of paraffin, mixed with the harsh aroma of his cigarette.

The boy disappeared for a few moments, returning with a tiny plastic cup of syrupy, bitter-sweet nectar. It was lethally strong and after three sips my head began to throb. On the screen the scene switched to Hebron where an Arab woman reporter described the mayhem before her eyes. She stood on a street corner, her hair blown about by the wind, visibly shaken. As I listened, my sense of shock turned to shame: for here I was having an easy time in Lebanon, while only 150 miles to the south, all this was happening. I would have been more use to the Palestinians at home, helping to organise protest demonstrations.

Behind me the man and boy clicked their tongues in anger.

11

'IN LEBANON WE LIKE BLONDS'

Beirut and Jbeil, April 2006

✧

To catch a *servees* to Beirut I had to climb onto the cardboard-thin
flyover that carried the coastal highway over Jbeil. At noon I stood
in the rain, watching the cars and lorries shoot past at seventy miles an
hour, feeling the flyover shake beneath my feet.

After less than thirty seconds an old, black mini-bus flashed its
lights, swerved off the road and stopped a few yards from me. I picked
up my haversack and ran towards it.

'Going to Beirut?' I shouted through the off-side window, over the
strains of a pop song on the radio. As the driver nodded, I saw that all
eight passengers were male.

The side door slid open. A single, bucket seat remained unoccupied,
beside a soldier in fatigues. I climbed onto it, clutching my haversack on
my knee.

No-one spoke as the minibus pulled away. I sat up straight, not
daring to lean back in case I landed on the knees of the man behind me.
A cool breeze blew in at the open window, spattering drops of rain on
my hands. The soldier sprawled beside me, tapping his boot in time with
the pop song. Every twenty seconds, a voice cut in with an advertisement
in French.

Was this an ordinary bus? I wondered. If so, why was I the only
female passenger? It was hard to imagine a Lebanese woman sitting
among these men. And why did nobody speak? Perhaps the Christian
Lebanese had acquired a European *froideur*. Elsewhere in the Arab world,
people travelling on public transport struck up long conversations.

After we had been going for about ten minutes, a convoy of
armoured vehicles rolled down the outside lane. Soldiers holding
rifles sat in the backs of trucks under open tarpaulins and the traffic
in our lane slowed to a walking pace. Not wanting to be stared at I gazed

at the floor, but I felt the soldiers' eyes upon me through the open window.

After the last truck had passed, the soldier seated beside me emitted a grunt and the bus pulled over to let him out. A young man moved forward to take the soldier's place. He was slight with a dark complexion and a boyish profile.

For several minutes we ground along at ten miles an hour. The radio went dead and the man behind me muttered under his breath and shuffled his knees against my back. When we passed a smashed up estate car on the hard shoulder, a murmur went around the bus. Seconds later, the traffic picked up speed again.

'That's what was holding us up!' the young man remarked to me in French. 'But where was the other car?'

'I only saw one.' I was glad to speak at last.

'Something must have hit it.' He smiled politely. 'You're a journalist?'

'No, I'm just visiting for a few weeks, from Britain.'

He smiled again. 'The reason I thought you were a journalist is that all the foreign women who came to cover the summit had short hair like yours.' An Arab summit had just finished in Beirut. 'Have you been to any other Middle Eastern countries?'

I named the countries I had visited and he asked me which of them I liked the best.

'Northern Iraq,' I replied without hesitating. The time I spent with the Iraqi Kurds in 1993 had been the richest and happiest period in my life. The man looked disappointed.

'I'd like to ask you a question,' he began again after a moment. 'Why does the British government support American foreign policy?'

I sighed and shook my head. 'Personally I think it's very stupid. Bush's policies are dangerous.'

He nodded. 'But the Arabs do stupid things, too.' He dropped his voice. 'You know,' he looked half embarassed, 'we often say bad things about the Arabs.'

'I've noticed that.'

'Particularly us Christians. But don't quote me!' He looked worried. 'Or I'll really be in trouble.'

A moment later the boy told me he was from Jounieh and a student of Computers, Communications and Engineering. When he finished his studies he hoped to visit Europe. I was seized by a sudden curiosity.

Here was a young Lebanese Christian, of reasonable intelligence, and one who could see the folly of both Arab and western politicians. 'Have you been to south Lebanon?' I asked.

The man looked uncomfortable. 'No,' he replied, smiling faintly.

'Why not?'

'No particular reason.'

'Are you afraid to go?'

He looked sheepish. 'A little. If I went, I would go with friends, not alone.'

'Why?'

'Oh... just it would be better to go with friends.'

'Have most young people from Jounieh been to the south?'

The young man shook his head. 'Of course not. All the houses in the south have been destroyed. There's nothing to go there for!' He paused. 'Unless you're in the army,' he added, 'and they oblige you to go.'

While I was mulling on this, he asked me which people in the Arab world I considered the best looking. I hesitated before answering. By my lights the Kurds were by far the most striking, with their sharp bone structures and thick, wiry hair, but I didn't want to hurt his feelings. 'I guess there are good-looking people everywhere,' I answered lamely.

He shook his head. 'The Lebanese are the best looking Arabs.' His tone implied that this was a matter of scientific fact. A moment later, his eyes lit up. 'In Lebanon,' he said, 'we like blonds. That's why the soldiers in the convoy stared at you.' I smiled to myself. My hair was reddish brown, but for years Arabs and Kurds had been telling me I was blond.

Rim had told me to wait for her on the corner of Rue Hamra by the Cafe Modca. I had not been standing there more than a minute when she pulled up beside me in a low-slung silver car. She looked small and fragile, wrapped in a grey coat with a shawl collar.

'It must be stressful driving in Beirut,' I remarked as we drove to her apartment.

'It's terrible!' She lit a cigarette on the dashboard lighter and wound down the window. 'There are no rules, everybody does as he likes.' A moped hurtled towards us. 'You see! This is a one-way street, but always somebody decides to come the other way.'

We parked below Rim's building and took the lift to the fifth floor. As we came through her front door, a slim boy in a black T-shirt and shorts opened a door halfway down the corridor.

'Hi Mum,' he called in Arabic, staring at me and then smiling. 'I ate lunch already. Dad's gone to work.'

'Okay, *habibi*. This is Teresa, from England.'

'Hi, Teresa.' The boy shifted effortlessly into English.

Rim ruffled her son's hair as he came to shake my hand. 'He's at a French medium school but his English is perfect. He learned it by watching TV! American cartoons, all day long. He never had a formal lesson.' Her expression suggested she was proud of her son's facility, but disliked the diet that had produced it. 'So, Teresa,' she ushered me into an L-shaped living room, the walls of which were lined with books. 'I'll show you some paintings and then we'll have lunch.'

I followed her into the base of the L, where thirty or forty canvases were stacked behind a cabinet. She pulled out four and propped them against the furniture. In each one a portrait of a woman was juxtaposed with a mask. The portraits were harsh, realist representations, whereas the masks were painted more suggestively, with loose brush strokes that blurred into one another.

'Are they self portraits?'

Rim nodded. 'I told you about these faces on the wall. This gave me the idea.' She was pulling out larger canvases from the back of the pile. In one a woman in a sleeveless red dress sat at a table with a glass of wine. 'Did you know that I was sick?'

'Yes,' I replied, 'Hassan told me.' The woman's arms looked firm and strong but her expression was pensive and uneasy.

'It was two or three years ago, I'm getting my strength back now. I was very, very sick. For three months I couldn't even sit up. So anyway,' Rim sped on before I could comment, 'the reason I'm telling you this is that I did a series of paintings about being in hospital.' She rested a large standing figure of a woman on a chair. In place of clothing, tiny paper tabs embossed with hospital numbers covered the skin. 'I did these paintings after I got better,' Rim explained. 'I didn't care whether anyone would want to look at them, or buy them. I did them *for me*, to help me digest the experience.'

'And then I had an exhibition, and in one week I sold twenty-five paintings.'

'You must have been pleased!'

'I don't know, I was so surpised that people liked them.'

After I had spent some time admiring the paintings, she re-stacked them and led me into a bare, white-washed kitchen, where the smell of meat fried in garlic lingered in the air.

'Look, I made a dish called Darwish's worry beads, can you eat this? It's from the south, it has a little bit of everything in it, rice, vegetables, meat. It's poor man's food!'

'It looks delicious.' I thought of my artist father, who had brought me up on poor man's food, and felt at home.

'Have you always lived in the centre of Beirut?' I asked as we sat down at the dining table in the living room.

'No, in '73, when I was nine, we moved to Dahyya. It wasn't a big Shi'a suburb then like it is now, it was a new area with small buildings. There were orange and lemon trees and some farms even, it was beautiful. We spent one and a half years there but when the war started we couldn't stay. For the two years of the first war, we spent some of our time in the south, in my mother's village near Armoun. And then we came back to Beirut.'

'Were you here right through the war?'

'Have some of these.' Rim pushed a dish of bitter, green olives towards me. 'Yes, I was here the whole time,' she went on, 'I never wanted to leave.'

I looked at her. Through her teens and early twenties she had lived with shelling, car bombs, kidnappings and the Israeli bombardment. It was hardly surprising that she seemed so full of nervous energy.

She returned my gaze. 'It wasn't how you would imagine it,' she said. 'There wasn't bombing all the time. Life went on. I continued with my studies, first at school, then university. Then I was painting. You lived your life and when something happened you went down to the shelter in the basement, and when it was over you came out and lived your life again.' I had heard the same from other people: Beirutis had shown an extraordinary resilience in the way they carried on with daily life.

'You see, if you wanted to survive you had to live normally; although of course it wasn't really normal.' She stopped with her fork in mid-air. 'And there were times when the tension became unbearable and you took to living to extremes: at one point I drank a lot, for example.'

The phone rang in the hall and Rim got up to answer it. When she came back I asked how much she thought about the war years, now.

'It's not like you sit at every meal and remember it,' she replied, picking up a piece of bread. 'But sometimes it takes just the tiniest hint or a small thing happening – a word, a smell, a scene – and it all comes back. Like you open a Pandora's box and all these things jump out.' Her deep, melodic voice filled the stillness in the room. 'I don't spend my life thinking about the past; but it hits me, suddenly. Like now, for example, I've been sitting in front of the TV these last 3 days seeing what's happening in Ramallah, and all I'm thinking about is what it was like here during the Israeli invasion, in 1982.'

Although the stated aim of the Israelis in 1982 was to drive the PLO fighters out of Lebanon, they deliberately inflicted heavy aerial bombardments on residential districts, first in Sidon, then in West Beirut. Thousands of civilians died in basement shelters when their five- or six-storey apartment blocks collapsed on top of them. In Sidon, more than a hundred died in a shelter beneath a primary school. As if that were not sufficient cruelty, the Israelis cut off the water supply to West Beirut during the hottest weeks of the summer.

'At that time I felt much stronger than I do now,' Rim went on. 'I was under siege and yet it was probably the only period during the war when I felt strong. During the Israeli invasion I felt clear that I didn't want to leave Beirut, that this was where I should be, although I was only 18. I was with my family, my sisters and my parents and none of us wanted to leave. We felt, *if the Israelis want to kill us, let them kill us, but we're not leaving, we're here.* We felt strong even without doing anything: just by being here we had a sense of meaning.' She let out a sigh of despair. 'But now, I feel meaning*less*, because I can't be there in Ramallah. I'm not a Palestinian, but you cannot see injustice and just sit back and do nothing!' Her voice filled with anger. 'I feel so weak and useless, because I can't do anything to help them. And I keep remembering 1982. Our apartment was destroyed by a rocket and we went to my aunt's house and sat there for a while, and then that house was destroyed, too. We changed apartment four times in Beirut, and each time, thank god, we were in the shelter when the apartment was hit. At that time, things were destroyed and you re-built them. They were destroyed and you re-built them.'

I listened to Rim's sing-song voice and recognised something that I had encountered before, in Iraqi Kurdistan: the deep sense of purpose experienced by people engaged in a collective struggle to survive.

Rim sat back in her chair. 'I always loved being in Beirut. During the war people were more tender with each other, closer, more real. I never wanted to leave the city.'

The door opened and Rim's son burst into the room. A look of surprise spread across his face as he took in that I was still here.

'Mum,' he began, 'can I use dad's computer?'

Rim smiled at him. 'Of course you can. I won't be long, *habibi*.'

'He's a good looking boy,' I said as the door closed again. I was trying to imagine what Dan would be like when he was nine.

'You know,' Rim began, 'the only time I thought of leaving was just recently. I started working on an application to emigrate to Australia. But my husband convinced me that it would be a mistake.'

'What made you want to go, when you'd never wanted to leave before?'

Rim pushed aside her plate and rested her chin in her hands. 'Probably because of my son. I wanted him to grow up to become a citizen, a human being, someone with rights. You see, even after all these years of war, Lebanon is in a mess politically. You can't trust any politician. Suddenly you see that the army is taking control of things... But it wouldn't have been easy to leave, because I'm very attached to Beirut. And with what's happening now in the West Bank... If I can be here in Beirut, not far from Ramallah, feeling so angry and depressed, imagine what it would be like if I was in Australia!'

'You'd feel very isolated,' I agreed. 'I don't think many people would be interested in events in Palestine.'

'Whereas at least here I can go to a cafe and talk about it. Also, I wanted my son to have another life, but who am I to judge what's best for him? He's nine years old now, and his memory is starting to flourish. He has his life here, his friends, his city, his school. He knows where he is and he knows he's Lebanese, he knows his village is Bint al Jbeil, he knows that his grandma is here, his friends are there. If I took him away it would be very difficult for him. Even to change school is difficult, but to go to another country, a different world? Who would be sure that when he was eighteen he wouldn't start looking for his roots and come back? So no, I don't want to make that kind of decision for him.'

12

SECRET MEETINGS

Jbeil, April 2002

The rain stopped an hour before dusk. Having spent the day cooped up in our attic salon, we were desperate for some fresh air. Wrapped in waterproofs and walking boots, we climbed down the spiral staircase and set off up the cobbled arcade of the reconstructed *souq*. The shops had already closed and there was hardly anyone about. The small, egg-shaped stones glistened with rainwater.

Dan walked a few feet from Paul and me, chattering to himself as he went and pointing to the sky. 'Blue guy up dere,' he kept repeating, 'Blue guy up dere.' He wore his trousers tucked into wellies, his grey and black anorak curving over his tummy and a blue woolly hat pulled down over his ears.

We were halfway up the *souq* when the sun broke through the clouds, casting a shaft of pure, sweet light on the cobbles. Turning I saw it fall, too, on the faces of a family who walked behind us. They were spread out across the alleyway, a man with plump cheeks and and a big belly, a woman in a black headscarf, a young boy and a small girl. I thought they had just come from the mosque across the way from Abi Chemmou.

We didn't greet each other but I noticed that the man was watching Dan with a look of delight. When we reached the steps at the top of the *souq*, we turned left towards the new city and the other family were about to turn right. But as I glanced at their backs, the man turned and walked purposefully towards Dan, his cheeks bulging in a smile of great tenderness. Dan stood on the top step, still talking to himself. When the man reached him he squatted down, framed Dan's face with his hands and kissed him on the cheek. Dan stared up at the man, non-plussed. Then the man beckoned to his little daughter. She came hesitantly and stood in front of Dan, but when her father bade her kiss him, she backed away.

We had all stopped by now – the wife, the children, Paul and I – and stood in the rain-sodden light, watching the exchange. The man, still smiling, stooped and kissed Dan again. There was something lovely in the way he did it, as if he felt a pure, uncontainable affection for this child who hailed from another world. Then he straightened up and walked away.

✧

Our five weeks were up and we were packing to go home. When I went downstairs to pay the bill, Elias was leaning on the bar, watching Ariel Sharon inform the world's press that he would continue his operations in the West Bank until the bitter end.

'Sharon came here once,' Elias announced as he turned towards me. His leather coat hung limply from his shoulders.

'What, to Abi Chemmou?'

Elias gestured at the terrace, where rain lashed the plastic sheeting that served as an awning. 'He had lunch at that table over there with Bashir Gemmayel, in 1982.'

I was taken aback. 'Before the invasion?'

'Before, yes.'

Sharon had had frequent contact with the Lebanese Christian right in the months leading up to the invasion. Together they had planned that Israeli troops would move up from the south to join Gemmayel's Lebanese Forces in East Beirut, cutting off the Syrians' supply lines to the city and encircling West Beirut.

'How did he get here?'

'Came by sea. Brought a unit of Israeli soldiers with him.' Elias gazed at me steadily and I had the feeling he was telling the truth.

'But why Abi Chemmou?' I inquired. *Did you want him here?* was the real question in my mind, but I managed to stop myself from asking it.

Elias scratched his chin as his eyes drifted to the spiral staircase, where Paul's boots were appearing from above. 'They all came here,' he said enigmatically. 'All the Christian leaders used that room upstairs for their political discussions.'

My mouth fell open. 'But I thought it was a wedding salon..!'

Elias smiled. 'In the last few years, I've used it for weddings. But this was during the war. I had the restaurant down here and I used to let out that room for secret meetings. I had them all here at one time or another – Dany Chamoun, Raymond Edde, Pierre Gemayel, Bashir Gemmayel, Samir Geagea.' He reeled off a list of famous names, including most of the leading figures of the Christian right.

'But how could the meetings be secret, with the restaurant just down below?'

'Easy. Nobody knew there was a room up there.'

'But the staircase?'

'Nobody knew where it led. The leaders stayed up there for hours on end. I used just one, trusted employee to make their refreshments, and he never left the room.' Out of the corner of my eye I saw Paul hovering discreetly with Dan, pretending to look at the oil paintings.

'Did you feel okay about hosting all these guys?' I asked bluntly.

'Look, politically I'm not with any of them, I'm independent.' Elias met my gaze. 'And personally, I don't like war, nor the idea of people carrying weapons. At the beginning of the war I thought we shouldn't fight. But in the end I saw that we had to, to prevent the Palestinians taking over the whole country. Do you remember Arafat's famous statement, "The road to Palestine passes through Jounieh"?'

'What did he mean by that?'

'He wanted to take the whole country. He'd have come here to Jbeil, with the Moslem Lebanese, if the Christians hadn't taken up arms against him.'

PART TWO

13

CHANGE

England, 2002–2006

We went back to Lebanon in the autumn of 2002, but the trip was a disaster. Dan picked up a virus on the day we arrived, and was sick for the following ten days. By the time he recovered, I was going down with the same bug and we decided to cut our losses and return home. From then on, my project seemed doomed, with one obstacle after another getting in the way. Each spring for the next three years I tried to book a trip to Leb-Leb, as Dan called it; but there were always powerful reasons militating against it. Some were to do with the political situation in the Middle East, while others were personal. In 2003, the Americans and British invaded Iraq on 20 March, creating a wave of fear and uncertainty throughout the region. In the spring of 2004, the situation in Iraq was deteriorating. The Lebanese friends from whom I sought advice said that we would probably be fine in Beirut as a western family, but that they couldn't be *sure*, especially as I would be going about asking questions, and that please if anything went wrong I mustn't hold them responsible. The tinge of anxiety in their voices was enough to put me off.

In February 2005, the assassination of Rafiq Hariri triggered mass demonstrations and a sit-in in downtown Beirut, with the twin demands of democracy and Syrian withdrawal. This was the birth of the so-called Cedar Revolution.

It would have been an interesting time to be in Lebanon; but by now Paul and I were in the process of separation. The decision had been mutual, but the process was painful nonetheless.

It was not until that summer that I was able to begin dreaming about a trip to the Middle East. By now we had re-established our lives in two separate households and Dan was getting used to the idea that he lived with me but made frequent visits to his dad. To begin with, dreaming was all I could manage. Life was demanding with a five-year-old to care for, a part-time job as a child abuse lawyer and the challenge of extracting myself from a long relationship.

In June 2005, Paul took Dan on holiday without me for the first time and I went to Cyprus for a week. I had spent many a happy hour there in my early thirties, painting the rocky hillsides and the sea and hanging out with my friend Nancy who lived there.

Although I found it hard to get on a plane without Dan, Cyprus was a good place in which to take stock of the changes in my life, and Nancy was still there to keep me company. I took my paints, hired a moped and soon began to enjoy myself. On the second morning, my short wave radio picked up the news in Arabic. Listening to the language made me think of Lebanon, a mere stone's throw away across the water. This in turn provoked in me a huge sense of dissatisfaction about my unfinished project there. Back in England a week later, I resolved to book a trip to Lebanon for spring 2006. By then, I hoped, Dan would be settled in our new arrangements and I would have more energy and mental space. I half wanted to take Dan with me; but after looking carefully at the risks, decided it would be unwise.

Through the winter of 2005/2006 I worked on my spoken Arabic and read books about Lebanon. I was excited about the prospect of a trip to Beirut, and only a little nervous. As the time drew nearer, however, my anxieties grew. Try as I might, I could not get out of my mind the idea that I might be kidnapped. There was little rational basis for this, since kidnappings had not occurred in Lebanon since the end of the civil war in 1990: it was in Iraq and Palestine that the tactic was becoming a daily occurrence. But fear is not a rational thing.

My anxiety was compounded by the guilt I felt about leaving Dan. Although I was only planning to be away for two weeks and Paul was keen to have him to stay, I knew Dan would feel hurt when I explained that I was going to Leb-Leb without him. We were very close and he generally wanted to go everywhere that I went.

I was determined that nothing should be said in his hearing that might suggest that I was taking any risk. I avoided mentioning my plans to many of our friends because I didn't want anyone to say, in Dan's presence, 'but is it safe? Are you sure?' This strategy made me feel even worse. For I was keeping a secret of something which, if it materialised, might turn his life upside down. In bad moments, usually in the middle of the night, I found myself imagining what it would be like to languish alone in an underground cell, knowing that my absence was causing torment to my son and family, and being unable to do anything to free myself. In the back of my mind, at these moments, was the thought of Margaret Hassan, the British woman married to an Iraqi who had been kidnapped and brutally murdered in Iraq in 2004. The facts that Iraq was not Lebanon, and I not her, provided little comfort.

14

HANAN'S AUNTS

Tariq al Jaddideh, Beirut, March 2006

The car journey through the darkness took only six minutes. Paralysed as I was by an unpleasant blend of weariness and anxiety, I barely had time to settle on the back seat beside Hanan and her five-year-old son Karim. The pain I had felt when I said goodbye to Dan in the school playground that morning was still ricocheting around my system and the only thing I felt sure of was that the sooner I arrived in Lebanon, the sooner I could leave again. I leant my tired, tear-choked head against the headrest and set myself to study the profile of Hanan's twenty-two-year-old brother, Jawad.

Hanan was twenty-five and lived near me in England. For the last six months I had been seeing her weekly to brush up my Lebanese Arabic, until by coincidence we had found ourselves flying to Beirut on the same day. Hanan's family were Sunni Moslems, her father Syrian, her mother Lebanese. She was taking Karim to visit her grandfather and aunts and had invited me to spend what remained of my first night in Beirut at her grandfather's home in a district called Tariq al Jaddideh.

Jawad sat twisting towards Hanan from the front passenger seat, his voice animated with excitement and laughter as they verbally continued the passionate greeting I had witnessed on the forecourt of the arrivals bay. Based on previous visits to Beirut, I was expecting the journey from the airport to take another twenty minutes; but, long before we could possibly have reached the city, the car left the motorway, sped down a handful of side streets and glided to a halt. I must have been close to sleep, for as we drew up I had the impression we were parking on sand, in a place where no vehicle had passed for weeks or months. As the doors cracked open and Jawad and his driver friend leapt out, a deep silence enveloped the car. I tensed instantly, suspecting that something was wrong. For no way was this the noisy, night-living city I remembered.

To confuse me even further, as I unfolded my legs and staggered out onto the 'sand', I saw a vast awning of faded, stripy canvas suspended from a building in front of me. On the far side of the narrow street another awning hung down, and another, the fabric utterly still in the breeze-less night.

'Why's it so quiet?' I breathed to Hanan, who stood watching her tall, denim-clad sibling pull her huge bags from the boot of the car. Karim lolled against her legs, his head resting on her stomach.

'Everyone is sleeping,' she replied. 'It's four o'clock in the morning, don't forget.'

When Jawad lifted my bag onto the ground, I followed Hanan and Karim towards the awning-clad building. We dragged the bags up a flight of grimy steps, towards a heavy wooden door.

'*Ma eindak al muftaah, Jawad?*' (Don't you have the key?) Hanan turned round and called to her brother, who was following with the rest of the bags. I sensed from the way she spoke that she had no compunction about making demands on him. As the oldest sibling and the wife of an Englishman, she felt it was Jawad's duty to be at her beck and call during her infrequent visits home. Judging from the adoring way he had gazed at her in the car, he clearly found her attitude acceptable. I watched as she took hold of the old-fashioned latch and rattled the door, making a noise which seemed disproportionately loud in the silence of the night.

'*Ma eindi muftaah,*' (I don't have a key). Jawad leapt up the steps and reached us as the door opened inwards. He gestured to me to enter ahead of him.

As we passed through the outer door into the apartment, I was dimly aware of a small figure in long johns disappearing through an inner door. We were in a small, dingy living room, lit by a single bulb which hung from the centre of the ceiling. Sofas and armchairs in faded, blue chenille crowded the walls.

'Have a seat.' Hanan waved me to a chair, flopped down on a sofa and began to remove her leather boots. I watched her slender figure, pretty in the chic black dress she had chosen to travel in, her thick black hair falling over her shoulders. I took off my coat, sat down and gazed around me. A large, ancient looking television sat on a piece of heavy wooden furniture at one end of the room. A low, battered coffee table occupied the centre of the floor. Hanan had told me her grandfather was poor. Behind the sofa where she sat, resting her legs over a bolster, an internal window opened onto another room, where the grandfather lay sleeping. I wondered that our noise hadn't woken him up.

'You like a tea?' Jawad stood over me.

'No thank you.' I forced a tired smile.

'Want to sleep?' Hanan swung her feet onto the floor. She had told me on the plane that she would be staying up all night to talk with her brother, but that I could sleep if I wanted to. She disappeared through a door and came back a moment later. 'You can lie down in there, next to my aunt.' She opened a door in the heavy piece of furniture and pulled out a thick blanket. 'Take this.'

I took the blanket, pulled my Dunlopillo pillow out of my suitcase and crept through the door, not wanting to wake the aunt. I carry this pillow with me everywhere, since to lay my head on anything else risks irritating an old whiplash injury in my neck.

Two large beds rammed together filled the centre of the room, leaving a narrow pathway between their foot and a tall, rickety wardrobe. The aunt lay curled on her side on the first bed, a blanket pulled up over her face. Her form was small and delicate and I felt no reluctance to lie down beside her. I kneeled up on the bed, took hold of the lumpy bolster which lay across its head, and moved it to a chair. If I laid my head on that, tomorrow my neck would be in agony.

While the aunt continued to sleep, I removed a few of my clothes, piled them on the corner of the bed and laid my pillow where the bolster had been. But just as I was about to lie down and wrap myself in the blanket, the aunt turned over, stretched out an arm and seized my pillow, uttering an incomprehensible string of words as she did so.

'*La, la, la,*' I whispered (no, no, no), taking hold of the other side of the pillow and tugging it away from her. In my disorientated state I couldn't remember the Arabic word for pillow, but one thing was clear to me: the pillow was not negotiable. As the aunt propped herself up on an elbow and peered at me through half-closed eyes, I dragged the bolster towards her with my free hand. 'You have this one,' I mumbled in Arabic, 'I need the one I brought with me.' By a miracle she seemed to understand my meaning, thrust my pillow back towards me and went back to sleep. Deeply relieved, I lay down two feet from her, wrapped my arms lovingly around my own delicious pillow and shut my eyes.

When I woke in the late morning, the bed beside me was empty except for a rumpled blanket. I sat up for a moment, then lay back down again, not ready for the day. When my eyes were fully open I stared at the ceiling, trying to make sense of the muted sounds that came my way. I could still hear no traffic, and wondered again if we were really in Beirut. Perhaps Tariq al Jaddideh was much further from the centre than Hanan had told me. From the next room I could hear the television, and the loud voices of two or three women. It sounded almost as if they were having a row, but every now and then I discerned a squawk of laughter.

Thoughts of Dan were pressing in on me, causing a pinched feeling around my heart. It felt so peculiar to have left the world that I shared with him and catapulted myself into this new and unfamiliar place. Did he understand how far away I was? I hoped not. I dragged myself up off the bed, searched in my bag for my mobile and sent a text to Paul to say I had arrived safely.

When I walked into the living room twenty minutes later, two women looked up. The small woman sitting in the chair nearest the door was dressed in an old-looking T shirt, a pair of leggings which ended just below the knee and a headscarf. It was an eccentric outfit and I wondered if she had just been doing the cleaning. She smiled, rose to her feet and stretched out her hand, leaving a cigarette smouldering in an ashtray.

'I am Ruhiyya,' she told me in a husky voice, 'Hanan's aunt. Welcome to Lebanon.' She darted towards me with noticeable energy and kissed me on the cheek, right, left, right. There was a sharpness in her features which gave the impression of impatience or intelligence, or a mixture of the two. I found it impossible to divine her age, but later that day after I had met several more of Hanan's aunts, I worked out that she must be forty.

As Ruhiyya sat down I turned to the woman who had risen from the seat beside her.

'I am Muna,' she announced with a smile. Muna was broad and buxom, about as different from Ruhiyya as it is possible for two sisters to be. She was dressed in a smart black trouser suit and wore a dark red bandeau across her forehead, lightening the severity of her black head scarf. 'You slept well?' she enquired as she sat down and lit a cigarette, leaning back in her armchair and regarding me with keen curiosity.

'Very well, thank you.' I was conscious of Ruhiyya scrutinising me, too, from behind a swirl of smoke.

'She didn't disturb you?' Muna jerked her head in Ruhiyya's direction.

I looked at Ruhiyya. This, then, was my sleeping companion of the early hours. 'Not at all, I hope I didn't disturb her.'

Muna slapped her thigh and burst out laughing. 'But she tried to steal your pillow! Ha, ha, ha! She told me all about it.'

Ruhiyya was laughing too. 'I was asleep when you came in, I was dreaming I found a handsome man beside me in the bed, I reached out to touch him and... you wrenched him away from me!'

As the laughter died down, Hanan came into the room, asking where her grandfather was. She looked remarkably alert for one who had not slept, still dressed in the black dress of the day before.

'He's in his workshop.' Ruhiyya gestured towards the street door.

Hanan had told me in England that her grandfather worked as a cobbler. 'He got up this morning just after I lay down,' she went on, yawning. 'It was seven a.m. and I was exhausted.' She pointed through the internal window to the adjoining room, where her grandfather had been sleeping when we arrived. Two old-fashioned iron bedsteads stood side by side. 'I was lying on that bed there. When he saw me, he was really upset. He stood by the bed, saying "how can you go to sleep now, when I have just woken up and want to see you? I want to kiss you, I want to hug you, and all you think about is going to sleep...!"'

'What a lovely grandfather!' I cried, thinking how lucky she was.

'All my family are the same, when I come from England.' She smiled. 'After I said hello to my grandfather, I slept about one hour and a half and then my aunties started to arrive.' She waved in the direction of Muna and Ruhiyya. 'They woke me up, and we went to drink tea at the house of my aunt Nadia. She lives just round the corner, opposite this building.'

Muna had got up and was making coffee in the kitchen. She came through carrying a tray of tiny cups and placed one on the low table in front of me. 'Where did you learn Arabic, Teresa?' She took a cup for herself and sat down heavily in her armchair. By English standards she was mildly overweight, but the taut brown skin of her cheeks and arms had an attractive, healthy glow. To the average Arab man, I thought, Muna would be voluptuous, not fat. She radiated good humour and I liked her a lot.

'A long time ago,' I began, 'I lived in Palestine.'

'Your accent is Palestinian,' Ruhiyya was still watching me from behind a fresh curtain of smoke. The pile of cigarette butts mounted up in the ashtray.

'Then I went to Iraq,' I went on. 'People laughed at me because I sounded Palestinian, so I had to learn the Iraqi accent. *Shlonich...*' I cited the Iraqi way of saying 'how are you?' to a woman, which brought smiles from Muna and Ruhiyya. 'And now I'm trying to learn to sound Lebanese...'

'Good,' said Muna with approval, 'good, you speak well. Arabic is difficult...'

I knew she was being kind, but I felt grateful. 'I always thought Lebanese Arabic would be the same as Palestinian,' I went on, 'but lots of words are different.'

'Ruhiyya should know,' Muna replied, 'She has Palestinian friends.' She lit a cigarette.

'Do you?' Hanan took a cup of coffee and sat down beside Ruhiyya. 'Teresa wants to meet some Palestinians. Can you introduce her to anyone?'

Ruhiyya wrinkled up her nose. 'There are lots of Palestinians in this area, it's not difficult to meet them.' She looked uneasy.

'How come there are so many?'

She made a gesture of disdain, pursing up her lips and thrusting her chin into the air. 'We are just a stone's throw from Sabra and Shatila. You can take her there, Hanan. Sabra's just down the road.'

'Do you know people in Sabra?' I wasn't going to give up easily.

Ruhiyya picked up her cigarette packet and pulled out another cigarette. 'Sure,' she replied, 'I have friends.'

'We used to live there,' Hanan added, 'when I was a little girl. When I was three in 1982, during the Israeli invasion, my parents abandoned our rented apartment in Sabra and fled to my father's parents in Syria. When we arrived, we turned on the TV and saw our old apartment block collapsing in a pile of rubble.'

I clicked my tongue. 'Do you still have family in Sabra?'

'Not now, we only lived there then because it was cheap.'

Muna was frowning. 'Sabra is a very poor area. Only very poor people live there. It is dirty, scruffy, the roads are just dirt, not tarmac.' I understood her to mean that Sabra would no longer be good enough for a member of her family.

'*I* didn't even go there when Hanan's mum was living in Sabra,' Ruhiyya added. 'I was in Brazil.'

I turned to her. 'What were you doing in Brazil?'

'I was there for nine years.' She reached up suddenly, removed her headscarf and tossed her head, so that her short brown hair fell out around her face. 'With my husband.' She spread the scarf across her knees, smoothing out the crumpled bit which had been tied beneath her chin.

'What was it like?'

'Poor. Very poor. Not like Sabra: much, much worse. But we did okay there, when my husband was alive. We had a shop.'

I gazed at Ruhiyya, wanting to know more but worried she might not like it if I asked too many questions. 'Have you just recently come back to Lebanon?'

She was folding the scarf, ready to put it on again. 'I came back in '93, after my husband was killed. I had three children by then, I couldn't live there alone.' She spoke without emotion, and I sensed that she didn't object to my questions.

'Your husband...' I began.

'Robbers. Gang of them came into the shop one day and shot him dead.' She glanced at me, wanting a reaction.

I breathed in sharply.

'Happened all the time in the area where we lived. People were poor, so they turned to crime.'

Muna shook her head, seemingly appalled that her sister could be so matter of fact. A moment later she stubbed out her cigarette and stood up. 'Excuse me, I have to pray.' She left her cigarette packet on the coffee table and walked into the bedroom.

'How old are your children now?' I asked Ruhiyya. Hanan had told me Ruhiyya lived with her grandfather in the apartment.

Ruhiyya thought for a moment. 'Fourteen, sixteen and nineteen. The younger two are in boarding school, the oldest one works.'

'It's because she's a widow and she doesn't have money,' Hanan explained softly, perching on the arm of a chair. 'The government pays for her children to go to boarding school. It makes life easier for her, she doesn't have to feed them. They come home every Saturday and go back on Sundays.'

✧

'Anything you need while you're in Beirut, please, I am happy to help you.' Jawad announced as we walked down the steps and into the street.

'Thank you, you're helping me already.' I blinked in the sunlight, which seemed bright after the gloom of the apartment. We were on our way to the phone shop, to get a Lebanese sim card for my mobile. 'How come you speak such good English?' Jawad had flat, pale cheeks with golden freckles, a long nose and grey eyes. He had grown up in Syria, and come to Beirut as a student.

'From the university. All our lessons are in English.'

We stepped off the pavement into the road to avoid a pair of women who stood resting their shopping bags against their shins, locked in animated conversation.

Small cars and mopeds were parked along the kerb, but the road itself was empty. High above both pavements, paint peeled from the stucco of the apartment buildings.

'What are you studying?' A drop of rain landed on my cheek, and another on my hair.

'Computer engineering. At the Arab university, not far from here.' He gestured behind us with a long, slender arm. 'How much d'you want to pay for the sim card?'

'As little as possible.'

We stopped at the end of the street, on the corner of a bigger road with moving traffic.

'Ninety units is sixty-five dollars; forty-five units, maybe forty-two.' He smiled at me, slightly anxious, as if he felt responsible for the outrageous prices. 'But we'll ask if they can give you a better deal. The man knows me.' I followed him along the pavement, glancing into the shops as we passed. They were small, neighbourhood businesses: an ironmongers, a bakery, a shoe shop. From every window, the smiling face of Rafiq Hariri gazed out at us, his pink cheeks pudgy, his pepper and salt hair neatly trimmed.

The massive car bomb used to assassinate Hariri on 14 February 2005 also killed twenty-two members of his entourage. Although the UN-backed investigation into the assassination was still going on, the background to the bomb was thought to lie in the Syrian perception of Hariri during the preceding few years as de facto leader of a movement opposed to its presence in Lebanon. The movement had the support of the USA, which in September 2004 had obtained, with France, the passing by the UN of a resolution calling for Syrian withdrawal (and the disarming of Hizbullah). Hariri's assassination had been greeted with excitement by the American government, which believed the moment had arrived to push the Syrians out of Lebanon. Meanwhile, in Lebanon, the 'opposition' – a loose coalition consisting of Sunnis, Druze and many but not all Christians, organised under the banner of the 'Cedar Revolution' – began to agitate openly for Syrian withdrawal and democratisation.

The Cedar Revolutionaries were only one tendency, however, in Lebanese politics: an equally powerful combination of forces would have preferred the Syrians to stay. Two mass demonstrations in March 2005 had given names to the new groupings. On March 8, some 400,000 supporters of the two major Shi'a organisations, Hizbullah and Amal, had come out onto the streets in a demonstration of support for and 'gratitude towards' Syria. By way of response, and in order to mark the passing of one month since Hariri's death, about one million supporters of the Cedar Revolution had demonstrated on March 14. From then on, the two groups were known as 'the people of March 8' and 'the people of March 14'. For the time being, the latter prevailed. On April 10, 2005, claiming victorious completion of their mission in Lebanon, the Syrian army departed.

'They all liked Hariri round here,' I remarked to Jawad.

'Oh yes,' he replied with feeling. 'Everybody loves him. This is a Sunni area, the people are big supporters of Hariri.'

'Did *you* like him?' I wondered if I, too, should have used the present tense, for the ubiquitous posters made one feel that Hariri was still a living presence. In Middle Eastern dynastic tradition, his son, Saad Hariri, had taken over the leadership of his supporters.

'I like him, of course,' Jawad replied, 'although I'm Syrian!' He forced a laugh. 'He did many good things for Lebanon. And specially for the Sunnis.'

'What d'you think about his death?' I knew Jawad might not feel able to tell me his real views, but I was curious to see what he would say. 'D'you think it was the Syrians?'

'Not necessarily. There are many possible explanations. Maybe the Syrians, maybe the Americans… who knows?' He raised his eyebrows with a trace of humour. 'Come, the shop is over there.' He stepped out into the road, where the traffic ground so slowly that it felt safe to dart in front of moving cars. On the far side, a crowd of men stood at the tall glass counters of the mobile phone shop. Jawad held up my phone until one of the bearded assistants took it from him and quoted a price. Then he turned to me. 'Sixty-two dollars, for the ninety unit sim card. And if you run out, you can recharge it.'

'Okay.' I took out the money and passed it to him. A moment later, the phone was back in my handbag.

Jawad hovered in the doorway of the shop. 'Hanan wanted me to buy her a *sandweech*.' He walked a couple of paces and stopped outside an open-fronted shop. 'You're hungry?'

Under a glass counter, ready-cooked *sandweeches* were laid out on display. They were a type of *menaish*, rounds of bread spread with cheese or *zaater* or roasted vegetables. A young man in jeans and a T-shirt stood at the door of a tall metal oven, wielding a spatula, while inside the shop another kneaded dough. When the oven door was opened, a wave of heat gusted into the street.

'The *khudra* is very good here.' Jawad pointed to a flat bread spread with roasted vegetables.

'Okay, I'll have one of those. And a cheese one too, I'm starving.' Jawad gave his order and we watched as the dough kneader shaped four lumps of dough and sent them through a set of metal rollers. At the back of the bar a gaggle of young men stood chewing on *sandweeches* rolled in paper, intermittently exchanging banter with the baker. Yet another Hariri gazed down from the wall.

'Jawad,' I asked in a low voice, 'is it a bit uncomfortable being Syrian around here?' I trusted that the rumble of the traffic would prevent anyone from overhearing me. A number of Syrian workers had been beaten up, even killed, at the time of the Syrian departure the previous year.

Jawad sucked his teeth and smiled. I couldn't tell whether his air of confidence was phoney or real. 'It's okay in this street, everybody knows me.'

'What about at your university?'

'*Yani*, mostly it's okay. Most people think I'm Lebanese. I speak with a Lebanese accent, I look Lebanese,' he reached up and stroked the stubble on his chin, regarding me with a trace of amusement.

'What would it be like if they knew you were Syrian?'

'I had a problem last year with one lecturer, when he found out I was Syrian. He had always assumed I was Lebanese, and then he got suspicious and asked to see my ID card.'

'What did he do?'

'Nothing, really. He was just very unpleasant. He threatened to fail me in my exam, but in the end he didn't.'

The baker handed our *sandweeches* to Jawad.

As we strolled back to the flat I asked how far it was to Hamra.

'Ten minutes by *servees*. You want to go there?'

I smiled. 'Not now, maybe another time.' My fears of the night before had been entirely misplaced.

15

'BEFORE THE WAR, LIFE WAS BEAUTIFUL'

Beirut, March 2006

✧

On the pavement beside the entrance to Hanan's grandfather's apartment, a group of old men sat on plastic chairs, smoking hubbly bubbly. Behind them, through a glass door, I glimpsed a small workshop set into the ground floor of the building. Jawad greeted the men as we passed, and they nodded and murmured in reply, glancing at me with veiled curiosity.

Inside the apartment, Hanan lay on the sofa watching TV. Muna and Ruhiyya sat opposite her, smoking, while a couple of teenage boys lolled in armchairs. Through the inner window I caught a glimpse of Karim asleep on a bed.

Hanan jumped up when we walked in. 'You brought the food? Thank god, I'm so hungry. I didn't eat anything since we got off the plane.' She seized the bag of *sandweeches* from Jawad, folded back the paper on a cheese one and sank her teeth into the hot bread.

As we sat down, the door creaked open and an old man entered the room. He was short, with broad, square shoulders. He moved slowly towards the kitchen, dragging one foot behind him, clearly unperturbed by the crowd in his living room.

Hanan winked at me. 'My grandfather, Abu Salim.' The old man wore an acrylic cardigan in dirty golden-yellow over grey, sagging trousers. A pair of spectacles with heavy square black frames dominated his face and I recognised him as one of the men I had glimpsed on the pavement. His right eye appeared closed.

Hanan stood up and I followed. '*Jiddi*,' she wrapped an arm around his shoulder with unmistakable affection. 'Meet Teresa. She came with me on the plane from London. This is her fourth time in Lebanon.'

Abu Salim stopped in his tracks, gazed at me through the thick lenses and held out his hand. His smile bore an unreserved warmth which instantly cut through the sense of displacement which had gripped me since I had stepped off the plane. My being away from Dan was at the root of the feeling, and it would not evaporate altogether until I got on the plane to go home, but the old man's kindness soothed and grounded me. The skin of his fingers was calloused and rough, reminding me of the feel of my father's hands.

'*Ahlan wa sahlan*,' he said simply, '*ahlan wa sahlan* (welcome).' Then, uncertain how to go on, he sank into an armchair and gestured to me to sit beside him.

'Teresa is writing a book,' Hanan announced, 'about Lebanon before and after the war.' This was somewhat imprecise, but it served as a good introduction. My intention was still to try to fathom how members of different Lebanese sects felt about each other and how they lived with their memories of the war.

Abu Salim peered at me and I wondered how much he could see through the thick lenses. 'Before the war, life was beautiful!' He shook his head slowly. 'Much better than it is now.'

'In what ways was it better?'

'In lots of ways.' He thought for a moment, rubbing his chin. 'Before the war things were cheap, and money went a long way. In those days you could buy a flat for 12,000 dollars! And of course in those days I was young... I was very active, I provided for ten children without even feeling tired. I never used to worry about money, whereas now I worry about it all the time. Even in the middle of the war, there was lots of work. I used to work for one month in Beirut and then we would flee to the Mountain, or to Syria, and live without working for six months! Now I have to work every day, just to keep going.'

'You're still working?'

'A little. I don't get a lot of work because these days, most people don't bother to get their shoes mended, they just go out and buy a new pair.' He leaned forwards as he spoke, resting his forearm on his knee and I noted again the breadth of his shoulders. That was another way in which he resembled my father.

'Do you mind me asking how old you are?'

'Eighty-two.'

I raised my eyebrows. 'I took you for seventy-five at most! Have you always worked as a cobbler?'

The old man sighed. 'I used to *make* shoes, but nowadays because shoes are cheap to buy ready-made, I only do repairs. In the old days, before I had my own workshop, I worked for a Christian in the centre of town.' He paused, wheezing a little. 'Worked for him for twenty years.'

Hanan perched on the arm of her grandfather's chair. 'Tell Teresa about the war, *jiddi*, she wants to know what you remember.'

The old man looked a little bewildered. 'What sort of thing? I have so many memories.'

'Tell her how you lost your eye.' She winked at me. She had already told me the story on the plane, but it would be interesting to hear it first hand.

The old man raised his right hand and adjusted the heavy frame on the bridge of his nose. 'One day, in 1975, a Palestinian *feda'i* (fighter) came to my workshop. He was from Fatah[3] and he lived in the neighbourhood. He wanted me to make a leather casing for a small bomb and he brought the bomb with him, in its old case. He sat down close to me and put the bomb on the table. But when he tried to take off the old case, the bomb started ticking.'

Hanan shook her head and clicked her tongue. She must have heard the story many times before, but it still upset her.

Grandfather spoke slowly, his tone matter of fact. 'The *feda'i* picked up the bomb and tried to disable it, but it was too late and the bomb exploded.' He paused, wheezing again. 'The *feda'i* was killed, and I was badly hurt. I lost my eye and my stomach was full of shrapnel. I had to have a lot of stitches.' He patted his stomach, which sagged a little through the yellow cardigan. 'My stomach's not really fat, the skin went flabby because of the stitches.' He glanced at me, to check that I had understood.

Hanan leaned towards her grandfather. 'Wasn't someone else in the workshop at the time?'

'My uncle. When the *feda'i* first came, uncle was sitting at the table where he put the bomb, but before it started ticking uncle moved to work over in the corner. If he hadn't moved, he would have died, too.'

'Was it common in those days for Palestinian fighters to ask the Sunnis to help them?' I was expecting the answer to be 'yes', because I knew that, of all the Lebanese, the Sunnis had felt the strongest affinity with the Palestinians – most of whom were also Sunni Moslems. But grandfather frowned.

---

3   Arafat's organisation within the PLO.

'The Palestinians were here against our wishes. We didn't want them here, they were like invaders.' He wiped his hand across his face in a gesture of weariness.

Ruhiyya stood before us, holding a tray with cups of coffee. The old man and I declined, but Hanan took a cup. 'Tell her other things you remember,' she urged her grandfather.

'The thing I remember most is the shelling by the Christians from East Beirut. It started at the beginning of the war in 1975. When they shelled us we used to go down to the neighbours' basement underneath the building. We spent hours down there. Sometimes we used to sleep down there. We were scared even to go out to buy bread.'

'Was it always shelling or did the Christians fight you in the streets?'

'No, the Christians didn't actually come here. If a Moslem went to the Christian side of town, he would be killed, and if a Christian came here, he would be killed.' He stared at the floor. 'Those were terrible days.'

I felt bad, because I was asking the old man to remember things he would rather forget. I fell silent, but after a few moments Abu Salim looked at Hanan and picked up a walking stick.

'I want to show your friend the Razmeh building.'

Hanan, Jawad and I accompanied him out of the apartment, across the road and fifty metres down a side street. Here the old man stopped and pointed at the back of an apartment building.

It was an extraordinary sight. The entire rear wall of the building was missing, leaving dozens of rooms gaping open like the cells of a honeycomb. The damage was clearly old, for weeds grew in the gaps in the masonry, giving the impression of a structure that was gradually returning to nature. Most bizarre of all was a red metal staircase, the remains of a fire escape, still in place between the second and third floors. A man stood with his back to us on the bottom step, his head thrown back, shouting to someone up above.

'People still live up there?' I asked in astonishment.

'The flats in the front of the building are occupied,' the old man said slowly. 'I'll tell you the story of why it was hit. In the summer of 1982, the Israelis heard that Arafat was hiding in the building. They were tipped off by someone who was with him. So they bombed it, but Arafat came down in the lift and left the building two minutes before the bomb landed.'

Jawad was at my elbow. 'I will tell you something else I heard. After this building was hit, Arafat was on the balcony of a different building, quite high up, and a group of his bodyguards were in the street below. He looked down and shouted "which of you betrayed me?" One of the guards looked up. Arafat shot him dead, there and then.'

I shuddered, telling myself that the story might or might not be true. In any event it served as a good illustration of the lawlessness of the time and the paranoia felt by Arafat. 'Do you know anyone living in the building now?' I asked. Washing hung from some of the balconies.

Jawad shrugged his shoulders. 'Not really. They are just ordinary families.'

We walked back towards the old man's apartment and I thanked him. He nodded, smiling, but I could see he was growing very tired.

'My grandfather needs to take a rest, now,' Hanan announced. She held open the front door for him, adding 'In a minute we'll go and sit with my uncle, I'll ask him to make us tea. But we have to take off our shoes, he's strict about that.'

16

THE CURTAIN MAKER

Tariq al Jaddideh, Beirut, March 2006

✧

Hanan opened the door adjacent to the one which led to her grandfather's flat. Inside, the layout was identical, but the walls were brighter and the carpets less worn. The uncle, a thin, smiling man of about fifty, stood in the centre of the floor, dapper in a white shirt and neatly pressed trousers. Two teenage girls stared at me from a sofa.

'Welcome, welcome,' he crowed. I removed my shoes, shook his hand and returned the welcomes. 'Please have a seat, make yourself at home.' He gestured at a long low divan upholstered in red and white damask that ran along the wall.

'My uncle is a curtain maker,' Hanan explained. 'He takes commissions from the neighbourhood.'

The uncle stood before me in his socks, a hint of mischief in his smile. His name was Salim.

'Do you work from home?' I enquired.

'On the balcony. Would you like to see?' I followed him through a doorway into a small, open-air sewing workshop, shaded from the elements on one side by an awning. Pairs of freshly sewn and pressed curtains, many adorned with tassles and satin rope, hung from a washing line. An enormously long Louis XIV-style stripy drape graced the back wall. Bolts of fabric were stacked neatly on the floor; and at the far end of the balcony, wedged into the corner, stood an old-fashioned treadle sewing machine and a wooden chair.

I ran my eye over the curtains arrayed on the washing line, resisting the temptation to run my fingers over the satin rope. The colours were drab sage greens and greys, the fabric suspiciously shiny; but, as a veteran maker of curtains, I felt a certain thrill as I surveyed them.

'Beautiful,' I murmured, 'very beautiful.' Of all the jobs on offer to a working class Beiruti, I thought, sitting on a quiet balcony sewing for your neighbours must be one of the most agreeable. Cold perhaps in winter, but delightful in spring and summer. Even though the fabric was synthetic, I could imagine the satisfaction the uncle must feel as he knotted the last loose threads of each commission, pressed it and hung it up, ready for collection.

'Thank you,' I said as I turned back towards the living room, 'you're making some lovely things.'

Uncle Salim regarded me with an air of contentment. 'Now, let me make you some tea.'

Muna had arrived while I was on the balcony, accompanied by Nadia, another of Hanan's aunts. Nadia was well-rounded like Muna, but more casually dressed in a long *gelabeyya*, with her hair pulled back in a pony tail. She greeted me warmly and we all sat down.

'We just went out to show Teresa the Razmeh building,' Hanan told them. 'Grandad was telling us about the day it was hit.'

'I can tell you about it, too,' Muna exclaimed, 'I remember it like it was yesterday.'

She settled herself on the sofa between the two girls and drew on an extra long cigarette. 'I remember the dead and the injured being carried out. Nearly all the people who lived in that building were killed. The street was full of ash and smoke.' She turned to Hanan. 'The windows of your grandfather's workshop were shattered. In fact every window in the whole building broke.' She grimaced. 'It was terrible. Really, there are no words to describe what it was like.'

'I was in your grandfather's flat,' Nadia interjected, 'when the bomb hit. The children were playing in the street. We heard the bomb land and a few seconds later the children ran indoors. Their hair was white from the ash and they were terrified out of their wits. The neighbours' little girl, who was six at the time, started to pray. I remember she said "please god, let me get married before I die!"' Muna and Nadia smiled.

'The bombing was always awful for the children,' Nadia went on. 'My friend's daughter was six months old. Whenever she heard a plane flying over she would curl up in her mother's lap, like a frightened animal.'

I was beginning to wonder how Hanan's family had felt about their Palestinian neighbours. Tariq al Jaddideh would have been targeted by the Israelis in 1982 due to the presence of its Palestinian population and its proximity to Sabra and Shatila refugee camps.

'Did you know many of the Palestinians who lived here then?' I asked Muna.

'Of course,' she replied, 'I knew lots. All the residents of the Razmeh building were Palestinian. The people on the top floors, that is. The lower floors were a prison.'

'Run by whom?'

'By the Palestinians. They were in control of the area at the time.'

'Did people know that Arafat was in the buiding?'

Muna sucked her teeth. 'Of course not. He moved about all the time, and nobody was meant to know where he was.' She ground out her cigarette and pulled another from the packet. 'A woman I knew was in her flat in the Razmeh building that day, on the fourth floor. When the building was hit, she jumped from the balcony and landed in the street without hurting herself.'

I gasped.

Muna looked at me. 'The bomb had hit the staircase so there was no other way to get out. It was not just this woman, quite a few people jumped.'

Uncle Salim came in from the kitchen with glasses of tea.

'Did you feel angry that by hiding in the Razmeh building, Arafat had put your street in danger?'

Muna looked puzzled. 'This whole area was controlled by the Palestinians in those days, so we couldn't get angry, it wouldn't have been safe.'

'But did you *feel* angry?'

'I felt angry, of course! We all felt angry. Not just because of the Israeli bombing: the different Palestinian factions used to fight *each other* in the streets round here, so that often it was too dangerous to go out. Say I wanted to go and buy meat: sometimes I'd get into the street and they would be fighting each other. That made me really angry!' She laid her cigarette in the ashtray and took a sip of tea. 'We used to say to the Palestinians, "look, your enemy is Israel, to each other you are brothers and fellow Moslems, so *why* are you fighting each other?"' She shook her head. 'That sort of thing used to make me *very* angry. And you know, I think that more often we were put in danger by them fighting with each other than by their conflict with Israel!'

I sipped my tea. It was too sweet but I was tired now and I thought it would help me to keep going. I asked Muna what her present-day feelings were towards the Palestinians.

She shifted towards the edge of her seat, resting her forearms on her knees and looking at me. 'I love Palestine as an Arab nation, but I hate a lot of what the Palestinians have done; both what they did then and even what they do now. You see, this is not their country, and they do not respect it. They steal, they shout and they try to control us. Wherever they live, they try to control the area. And because they believe they are just visitors here, they don't care who may be hurt by their bad behaviour. I'll give you an example. If a Palestinian steals from a shop, he doesn't stop and think "oh, it's my brother's shop, I'd better not do this" – as he might think if he were in his own country.'

I nodded.

'Here's another example. Not long ago, a Palestinian murdered a Lebanese. Immediately afterwards the Palestinian fled into Shatila camp, knowing that he could not be arrested there by the Lebanese police, because they do not enter the camp.'

'Why don't they enter?' I assumed she was referring to the Cairo Agreement, but I was interested to see what she would say. The Cairo Agreement was negotiated between the PLO and the Lebanese army in 1969, with the aim of setting parameters to the burgeoning military activities of the PLO within Lebanon. Under its provisions, the PLO commandos were to be restricted to certain areas and their operations against Israel were to be secretly co-ordinated with the Lebanese army. An additional feature was that the Lebanese security forces would not enter the refugee camps, leaving the Palestinians to run them autonomously.

'They can't,' Muna went on. 'The camp is controlled by the Palestinians. This is a huge problem. Look, a Palestinian steals a car and drives it into Shatila. No-one can even go and get the car back, let alone arrest the Palestinian!'

I was surprised to learn that the Cairo Agreement was still being adhered to, some thirty-seven years after coming into force, and sixteen years after the end of the civil war. Back in 1969, the Agreement had outraged the Maronites, who generally resented the Palestinian presence and saw the Agreement as weakening Lebanese sovereignty for the sake of appeasing Moslem opinion. Lebanese Moslems had generally favoured the Agreement, because they supported the Palestinians' attempt to combat Israel from Lebanese soil.

In the early years following the Agreement, the divergence of interests between the Maronites on the one hand and the Moslems and

Palestinians, on the other, grew greater. In 1970, the PLO was turned out of Jordan and transferred its centre of activities to Lebanon. This attracted Israeli raids against Lebanese border villages, which in turn led to an exodus of Shi'a peasants towards the shantytowns and Palestinian refugee camps that ringed Beirut, where a 'comradeship in misery' grew up between the two communities. Meanwhile, the PLO exploited the weakness of the Lebanese state to the full, so that by the mid 1970s it was effectively operating its own 'state within a state' in the camps and, later, in much of West Beirut.

I found it interesting that now, thirty years on, little love was lost between Muna and her Palestinian neighbours. 'What about this area?' I asked. 'Do the Lebanese police have control here?'

'Nowadays, yes. But during the war, no. During the war this area was controlled by the Palestinian militias.' Muna smiled. 'I love Lebanon,' she went on. 'And I see the Palestinians as invaders here, just like all the other invaders we have suffered at the hands of. I cannot like anyone who invades my country.' She sighed. 'You see, we Lebanese still don't feel we are in control of our own destiny. We've been invaded countless times: by the Palestinians, the Syrians, the Israelis. I hate *all* of them!'

I asked if she had any Palestinian friends.

'No. Even during the war, when there were Palestinians living in this street, I didn't have any. The woman I knew who jumped from the Razmeh building wasn't really a friend, just a neighbour.'

'Have you been to any of the Palestinian camps?'

'Shatila.'

'What are the conditions like?'

Muna pulled a face. 'Very bad. The people are very poor, their lives are very difficult. They don't have many legal rights: they can't get the same medical treatment as us and they can't work in a whole list of professions; they can't even buy property in their own name.' She paused to light a new cigarette. 'Of course I can see that their circumstances lead them to behave badly. When they see, for instance, that the Lebanese own their own homes, they feel hard done by and they go out and do things they shouldn't do.' She paused. 'But from our point of view, as Lebanese, we don't like them because we are on the receiving end. They've been here since 1948, which is a long time now. And for all that time we Lebanese have felt we are not really in control of our country. We've had the Syrians here for a lot of that time too, you know.'

I began to wonder how Hanan was feeling as she listened to Muna. Hanan had led me to believe that the Lebanese part of her family were broadly pro-Syrian, but it was clear that this was not the case.

'Look,' Muna went on, 'I love all the Arab peoples, without exception.' She held the fingers of her right hand to her mouth, kissed them and flicked her fingers wide open in an extravagant gesture which I found unconvincing. 'And in every people, there are good elements and bad ones. Okay. Despite the bad elements, I love them all: Palestinians, Syrians, Egyptians, Iraqis...' She nodded her head as she enunciated each name on the list. 'But when you find the people of a different country living in your country, fully armed with heavy weapons, of course you start to hate them!'

She lapsed into silence. Salim had left the room and I could hear the hum of his sewing machine from the balcony. After a few minutes I asked Muna if she thought it would be safe for me to visit Shatila.

'You'll be okay.' She paused. 'I live in an area called Hayy Sulum. It's a Shi'a area, very poor, not unlike Shatila.'

I raised my eyebrows, for I was keen to visit some poor Shi'a areas. 'Can I visit you there?' I felt Muna was sufficiently up-front to say 'no' if she didn't like the idea.

To my surprise, she frowned. 'I don't know anybody there, I've only been in my apartment for a month and I try not to mix with the neighbours.' She looked decidedly uncomfortable, but after a moment she added, 'Yes, all right, I'll take you there if you want.' She inhaled deeply before grinding another butt into the ashtray.

'I'd be very grateful if you would.' I smiled as warmly as I could. 'Why don't you mix with your neighbours?'

Muna thought for a long time before answering. 'They are very poor and very rough. I don't like the way they behave.'

Hanan, who was seated beside me, was becoming uncomfortable. She turned to me and murmured in a low voice, 'Muna was telling me earlier that the Shi'a in her area shout a lot and have very bad manners. They really are rough.'

Salim appeared in the doorway as Muna untied her headscarf and stretched it across her lap. Beneath it, the red bandeau held her hair in place. 'Hayy Sulum is very, very poor,' she went on, 'and, being Shi'a, most of the residents are extremists. They don't like Sunnis.' A moment later she re-tied the headscarf. For the second time that day I felt a wave of liking for her, despite her negative feelings towards the Palestinians and the Shi'a.

'Why don't the Shi'a like Sunnis?' I enquired.

'The Sunnis are happy to talk to the Shi'a, but the Shi'a don't feel the same way.'

Muna adopted an air of hurt, as though she took the Shi'a's antipathy personally. Hanan lowered her voice again. 'She just doesn't want to mix with them, really. She has a kind of prejudice against them...' I could tell from her tone that Hanan felt embarrassed.

I pretended not to have heard. 'How long have you lived in Hayy Sulum?'

'Only a month.'

'Do your children go to school there?'

'No, they come over to this area to go to school, by *servees*.'

I was conscious of Salim becoming restless.

'What does your friend want to know?' he whispered to Hanan.

'About the Shi'a,' Hanan replied.

He sucked his teeth and turned to me. 'The Shi'a are troublesome people! Stubborn, snobbish, not worth talking to.'

Muna forced a smile. 'Listen, Teresa, everyone in Lebanon has a different opinion. If you go to Hamra you'll see foreigners like yourself. If you go to Hayy Sulum, you'll see people who are very poor and rough. And everyone will tell you something different. You'll hear a lot of bad stories while you're doing your research, that's for sure, and you'll end up with a lot of white hairs on your head!'

We both laughed.

'But to answer your question, you're welcome to come to my house one day. I'll take you to visit the neighbourhood. I don't know anybody there, but at least you can see what it looks like.' She stood up. 'Excuse me for a few minutes, I have to go and pray.' She beamed at everyone, determined to mask the last of her discomfort, walked to the door and put on her shoes.

Hanan jumped up. 'I have to pray, too. Wait for me, Teresa, I'll be back in ten minutes.'

After they had left, Salim brought more tea and sat down beside me on the divan.

'We don't like the Shi'a,' he began, 'because they don't like Hariri.'

A year after Hariri's murder, the deepest cleavage in Lebanon's politics remained that between the people of March 8, consisting principally of supporters of the pro-Syrian Shi'a organisations Hizbullah and Amal, on the one hand, and the people of March 14, consisting of the Sunnis, many Druze and many Christians, on the other.

'Did you know,' Salim went on, 'Nasrallah has only *just now* read the Quranic verses that observant Moslems have to read for Hariri's death?' Sayyid Hassan Nasrallah was the cleric who lead Hizbullah. 'It took him thirteen months!' He clicked his tongue and shook his head. 'And did you know that the Christians and the Sunnis get on much better with each other than the Sunnis do with the Shi'a?' He smiled, as if this were a piece of information which should please me.

'What about the Christians and the Shi'a? How do they get on?' I was pretty sure I knew the answer, but wanted to see what Salim would say.

He shook his head with an air of doom. 'They don't.' This was not quite accurate, certainly at the political level, for in May 2005 Hizbullah and Amal had entered into an alliance with the Christian politician Michel Aoun,[4] who had just returned to Lebanon from exile in France, with his sights once again set on the Lebanese presidency. Aoun had a large following among a certain section of Lebanese Christians, and even among some Moslems. Most bizarrely, given his wartime history, he had now adopted a pro-Syrian stance – presumably a requirement of his alliance with Hizbullah.

But I deliberately took Salim's words at face value and enquired why the Christians and Shi'a did not get on.

'Oh, there are lots of reasons. The Shi'a have huge families, they are very backward in this respect....'

---

4   In 1988, Aoun was nominated prime minister by the outgoing president Amin Gemmayel, in breach of the National Pact, which required the prime minister to be a Sunni. When the incumbent Sunni prime minister, supported by Syria, refused to give up his post, severe fighting broke out between Aoun and his supporters on the one hand and the Syrians and their supporters on the other, in the summer of 1989. In November 1989 Aoun declared himself president, opposing the Taif Accord negotiated in October 1989 in Saudi Arabia to bring an end to the war. From then on, armed by Iraq, Aoun and his supporters held out in their virtually separate state in East Beirut until autumn 1990. By then, the flow of weapons had ceased, due to Iraq's invasion of Kuwait. When at last he left Beirut, Aoun went into exile in France.

I was hoping to learn more, but at that moment Hanan reappeared at the door and bent down to take off her shoes. 'Teresa,' she said with an air of embarassment, 'Muna has thought it over and she is sorry but she does not feel it would be safe for you to visit her in Hayy Sulum.'

'Oh,' I said, disappointed but intrigued. 'Why's that?'

But before Hanan could reply Salim stood up and wagged his finger at me. 'No,' he began, 'You must definitely not go there. Hayy Sulum is in Dahyya, and if you go to any part of Dahyya it is very likely you will be kidnapped by Hizbullah.'

Kidnapped. It was not a pleasant word, and much less so when used to describe something that might happen to me. But I thought it highly unlikely that Salim's prediction was accurate.

'What would Hizbullah want with me?'

'You are a foreigner, they would want to question you, to interrogate you!' He stood in the middle of the floor, regarding me with exasperation.

'Really? Are you sure?' I knew that Hizbullah had condoned and probably participated in kidnappings of westerners in the 1980s. But given that they were now full participants in Lebanon's political system, with deputies in parliament and ministers in the government, I thought it improbable that they would seize a foreigner off the streets.

'For sure! No doubt about it! If you go to Dahyya they will interrogate you, torture you even, and it will be very difficult for us to get you out!' From the energy in Salim's voice I deduced that, even if wrong, he was sincere. Exhausted by the effort of trying to convince me, he sank down on the sofa and rested his forearms on his knees. I decided that it would be tactful to pretend I took him seriously.

'Well, thank you for warning me, I certainly don't want to go through that!' I nodded and raised my eyebrows. 'It's a shame, because I had hoped to meet some people from Hizbullah, but not if it would be dangerous.'

The door opened again and Muna entered the room. 'Teresa,' she said, 'I am so sorry, but it would not be safe for you to visit me in Hayy Sulum.' She shook her head, polite but firm.

'Yes,' I said, 'Salim has just explained. Don't worry, I won't go there.' I hesitated. 'Why are Hizbullah so jumpy? Is it particularly at the moment, or are they always funny about foreigners?'

Salim regarded me with the air of an adult trying to explain something to a wayward child. 'Dahyya has always been a problematic area. The Shi'a are trouble, they are not people to mix with. And especially now. The Americans are trying to dis-arm Hizbullah, I'm sure you've heard about that. So if they see you walking about, they will think you are a spy.'

'Okay,' I nodded at Salim and Muna. 'Don't worry, I'll take your advice.' I could see it would be fruitless to press the matter further. Later I would phone Hassan Daoud, I decided, and see what he thought about what they had said. I was pretty sure he would laugh.

At the end of the civil war, when all the other militias had laid down their weapons in accordance with the 1989 Ta'if Accord, Hizbullah had refused to do so. It argued that its armed forces were not really militias but rather 'Islamic Resistance' groups committed to ending the Israeli occupation of the south, and badly needed to defend the country against the SLA. This argument was accepted by many, though not all, Lebanese, for the continuing Israeli occupation could not be ignored and was clearly an obstacle to the country's post war recovery. The newly established government allowed Hizbullah's forces to remain armed and operational.

During the 1990s, Hizbullah continued to mount highly professional raids against Israeli military and SLA targets in the occupied southern security zone and, on relatively rare occasions, in northern Israel. For their part, the Israelis launched a number of aggressive incursions north of the security zone, most notorious of which was the 'Grapes of Wrath' operation in April 1996. Fleeing from both air and ground attacks by the Israeli Defence Force (IDF), a group of 106 civilians took refuge in the UN base in the village of Qana, only to die when the Israelis deliberately shelled it.

When in May 2000 the Israelis unilaterally withdrew from most of the southern security zone, Hizbullah claimed the credit. The only slice of land which the Israelis refused to cede was the Shebaa farms area, a hilly strip some two miles wide by nine miles long adjoining the Golan Heights, which the Israelis claimed was the subject of a territorial dispute between Lebanon and Syria. The Lebanese regard the area as indisputably part of Lebanon.

Following the Israeli withdrawal, rather than focussing purely on internal Lebanese politics, Hizbullah decided to maintain its role as a resistance organisation in the Arab-Israeli conflict. Israel's continuing occupation of the Shebaa farms area provided the perfect pretext. For the next six years, Hizbullah harassed the Israeli soldiers occupying the

Shebaa area and they, in turn, harassed Hizbullah. Casualties occurred on both sides, but the figures were dramatically lower than during the years prior to May 2000.

Israel, however, was not happy with Hizbullah's continuing activities and neither was the US government. Thus UN resolution 1559, passed in 2004, not only required the Syrians to withdraw from Lebanon but also required the Lebanese government to disarm all militias and extend its 'full sovereignty over all Lebanese territory'. Given Hizbullah's strong links with Syria and the struggle between pro- and anti-Syrian forces which was taking place in Lebanon at the time, it was hardly surprising that the Lebanese government failed to comply with the resolution.

17
On the 'Bloody' Coastal Highway

Beirut, March 2006

I stood on the corner by *Helouyaat Dimashq*, the pastry shop which Hiba had suggested as a landmark, round the corner from Hanan's grandfather's building. Hiba was a Lebanese friend who until recently had lived near me at home. She had returned to Beirut the previous July after fourteen years in England. On the phone all she had told me was that she now wore a headscarf, and that she had installed herself and the family in a huge apartment outside Beirut, with wonderful views of the sea. I was welcome to stay for as long as I wanted.

While I waited, I took out my phone and dialled Hassan Daoud's number. After we had exchanged greetings I told him about the dire warnings I had been given by Muna and Salim about the dangers I would be facing if I were to set foot in Dahyya.

He chuckled. 'It's absolute rubbish. Hizbullah are a parliamentary party these days, they are not in the business of interfering with foreigners. Feel free to go to Dahyya and walk around the streets there. Nothing will happen to you!'

'I won't be kidnapped?'

'Kidnapping of westerners was a political strategy used in the 1980s, during the war, in order to achieve particular political goals. It's finished, over.' He paused. 'But it's funny they said this to you.' He chuckled again. 'Or perhaps not. All the Lebanese sects are in the habit of saying derogatory things about each other.'

As I put away the phone, a white four-wheel drive rounded the corner and I saw Hiba waving at me excitedly from the wheel. Except for the blue scarf which framed her face, she looked her usual, exuberant self. In England, she had worn her hair in a pony tail.

'Goo-od, I found you, Teresa!' she cried as she leapt out of the driving seat and kissed me three times. In place of her usual jeans she wore a full length cotton skirt and a long, figure-hiding cardigan. 'But the traffic is so terrible today! You will not believe it.' She seized my bag and lifted it into the boot, brushing aside my attempt to help her.

'Where are the children?'

'Basma is here,' she pointed through the window at the tousled head of her daughter, who lay sprawled in a car seat, fast asleep. At five and a half, Basma was only six months younger than Dan.

'She is so-o tired, poor girl, since she started school. Every afternoon she falls asleep in the car.'

'And the boys?'

'I left them in the flat!' Hiba smiled with exaggerated glee. 'They are big boys now, I don't have to worry about them so much any more. Mustafa is fourteen!'

She climbed back into the car and I got in beside her. I could still remember Hiba's warm, bubbly welcome the night a mutual friend had taken me to meet her for the first time in 1993. She had been a pretty young woman of twenty-one, struggling to find her feet in a provincial British city and nursing Mustafa, who was the most beautiful baby I had ever seen. Hiba's Lebanese husband, who was ten years her senior, had lived in England since the early 1980s, but she had only joined him when they married the year before. It was a situation which might have daunted some young women, but Hiba was stronger than most, with an extraordinary gift for making friends. Born in 1972 to a Sunni merchant family, she had survived a wartime childhood in Beirut, coming to England only shortly after the last bullets were fired.

I hadn't seen a lot of Hiba during her first ten years in England. By the time we began to meet regularly, after Dan was born in 2000, she had a bigger group of friends than I had. She was the mainstay of the parent teacher association at the primary school which Mustafa and her second son, Walid, attended, and she seemed to know everyone in her local community.

'So!' Hiba started the engine and adjusted her rear view mirror. 'You made it to Beirut!' Her English was fluent and idiomatic, but her voice had a sing-song tone that made English words sound less flat and more interesting than when an English person pronounced them. 'How's Dan? Is he with his dad?' She smiled brightly, but I had to wipe my eyes. Hiba patted my shoulder. 'He'll be fine, he'll be fine. It's you who will suffer more than he will!' She laughed. 'When you miss him too much you can cuddle Basma, she always likes to be cuddled.'

I twisted round to look at the sleeping girl on the back seat. She was all legs and arms, and thick, chocolate brown hair.

'She's got so much bigger! I can hardly believe it.'

'Well, yes, they do. You would notice more than me, after – what is it? Eight months?'

We were crawling in a queue of cars towards a flyover. On one side of the road, a stream of young people flowed in and out of a doorway in a high white wall. Hiba followed my gaze.

'That's the Arab university. Now, I hope you remember the way the Lebanese drive! This is not England, Teresa, this is not England.' She wiggled her eyebrows with a show of mock hysteria.

'Are we going on the motorway?'

'I think not, it is just too dangerous. You know what I call it? The "bloody" coastal highway. I use it when I have to, but no, today we will take the old coast road. It's a little slower, but our chances will be better. I don't like to risk my life every day of the week.'

'Are there lots of accidents?' I already knew the answer.

Hiba pointed to her ear. 'Pardon me? Remember, when I am driving it is not so easy for me to lip read.' Hiba had a hearing problem. Her consultant in Britain had concluded that she had suffered permanent damage to her ears due to exposure to extreme noise during the war. Hiba herself dated it from an incident when a bomb had landed on the next-door building when she was a teenager. 'I don't wear my hearing aids now we are living in Beirut,' she smiled. 'When I am with Lebanese I don't need them, because almost everybody shouts!'

I laughed. 'I was asking if there are lots of accidents on the coastal highway,' I repeated, raising my voice.

'Oh! Every day the coastal highway gets painted with blood. That's why I gave it this name. Sometimes I take it when I am going to visit my parents. You are speeding along and then suddenly, bam! In front of you there is a huge traffic jam and an ambulance screaming to get through. All because some lunatic has done a U-turn.'

I shook my head. 'Please, let's take the old coast road!' For all my worries about political violence, I had known, when I planned the trip, that the most likely mishap was a car crash.

'We will, we will,' Hiba smiled. 'We are mothers, we do not wish to die today.'

We passed under the flyover and were soon chugging south in a line of slow-moving buses, cars and lorries. To either side the road was lined with decrepit buildings in sand-coloured concrete with shops at street level and accommodation above. The sides of the road teemed with imperilled life, for in many places there was no pavement as such. I saw a man pushing a barrow laden with apples, little boys running, a pair of headscarved women in long robes carrying bags of shopping, and an old man standing beside a handcart piled high with *ka'ik*, the Levantine bread encrusted with sesame seeds. Every few hundred yards, the buildings gave way to stretches of waste ground overgrown with weeds and yellow flowers. Then the shops began again, followed by a car breaker's yard, more shops, children, barrows, motorbikes and women carrying shopping.

'These are the southern slums,' Hiba explained. 'The people here are very poor. Mainly refugees from the south, who migrated to Beirut during the war.'

We were passing a stretch with a raised pavement at the side of the road, where every other shop sold furniture. Cheap-looking wooden framed sofas, chairs and dining tables spewed over the pavements, and the words 'Gallery' this or that were painted above the shops. I caught a glimpse of a small booth selling plants in terra cotta pots, oddly out of place amid the traffic fumes and filth.

'So how do you find me in the headscarf?' Hiba shot me a smile.

'Actually, I think it suits you. I know that's not the point, but you look very good in it.'

'Some of my friends in England were so worried when I told them I was going to adopt it! They seemed to think I was giving up my rights, as if I was wearing it to please my husband, or some such nonsense...'

'It wasn't Omar, was it?' I couldn't imagine Hiba 's mild-mannered husband making such a request of her.

'Not at all, not at all.' She paused, driving with just one hand on the wheel. 'Actually the big thing for me was...' she slowed as a vehicle shot out of a side road in front of us. I assumed she was going to say September 11th, but I was wrong. 'The big thing for me was the *tsunami*. I found it so shocking, that so many people should be killed in this way, and it made me think maybe god is very angry with us. I looked at my life and I felt up till now I have not been such a good Moslem. So I decided I should no longer take just the parts of the religion which I find easy. From now, it's either all or nothing, I decided. Wearing the headscarf is part of the religion, so from the day we arrived in Beirut, I have been wearing it. And I try to pray the full five times a day.'

We had been grinding along in the fumes for fifteen minutes when, across a patch of waste ground, I caught a glimpse of the sea. Juxtaposed with the urban grime all around us, it looked extraordinarily fresh and clean.

'Nearly there now.' As Hiba spoke, Basma wailed from the back seat. 'And the little lady is waking up.' A moment later the road swung out in an arc, bordering a stretch of empty beach. I felt an intense sense of relief, as if an invisible hand had been clutching at my throat and had suddenly released me. My gaze travelled across the sand, over a series of small breakers and out across the calm, blue water.

A couple of miles further on, tall apartment buildings stood between the beach and the road. We were no longer in the slums, for the buildings were newly constructed with crisp new awnings hanging from their balconies. At street level, expensive-looking supermarkets stood beside pastry shops and restaurants. Hiba turned down a side road and parked at the foot of a ten-storey block.

'Welcome, Teresa,' she cried as she pulled the keys from the ignition and turned to Basma in the back. 'This lady wakes up very cross from her afternoon nap. Come, Basma, if you stop shouting you can press the button for the lift.'

I dragged my bag from the boot and followed Hiba and Basma through the glass door of their building.

'Hopefully the electricity is on,' Hiba frowned. 'Otherwise we'll leave your bag with the porter. Six storeys is a long way to walk, I can tell you!'

'You get power cuts?'

'This is the down side to not being in Beirut, but generally they are in the morning. My main form of exercise is walking up the stairs with the shopping!'

'It's working, it's working!' Basma cried in Arabic as the button on the lift door illuminated. The previous summer she had been bilingual but now, it seemed, her mother tongue came more naturally.

'Are you happy with the new school?' I asked as we squeezed into the lift. Hiba had put the children into an international school, where the teaching medium was English.'

'*Yani*, yes and no.' She moved her eyebrows very slightly. This was a subject for later, I sensed, after Basma had gone to bed.

Two stout front doors faced each other across a large lobby on the sixth floor. Basma ran on ahead and was already seated in front of a giant television when I wheeled my bag into the apartment. Mustafa came to the door, smiling and holding out his hand, while Walid grinned at me from a sofa in the living room. Behind him, I glimpsed a salon of breathtaking dimensions.

Both boys had grown taller, but it didn't seem long since I had last seen them in England. I delved in my bag for the chocolate I had bought them in the duty free.

'I hope you don't mind...' I glanced at Hiba.

'Not at all!' She had kicked off her shoes and was pulling the inner layer of her headscarf over her head, a tube of white cotton jersey which fitted snugly over her head and neck. In the car she had worn a blue lawn scarf over the top. Tube removed, she shook out her hair, hung the tube on a hook inside the front door, and thrust her shoes into a crowded shoe rack.

'See our latest acquisition!' she cried with mock pride, pointing at the shoe rack. 'Mustafa helped me to assemble it last night. We're getting very good at DIY, Mustafa and I, now that Omar isn't here to help us.' For the last few months Omar had been working in the Gulf. 'You see how we're rattling around in these huge rooms,' she went on. 'In England the flat was so small we had no space for furniture, and now, we have too much space and almost no furniture! Now, Teresa, I expect you would like a cup of tea. Let me put the water on to boil, and I will give you a guided tour of the palace!'

And a palace it was. The salon must have measured forty feet by twenty, with a fake marble floor and two sets of giant French windows opening onto a vast balcony. Mugs of tea in hand, we stood at the parapet, watching a pink sun slide into the pale blue sea. 'It's fantastic,' I told Hiba. 'Lucky you!'

She rubbed her hands together and giggled in delight. 'My family wanted me to take an apartment in their building, in town, but I said 'no, I want my independence!' She shivered. 'In the evenings it is still a little chilly, especially with the breeze off the sea. But in the summer, imagine! Every day after school, we go to the beach! The children love it.' She stepped back into the salon. 'Now, would you like to take a shower? Come and see, you have a choice of three bathrooms!'

By the time I had showered, unpacked and sent an email to Paul and Dan, my short night was catching up with me and I was ready for my bed, but Hiba called me into the kitchen. A delicious smell wafted from the oven and the table was laid for two.

'I hope you have a good appetite, Teresa! My brother-in-law is a fisherman, and he caught me two large fish this morning. I don't know what you call them in English, but the flesh is juicy and succulent and especially good with rice!' She opened the oven door, bent down and lifted a sizzling casserole onto the table.

'I thought he was a dentist?'

'*Yani*, he makes his money as a dentist, but when he has finished with his patients, he goes straight to the sea wall! My sister complains because she never sees him.'

'Aren't the children going to eat?'

'Don't worry, they ate while you were in the shower. Basma is asleep and the boys are watching James Bond.'

When I sat down at the table I realised that I was absolutely ravenous. Hiba removed the backbone from the fish with a few deft movements, and placed a large fillet on each of our plates.

'Help yourself to rice,' she instructed. 'You're not going to lose weight while you're in Lebanon, that's for sure. Oh, I do so like this fish!' Her eyes swam as she picked up her knife and fork.

When we had each cleared our first plateful I asked her again about the school. She was on her feet, filleting the second fish. 'Academically, the standards are very high. So high, in fact, that Mustafa has found it a shock. He has to work much, much harder than he did in England. He is very bright, and yet it has taken him the whole of the first two terms to get the results he should be getting in the tests.'

'Tests?'

'Oh, tests and tests and more tests! At the end of every week they give them tests. And absurd amounts of homework.'

'Even for Walid?'

'Even for Basma! This is why she becomes so bad tempered in the evenings. School begins at ten to eight in the morning and finishes at 4 o'clock, even for the youngest ones. She is exhausted, poor child. More rice?' I shook my head. 'So,' she went on, 'academically it is tough, but at least they are not wasting their time. For me, the biggest problem is the way they discipline the children.'

I raised my eyebrows.

'They hit them if they misbehave. Mustafa told me the first week he was there. I was so angry! A boy in his class was hit across the knuckles with a ruler, for doing something wrong, I can't remember what it was. I went to see the director. He denied that they hit the children, but I don't believe him, I believe Mustafa.' She picked up her fork. 'Besides, other parents have told me about children being hit. I have told Mustafa and Walid, that if any member of staff lays a finger on them, I will personally beat up the director.'

'Are you going to join the Parent Teacher Association?'

Hiba rolled her eyes. 'Chance would be a fine thing! They don't have one. I went to the director to suggest that we start one and he said "No, thank you very much, we don't need the parents to help us run the school." This is the attitude, very closed. Even to get an appointment with your child's teacher is a battle, often you have to wait a week.'

I slept deeply that night, waking only briefly at seven a.m. as Hiba left the flat to take the children to school. It often took her half an hour each way, she had said, battling through the early morning rush hour. At eight thirty I opened my eyes, suddenly conscious of the roaring of traffic. I crossed the room, lifted the blind and stared out at the coastal highway below. Two lanes of cars and trucks sped south towards Sidon, and another two sped north to Beirut, causing a vibration which made the window rattle. Beyond the road, a chaos of concrete apartment blocks straggled up the rocky hillside, thrown up in anarchic post-war haste with the same disregard for for the environment which had shocked me in Jbeil. Dropping the blind I padded across the hall in my bare feet, making for the back of the building to get a view of the sea.

I opened the French window and walked to the edge of the balcony, hoping no one could see me in my pyjamas. A soft morning sun was shining on the water. Across this stretch of sea and a few miles of land, I mused, my friend Nancy would be unlocking the door to her pottery, in her hill village in Cyprus. It was nice to think she was so close. Many, many miles further west, Dan would still be asleep in his bed in Paul's new house. I still felt upset when I thought of him, but I was beginning to feel excited about being back in Lebanon.

18

'IN THOSE DAYS, THE LEADERS OF LEBANON WERE LEBANESE'

Tariq al Jaddideh, Beirut, March 2006

Hiba had told me where to stand to take the *servees* into Beirut. I walked beside the beach for a couple of hundred metres, passing the entrance to a swimming club which was closed for the winter, and took a side street which led through a tunnel under the main road. On the far side I climbed up onto the hard shoulder and stood facing the stream of fast moving cars, steeling myself against an unpleasant sense of vulnerability and exposure. I had only been waiting three minutes when a car swooped out of the fast lane and drew up a few feet from me. I opened the door, checked that the driver was bound for my destination and climbed in, murmuring a polite '*Salaamu a leekum*' to the passengers in the back. After hurtling for ten minutes along the 'bloody' coastal highway, we were at the Cola intersection. From here it was a short walk to Hanan's grandfather's apartment.

The door to the apartment stood ajar. Hanan greeted me as I pushed it open, signalling to me to come and sit beside her and Karim on the settee. Through the internal window I caught a glimpse of Ruhiyya moving about in the back room, talking to a woman I didn't recognise, who was changing the nappy of a small baby. In the armchairs opposite, Nadia sat talking with an older woman whom I had not met before. She wore a full-length grey wool coat-dress and a synthetic headscarf. Her pale face was heavily lined, and she was sobbing into a handkerchief.

'My aunt Nahla,' Hanan murmured, inclining her head very slightly. 'I'll introduce you when I can, but she's a bit upset.'

'Has something happened?'

'Her son's been arrested.' Hanan looked at me, and I guessed she was remembering that in my English existence I worked as a lawyer. 'It's a bit odd. There were two men in the neighbourhood, nobody knew them. They had only been here a few days, and they asked Nahla's son to work with them. He was out of work, so he said "yes". I think they were paying good money. They had an apartment upstairs, on the fifth floor of this building.'

'What sort of work?'

'I'm not quite sure. Normally my cousin works as a plumber's assistant. Anyway, at five o'clock this morning, the police raided the flat. They took the two men, and they took Nahla's son.'

'Did they say why?' It was years since I had practised in criminal law, but the obvious questions still sprang to mind.

Hanan's face betrayed no emotion. 'They said the two men were making a bomb.'

My mouth fell open.

'I don't know if it's true.'

'Has your aunt asked to see her son?'

'She's just come back from the Gendarmerie. They said she can't see him yet, but probably tomorrow. First, they have to question him.'

I tried not to grimace. Judging by the Amnesty International reports I had read, interrogation by the Lebanese Gendarmerie was unlikely to be a pleasant experience. 'So who were the two men?' It was unsettling to learn that there might have been bomb makers at work in the building only yesterday.

'Nobody knows. I saw them in the street yesterday afternoon. They wore long white robes, like the *Ahbash* wear.' The *Ahbash* were a Sunni Moslem fundamentalist group who had been active in Lebanon since the 1980s. 'They were definitely not from round here. My grandfather noticed them a couple of times last week. They were strangers.'

As Hanan finished speaking, Nahla blew her nose loudly and stood up, clutching a grey plastic handbag. She nodded gravely at me and made for the door.

'Are you off, Auntie Nahla?' Hanan jumped to her feet and followed her aunt to the door. She kissed her on both cheeks, uttered a string of farewells and hopes for the swift return of her son, and held the door for the older woman to pass through.

Half an hour later Hanan and I were chatting idly with Nadia and Abu Salim, who had come in from his workshop, when the door opened again. This time Muna walked in, smart as ever in her black trouser suit, followed by a short man in his sixties with a square head and neatly trimmed moustache. In the split second before she leapt to her feet to perform the ritual of greetings and introductions, Hanan managed to nudge me in the ribs. 'Nadia's husband,' she whispered. 'Remember?'

Luckily, I did remember. In the early hours of the previous morning, as the lights of Beirut began to twinkle through the darkness below us, Hanan had told me about the curious terms on which Nadia had contracted her third marriage. After Nadia's first husband had died, leaving her, like Ruhiyya, alone with three children, she had met and married a Jordanian. Sadly, the marriage had been doomed, for Nadia had not sought her father's consent. When Abu Salim found out about the new husband, he had become so angry that she had felt obliged to divorce him.

Some years later, a Lebanese friend of Abu Salim's, a widower named Mohammed, had fallen in love with Nadia. She was just under forty at the time, and working hard as a seamstress to support her children, who, like Ruhiyya's, boarded in a government school during the week. When her father's friend proposed to her, she decided to accept him, but on the strict condition that this time the marriage should remain a secret from her father. This could only be achieved by the couple living separately, an arrangement which seemed to bother neither Nadia nor Mohammed. After the marriage, Mohammed took to visiting Nadia several nights a week, but was always careful to leave before dawn.

When I asked Hanan why Abu Salim had objected so strongly to Nadia's marriage to the Jordanian, she had replied that she didn't know. 'I think he just didn't want her to be married to anyone. She was always his favourite daughter. Probably he just wanted her to be free to look after him in his old age.'

I had taken a liking to Nadia, who struck me as a warm, kind-hearted woman with a softer disposition than those of her sisters Muna and Ruhiyya. When it dawned on me that I was about to witness a three-way meeting between Nadia, her new husband and her jealous but unwitting father, I felt a passing anxiety on her behalf, and an irrational fear that I might somehow say the wrong thing and give their secret away. My anxiety mingled, however, with a degree of amusement, for I felt sure that both Nadia and Mohammed must be well-practised at handling such situations, given the close-knit social world in which they moved.

When Hanan had finished greeting Mohammed, I stood up and held out my hand. This was an error of etiquette, for, being a minor

Sheikh, he never shook hands with women. Only slightly embarassed, he held out his right arm for me to grasp through the protection of his pale green anorak. I duly did so, feeling a bit of a fool for my gaffe, and sat back down on the sofa. Meanwhile, Mohammed went on to greet Nadia and Ruhiyya in a manner that implied that he had not seen either of them for an equally long time, before embracing Abu Salim with warmth. He then sat down heavily in an armchair beside Abu Salim, and at a safe distance from Nadia. He was a broad, bulky man and his short stature made his large head seem all the larger.

While Mohammed and the old man exchanged news, Nadia stood up, the picture of composure, and went into the kitchen. She returned a few minutes later bearing a tray of tea glasses and proceeded to offer them around the room.

Muna was seated in a large armchair between Mohammed and the door, smoking and listening to the conversation between the two men. When they fell silent for a moment she glanced at me, leaned towards the low table in the centre of the floor and stubbed out her cigarette.

'Teresa, you remember the conversation we were having yesterday, about the Palestinians? You should ask Mr Mohammed some questions. He knows a lot about the Palestinians, because he used to work for the police.' She turned to Mohammed and explained to him briefly that Hanan's foreign friend was writing a book about the way the Lebanese felt about the Palestinians. I cringed, feeling the poor man would think I was very odd indeed, if not downright suspicious. But Abu Salim leapt to my rescue.

'No, her book's about Lebanon before and after the war,' he corrected Muna. 'She was asking me yesterday what life was like before 1975.'

Mohammed took a glass of tea from Nadia, nodding at her politely. 'Before 1969, life was wonderful,' he announced in a tone of surprise, as if this were such an incontrovertible fact that everyone should be well aware of it. 'Lebanon was free, it was a beautiful country, and we were in charge of our own destiny.' He regarded me across the room.

'In what sense were you in charge of your own destiny?' I smiled politely, as if I had never heard this said before.

'What I mean is that, in those days, the leaders of Lebanon were Lebanese.' He paused, allowing time for the weight of his words to sink in. 'It was before the Palestinians started to sabotage our sovereignty.'

'Mr Mohammed worked in Dikweni before the war,' Abu Salim butted in. 'He had to deal with the Palestinians a lot in his work.'

I took a glass of tea from Nadia. She seemed admirably at ease, I thought, as she deposited the empty tray on the coffee table and settled back into her armchair.

'I worked for Dikweni town council,' Mohammed went on, 'I was a clerk in the local police force.'

Dikweni was a little town in the Mountain, about five kilometres from Beirut, with a mainly Maronite population. It was close to Tell al Za'atar, the Palestinian refugee camp which had been besieged by Maronite militias in the summer of 1976.

'What were relations like between the Maronites and the Palestinians in Dikweni before the war?' I asked.

'Until the Cairo Agreement, they were good. The leader of the town council was a Maronite. He used to help the Palestinians sort out their paperwork when they had bureaucratic problems. He would help everyone, Maronite, Lebanese, Palestinian, without taking money from them. But once the Palestinians started to stockpile weapons in the camps, in the late 1960s, relations deteriorated and the situation changed. After the Cairo Agreement, the Palestinians no longer allowed the Lebanese police to enter the camps, so the camps became no-go areas.' Frown marks formed across Mohammed's broad forehead.

'Palestinians would get up to no good outside the camps,' he went on, 'and then run into the camps to hide. We couldn't follow them, so we were unable to bring them to justice.'

'What would have happened to the Lebanese police if they had entered a camp?'

'There was no way Lebanese police could enter, because the Palestinian militiamen were in control. If the militiamen didn't like the Palestinian whom the Lebanese police were pursuing, they would hand him over; but not otherwise.'

'Do you remember the Maronite attack on Tel al Za'atar?'

'I wasn't there when Tel al Za'atar was attacked, but I heard about it on the news and I saw what had happened afterwards.' It was hard to tell from Mohammed's tone what he felt about the fate of the Palestinians of Tel al Za'atar. Three hundred babies and young children had died of dehydration during the siege. On the day the camp was finally evacuated, 1,500 camp residents had been killed, while the Syrian army sat idly watching from a nearby hilltop. I decided the subject was best abandoned.

'What was life like for you once the war started?'

'My wife was always afraid, but I was not.' Mohammed was referring to the wife from his first marriage, whose fate I didn't know. 'I am never afraid of anything!' He chuckled, producing admiring smiles from Muna and Nadia. 'Our house was between Dikweni and the refugee camp. My Maronite neighbours always treated me well: I was a clerk in the police force of the town council, after all. It was the Palestinians from the camp who behaved badly.'

'Did that affect how you felt towards them?'

'Of course, it made me not want to help them, and I didn't help them, because they didn't stick to the Cairo Agreement. They were operating against Lebanese national interests.'

Nadia leant forward and placed her empty tea glass on the table. 'I never liked the Palestinians,' she announced.

Mohammed was frowning again. 'Look,' he began, 'I support the Palestinians' right to fight the Israelis *inside* Palestine, I am not a supporter of Israel. But I don't like what the Palestinians have done in Lebanon.'

'No,' I said, 'I can see that. Can you tell me more about how the Palestinians behaved in Dikweni?'

'Ok, I'll give you an example. Sometimes the town council would give a Palestinian permission to build a *one*-storey house, *outside* the camp. So what does the Palestinian do? He builds a *three*-storey house. And so that the council can do nothing about it, he gets the Palestinian fighters to defend his new house. This sort of thing happened all the time: the Palestinians used to take no notice at all of the Lebanese authorities. They were always trying to show us that we had no control over them and that they could do whatever they liked.

'I could give you other examples. Whenever a Lebanese soldier or policeman tried to pass through a Palestinian area, they would be stopped by the Palestinian forces and told to leave and never return. I myself was stopped many times by members of the Palestinian forces. They would tell me to leave because the area was under their control.' He glanced around the room with an air of indignation.

'Thanks,' I said slowly. 'Now I understand better why you dislike the Palestinians.'

Mohammed's response was a burst of raucous laughter. 'Lebanon, Lebanon,' he said in English, shaking his head in acknowledgement of the perversity of his own people. 'Here in Lebanon,' he went back to Arabic, 'there are Moslems and Christians, Palestinians and Lebanese, lots of different sects, and we spent fifteen years fighting with each other. Before the war there was a lot of affection between the different sects, but that didn't prevent us fighting.' He shook his head again. 'But you know, we Lebanese are a funny lot. Even during the war, as soon as we went abroad, as soon as we left the country, the affection would return and we would stand up for each other. And that hasn't changed, it's the same now.'

Mohammed seemed to be enjoying the conversation, so I asked him what other memories of the war lingered in his mind.

He thought for a few moments. 'Eventually I couldn't continue with my job in the police, so I worked as a taxi driver. One day I was returning to Beirut from the Bekaa, with a passenger. It was during the fighting between the Syrians and General Aoun, in 1989. In our hearts we supported General Aoun, but it was too dangerous to say so publicly, we would have been killed by Syrian *mukhberaat*.' As Mohammed drew breath, everyone in the room began to talk at once, in loud voices. Hanan remonstrated with Nadia and Muna, asking them to be quiet so that we could hear what Mohammed was saying. 'During the journey,' he went on, 'about ten kilometers from Chtaura, I had to stop at a Syrian checkpoint. A Syrian *mukhaberaat* man beckoned to me and I thought he meant me to drive forwards, but he followed me with a gun and told me to stop. He would not let me get out of the car and started to beat me up through the door. Then he dragged me out and took me to the *mukhaberaat* office and left me there. When the man in charge asked me why I was there, I said "one of your men picked me up at the checkpoint and brought me here". He asked why I was covered in bruises and I explained that I had been beaten. The man apologised and let me go.'

'Did you get back to Beirut safely?'

'Yes.' He paused. 'That sort of thing happened a lot during the war. Another time, I was driving through Dweirish, between the Bekaa and the Mountain, with a passenger, when one of Aoun's bombs landed on the road in front of us. A fragment of shrapnel came flying through the windscreen above my head, only missing me by a hair's breadth. I was covered in cuts and scratches.

I shook my head. 'And did you ever see people being kidnapped, at check points?'

Mohammed grimaced. 'I often saw people being taken out of their cars, but you never knew if they were being kidnapped. They could simply have been taken out, asked a few questions and then allowed to go. When people were kidnapped, a lot of care was taken to make sure that nobody saw what was happening.'

19

A WARTIME CHILDHOOD

Beirut, April 2006

'As children we were always frightened of the Syrians; always, always.' Hiba wrapped her hands around her mug of tea and gazed at me across the lounge. I had just arrived back from the sit-in for the disappeared in Syrian gaols and was telling her how upsetting I had found it.

'When I was a teenager, the Syrians had checkpoints all over Beirut. You could never go more than a kilometre without coming to one. It was terrifying, because everybody knew that the checkpoints were where the Syrians kidnapped people.' She took a swig of tea, looking down at the floor. I could sense her fear, even now. 'One day, our car broke down at a checkpoint. A Syrian soldier shouted at us to move. Luckily, a man we didn't know helped us by pushing the car out of the way with his car.' She paused. 'There was even a Syrian check-point at the corner of our street. The soldiers used to help themselves to timber from my father's timber yard, and to meat from the local butcher's.'

'Did they offer to pay?'

Hiba sucked her teeth. 'They used to say, "We are your protectors and we need these supplies."'

'Whereabouts did your family live during the war?' Hiba had been only three when the war started, and had spent her entire childhood in Beirut.

'In the same building where my parents live now, close to the port. You can see the beach and the docks from their apartment.' Hiba's father was in the food import business. 'Wait a minute, I want to adjust the blinds.' A dazzling sea light was flooding the room, making it hard for her to see me. She stood up and went to the window.

'Do you remember the beginning of the war?'

The first thing I remember is Black Saturday, in December 1975. That was the day the Christians went to the port to slaughter Moslems. Some people jumped into the sea, to save themselves.'

'I'm amazed that you remember! You were so young.'

'But I do.' She sat very still, as if searching for other memories. 'In the summer of 1982, when the Israelis came, I remember two days of aerial bombardment. Our building was close to a petrol station and my father's timber yard, so the risk of fire was very great. We spent those two days in the basement shelter beneath our building, with at least twenty other families from the neighbourhood. It was like being in a grave. There was only one toilet for all those people and it didn't flush. The weather was very hot and we were short of drinking water. And there was only one exit. We didn't want to open it in case the fighters came in, but we had to, for ventilation.' She drew breath. 'I remember the smell of burning when the petrol station was hit. Everyone was screaming because we thought it was the end.' She took a sip of tea. 'In my memory, it's as if we were in that shelter for months and months. At night we slept on mattresses and in the day time we rolled them up. My mother used to go up to the flat in the morning to cook on a paraffin stove.'

'Was there enough food?'

'*Yani*, we didn't go hungry. We ate endless rice with tinned vegetables. And the owner of Idriss supermarket had out-of-date meat in his freezer, which he sold to us.'

'Did you stay in Beirut throughout the siege?'

'I did, but my father sent my older brothers and sisters to our apartment in the Mountain. Because I was the youngest, I stayed in Beirut with my parents. I remember the day my brothers and sisters left. I cried and cried.' Suddenly Hiba's nose turned pink and she dabbed at her eyes with a tissue. 'I was so upset that my mother walked with me from one shop to another in the heat, to find me a Bounty bar and an "Extra", a fizzy drink made from pineapple juice. I always remember that. When we got home she let me drink it from one of her most expensive glasses.' Hiba shook her head, as if trying to rid herself of the pain associated with the memory. 'A few days later, we heard that a bomb had gone off in a restaurant in the village where my brothers and sisters were staying. It was a devastating moment, because we didn't know whether or not they were in the restaurant at the time. The phone lines were down, and we simply had to wait for someone to drive down to Beirut from the Mountain. Luckily, they were okay.

'Another thing I remember is when my grandparents' house was hit. They lived quite close to us, and they kept pigeons on their roof between the oil tank and the water tank. One day from our balcony we noticed that the pigeons were going mad and we knew that the house had been hit. Thank god, my grandparents were out at the time. It was an old house, but only the roof and the pigeons were damaged. The storey below was fine and my grandfather, who was a carpenter, was able to repair the roof. But my grandparents were very upset about losing the pigeons.' Hiba rested her chin in her hand. 'Now that I'm talking about the war, so many memories are coming back! Things I've not thought of for years.

'We children were fascinated by the Israeli soldiers, especially the women. We used to crowd round them in the street, until my parents called us to come back to the shelter.

'Being in the shelter was not always so bad. There was an old lady who lived in our building, called Hajji Wisal. She had a very white face and I thought she was beautiful. Sometimes when we were in the shelter she would spend hours telling us stories. We listened so intently that we forgot there was a war going on. They were like fairy stories – about marriage, kings, poverty and riches. Surprises of fortune, that kind of thing.

'I think we had a good childhood, despite the war. We were very close to one another and we got a lot of attention. And you know, people helped each other a lot in those days, much more than they do now.' Hiba put her mug down on the floor and shifted in her seat. 'There was a Maronite farmer, Abu Marun, who used to supply my father's shop. One day he drove into Beirut to the shop with his boot full of vegetables. My parents begged him to leave because they feared he would be killed. But when he saw the vegetables, my father wept. Abu Marun had risked his life to bring them to us and check that we were alright.' She smiled. 'In those days, Teresa, business was about friendship as much as it was about making money. Nowadays it's different, people are more materialistic.' She fell silent for a moment.

'I remember the day Bashir Gemmayel was elected president, in September 1982. That was a terrifying moment for Moslems. People were in the streets running and walking – there were no cars. It was between late afternoon and sunset. Some people were in their nightgowns. In our neighbourhood everyone was screaming "the Christians are coming to get us".

[165]

'My father gathered my sisters and brothers and showed them how to use a hunting rifle. My sisters were crying because they didn't want to learn. My father said "you have to be able to defend yourselves". I was too young to fire a gun, but on the balcony we had potted plants and rocks which normally we used to block the drains to stop rats from coming up the pipes. I was planning to use these to defend myself.

'After the Israelis left Beirut, and my brothers and sisters came back from the Mountain, my sisters and I attended a private school for Moslem girls, in Barbir. Because it was near the Green Line, there were snipers and when they started firing we had to go down to the cellar. My father would come and get us in his car. He would cram us in with as many of our friends as possible, to get us to safety. The school owned lots of buildings, and when it got too dangerous in Barbir they moved us to a different location, and then another one.

'After the Israelis left, I remember long nights of bombing and shelling. The militias of Amal and Hizbullah and the Druze Socialists were fighting with each other for control of West Beirut. They only fought at night, which made it impossible for us to sleep. We used to go down to the shelter and wait for it to stop. Bombs were being fired from across our street and a lot of residents were killed.'

By the 1980s, the Shi'a were beginning to play a bigger part in Lebanese politics. Amal was the militia attached to the *Harakat al Mahrumin*, or Movement of the Deprived, which had been founded in the early 1970s. The original goal of the Movement had been to promote the social and economic development of the Lebanese Shi'a. However, from the late 1970s, Amal had led a campaign of resistance against the Israeli occupation of the south, and by 1984 it had taken control of much of West Beirut.

Hizbullah had first appeared in 1982 in both Beirut and the Bekaa, one of a number of Islamic fundamentalist groups to emerge in Lebanon at the time. In general, such groups were inspired by the Islamic revolution in Iran in 1979 and fuelled by a general disillusionment with the failings of secular Arab nationalist and leftist political movements. But, as a specifically Shi'a fundamentalist group, Hizbullah had particularly strong links with Iran. Its formation was formalised in 1985 when it issued its 'Open letter … to the Downtrodden in Lebanon and the World', setting out its strongly anti-Zionist ideology. In a sense, Hizbullah came into being as a result of and in response to the Israeli occupation of south Lebanon.

But although it dedicated much of its efforts to resisting the Israelis, Hizbullah also became embroiled in battles for control of West Beirut.

'In 1986,' Hiba went on, 'when my sister got engaged, one day I was sent out of the shelter during a lull in the fighting to buy food at the supermarket. I was fourteen at the time. My mother said, "you are small and can run fast, so you should go." It was early in the morning and when I arrived, the supermarket was still closed. I had to stand outside, waiting in the street. Women were gathering, talking about the nearby buildings which had been hit in the night.

'Another time, my mother sent me to a shop opposite and the bombing started after I got there. It was the same three: Hizbullah, Amal and the Druze. I had to stay in the shop until it stopped.'

'Did you understand the differences between all the groups and what they were fighting about?'

Hiba rolled her eyes. 'As children we didn't understand at all. We used to ask our parents, "who are Hizbullah fighting for? and who are Amal fighting for? And who are we with?" They would say "we are with no one, just with Allah." I remember, when the Israelis came, seeing Bashir Gemayyel on the television. I was ten at the time. He was so good looking that he became my hero for a while – because I didn't understand who he was!' She laughed.

'Another job given to us as children was to carry water. We used to use those plastic urns like the one I have in the kitchen.' I had seen a green plastic urn sitting on the fridge. 'We would put a stick through the handle and two of us would carry it between us. Sometimes we had to walk a long way, in the heat, to the water company. It was very tiring. And when we got home we had to go up four flights of stairs.' Hiba wrinkled up her nose. 'When I look at that urn in the kitchen, it reminds me of those days, and I hate it.'

'When I was sixteen, in 1988, there was a lot of bombing. I was getting rebellious at that stage and refusing to go to the shelter. One day I was in our apartment, making coffee. It was late morning and I wanted hot milk in it, so I was about to step out onto the balcony to fetch the milk powder. At that moment I heard a bomb wheezing but not landing. That was unusual because usually after you heard a bomb wheezing, you would hear it explode. A few seconds later, it hit our building. We were on the fourth floor and it hit a kitchen wall on the sixth floor. All the shrapnel fell onto our balcony.

'After the noise, all I can remember is running down a long dark corridor in a cloud of black dust. My mother said I was screaming. She came up the stairs to meet me.' Hiba grimaced. 'After that, I went to the shelter more often.'

'During the war between Aoun and the Syrians, my cousin and I used to sneak magazines into the shelter so that we could sit there reading about sex. And at around that time, when I was seventeen, I used to lie to my parents by saying I was going to meet a friend in the next block. My friend used to tell her parents the same thing, and we'd meet and walk around the streets. Sometimes we went to Barbir to meet the boys who ran the Civil Defence. They drove ambulances and it was their job to go and collect bodies during breaks in the fighting. We thought they were very cool.'

'Were they armed?'

'No, they weren't armed. They were volunteers, and what they did was very dangerous, although we didn't see it that way at the time. They used to have their bases in the car parks of hospitals and schools.' Hiba stretched her arms in front of her. 'And if we didn't go to meet them, we went to the Corniche to sit in a café and drink Nescafe.'

'Was it safe to be on the streets?'

'It wasn't safe at all! One time when we were on the Corniche, the cannon started firing.' Hiba rolled her eyes. 'We had a lot of adventures that year!'

I had often wondered what it was like for Hiba when she left Beirut and came to England, aged eighteen, in 1990.

She smiled. 'It was very difficult to adjust, at first. I used to ask Omar whether we should store water and when there would be power cuts. He would laugh at me. Once, I was walking down Kingston Road, and I heard the sound of a demolition gang at work. I thought it was a bomb.

'Another time I was alone at home and I heard an ambulance siren. I was so terrified that I hid under the stairs. And the first time I was invited to a big firework display, I found it so scary and upsetting that I was desperate to go home.' She looked at me. 'You know, I used to wonder why people in the UK should not be fighting with each other. I thought it was very odd.'

20

FORENCE RAAD

Mount Lebanon, April 2006

✧

I was dreading going to meet Florence Raad's relatives.

In the photograph I had seen on the display board at the sit-in, Florence had looked young, and her features had radiated health and wellbeing. She wore her thick black hair coiffed in a 1960s-style bouffon and a pair of large eyes returned the gaze of the photographer with the confidence, almost impatience, of a woman who knew her place in the world.

The family had given me directions over the phone and told me to be at their house at seven p.m. It was a long ride from Hiba's place. The taxi climbed into the Mountain as the spring evening waned, and when it turned off the main road onto a narrow, twisting side street we passed a pair of ficus trees in full leaf wedged against the wall of a small church. They were a beautiful sight, being almost the first greenery I had seen since stepping off the plane. A minute later, the taxi pulled up in front of an apartment block.

I paid, got out and adjusted my handbag on my shoulder. Then I walked to the door and pressed the buzzer.

'Miss Thornill?' a pleasant male voice greeted me. 'Please come up to the second floor.' He spoke in French.

I walked across the hall and opened the door of the lift. Dusk was falling and I could only just see my way. When I stepped out on the second floor, a middle-aged man in smart trousers and a white shirt stood waiting for me in front of a polished mahogany door.

'Welcome, welcome, we are very happy to see you. I am Emile, we spoke on the phone.'

As I took his hand, two middle-aged women stepped forward to greet me. I was ushered into a large, comfortable living room and invited to sit down.

'We were excited when you called us,' Emile began. His formal manners and trim appearance made me imagine he might be a doctor or a lawyer. 'We thought perhaps you had some information concerning Florence.'

I had realised there was a danger that the family would jump to that conclusion, but had not seen a way to avoid raising their hopes. 'I'm so sorry,' I said, looking from Emile to the women and shaking my head. 'You must have felt very disappointed when I explained why I had rung you.'

'Ah, but we were pleased to hear from you in any case. It's good that someone should wish to write about our aunt. You are British?'

As I explained a little about myself and what I was doing in Lebanon, a slim young Asian maid padded into the room with a tray of coffee cups. She kept her gaze very low as she moved between the pale beige armchairs and sofas, treading softly on the carpet in her slippers. A rope of thick brown hair fell down her back, luxuriant against her pink gingham uniform.

'We will tell you what we remember about our aunt's case.' Emile turned over in his hands my book about Iraqi Kurdistan, which I had brought with me as proof that I was in good faith. 'I am Florence's nephew, and these two ladies are her nieces. This is Miriam,' he gestured to the woman seated nearest to him. Her face was clean of make-up and she wore her fair hair pulled back in a bun. She was dressed in black. 'And this is Georgette.' Georgette sat at the opposite end of my sofa. She was a little younger than Miriam and more fashionable in jeans, a blue chenille jersey and elaborate purple eye shadow. 'I called the whole family after you contacted me,' Emile explained, interlacing his fingers as he spoke. 'The others will be here shortly. You see, we all remember different things about our aunt. So it's better if you hear from all of us.' As he spoke we heard voices in the hallway. The door swung open and half a dozen young people, an older man and two older women burst into the room. I was introduced to them all, but afterwards I found it hard to recall the names. The older man was the brother-in-law of Florence, the women were more distant relatives and the younger ones were second cousins.

When everyone was seated, the maid began a second tour, this time bearing biscuits and glasses of mango juice.

'Do you prefer to speak in French or English?' Emile asked me. 'I can speak English, but for my cousins French is easier.'

'I can manage in French,' I replied. 'Can I just ask, I know you're Christians, but –'

'We are Maronites. So we should tell you the story of what happened to our aunt.' He paused, pushed his elbows into the arms of his chair and straightened his back. An expression of anxiety settled over his features.

'Florence was a journalist. From 1978 she was based in France. She wrote mainly for *al Sharq al Awsat* newspaper, in both French and Arabic. She was very pro-Palestinian in her writing.

'She wrote about the civil war, and other subjects. She was based in Paris, but she used to come and visit regularly. Through her work she had a lot of contacts in Lebanon. And because she had a press card, she was able to cross through areas of the country where we couldn't go, because of the fighting. She was a remarkable woman, confident and fearless. Sometimes she was able to use her contacts to help arrange exchanges of people who had been taken hostage by the different sides.'

'So she was very brave,' I said, looking from Emile to Miriam. The room felt crowded now, but mostly the new arrivals listened in silence, the older ones chipping in a comment from time to time.

'Yes, in a way,' Miriam replied, 'but really Florence was without fear.' I thought I sensed a tinge of criticism, and wondered what was to come.

'What sort of age was she?'

'She was forty-two when she disappeared.'

'I thought she looked much younger.'

Miriam smiled. 'She was very young when that photograph was taken… But at forty-two she was still young.'

'Did she have children?' I had wanted to know this from the moment I saw the photograph.

'No, she wasn't married. Thank God.' Miriam and I exchanged glances.

'In those days,' Emile went on, 'Florence's part of the family lived in an area known as East of Sidon. This is in the mountains between Sidon and Jezzine, and at that time the inhabitants were mainly Maronite. In April 1985 the whole area was evacuated by the Red Cross, because the Palestinians were attacking and it wasn't safe to remain. Not one person was left behind in the villages. Florence's family was evacuated to Jezzine.

'When her newspaper learned about the evacuations, they decided to send her to Lebanon on a reporting mission. So, just after Easter, she flew from Paris to Beirut. Now, Florence's mother and some of her brothers and sisters were in Jezzine, as I said, but the rest of the family lived in Beirut.'

Miriam leaned forwards. Her voice was deep and rather beautiful.

'I was already married and living in Beirut; my mother, Florence's sister, was in Jezzine. At that time we had had *no* news at all about my mother and the family, we didn't know what condition they were in, we didn't even know *where* they were. All we knew was that they had been evacuated by the Red Cross, and we heard bits of news on the radio. There was no way of finding out what had happened to individuals, because the telephone lines were down and all the roads were closed. From our point of view, in Beirut, we didn't know if members of our family had been killed, or if they had been caught up in fighting, or what. The Red Cross brought the old and the sick to Beirut; but there was no information about anybody else.'

'So the Palestinians had attacked the region prior to the evacuation?' I addressed myself to Miriam.

'There hadn't actually been an attack. From what my mother told me, the Red Cross had warned that the Palestinians were about to come and commit a massacre, and had therefore advised people to leave.' She paused. 'You can imagine what it was like for my mother and Florence's family. They had lost everything and were living as refugees in a rented house in Jezzine.

'When Florence arrived in Beirut, she decided to use her press card to travel to Jezzine. If she hadn't had a press card, she couldn't have got through. When she arrived, she found the family and stayed with them for two nights. Thank god, everyone was safe.' Miriam caught her breath.

'During her visit, she borrowed her brother's car to drive down to her parents' village in East of Sidon, to see what had happened there. She took my mother with her, and the mayor of the village. When they arrived, they found Hizbullah in control of one sector of the village and the Palestinians in control of another, and some other pro-Nasser militia in control of a third sector. But the point is, she went down and came back up to Jezzine safely.'

Georgette spoke next. 'Florence was worried while she was with us. She told me that she felt she was being followed.'

'By whom?'

'The Israelis. She had written a lot of articles that were very pro-Palestinian, as Emile told you. She told me that she felt the Israelis were after her.'

'Were the Israelis in Jezzine at the time?'

Georgette nodded. 'But we don't know for sure that they were following her.'

Emile began to speak again. 'It was when she tried to return to Beirut, that she ran into problems. She had three interviews planned: one with the Druze leader Walid Jumblatt, in Moukhtara in the Shouf; one with Fadlallah, in Beirut, and the third with... I forget.' Fadlallah was a senior Shi'a cleric and the spiritual mentor for Hizbullah. Emile rested his chin in his hand for a moment and looked down. 'Possibly it was with Amin Gemmayel.'

Amin Gemmayel had assumed the presidency in 1982, after the assassination of his brother Bashir.

Emile looked up again. 'Anyway, she insisted on going alone.'

'She was advised against it,' Georgette added. 'I remember that Jean Aziz, the parliamentary deputy for Jezzine, told her to wait. The day after the day she wanted to travel, a convoy was due to set off on the same route. He felt she would be much safer if she travelled with the convoy.'

I was starting to feel very cold, although the temperature in the room had not changed.

Georgette shook her head. 'But she refused to wait. She felt that she would be okay driving alone, that nothing would happen to her. Jean Aziz tried to explain to her that in Lebanon a press card is worth nothing, it does not protect you one iota. But she didn't listen to him. As Miriam said, she was without fear.'

Emile went on. 'The morning Florence left Jezzine, one of her brothers followed her in a separate car as far as the bridge at Joun, over the Awali river. The river was the border between the Christian-controlled areas and the Druze-controlled areas. At the bridge they said goodbye, and Florence drove on alone.' He paused. 'That is the last time anyone saw her.'

I hesitated. 'Do you know what happened?'

Miriam broke in. 'We did everything we could to find her. We made every possible enquiry, but no-one had seen her, no-one knew anything about her.'

'Was the car ever found?'

Emile clicked his tongue. 'No, but during the war cars disappeared all the time. Cars were stolen from the forecourts of people's houses. It was easy to make a car disappear just by changing the number plates.'

'Do you know if she arrived to see Walid Jumblatt?'

Miriam shook her head. 'He said he wasn't holding her, and that he hadn't seen her.'

'And Fadlallah?'

'He said the same thing, that he hadn't seen her.' She paused. 'We also tried to find her through the Lebanese Red Cross, and the International Red Cross, but they had no news of her.' She paused. 'There were always people offering to act as intermediaries, at that time, for money. People who claimed to have connections with the Syrians would approach my uncle, Florence's brother, and say 'We have seen her. If you want to see her, you must give us money and we'll bring news of her...' My uncle was taken for a ride like that, several times. Eventually he told the intermediary that he must tell us something about her that only *we* knew, so that we could then be sure that he had really seen Florence. But the man didn't bring any tangible proof that he had seen her and my uncle stopped paying him.' Miriam let out a sigh of despair. 'At that time, our whole life was askew; the whole family was without money, homeless, having to re-build their lives.' She looked at me. 'Florence's kidnapping was very difficult to deal with: one couldn't contact anyone, the war was going on, everything was uncertain.'

I was struggling to make sense of the story. 'So, unlike the other people at the sit-in, you can't be sure Florence was taken by the Syrians?' I addressed myself to Miriam.

'That is why I didn't join the protest straightaway, because I knew that most of the people involved were sure that their missing relatives had been taken by the Syrians, whereas we can't be sure. Now the reason why we eventually decided that she was probably in Syria, is this. Two and a half years ago, it was reported in a Beirut newspaper, *an Nahar*, that a Syrian who had been released from a prison in Syria, had gone to France and had a meeting with the Maronite patriarch in Paris. The man gave the patriarch a list of names of people he had met as detainees in Syria, and Florence's name was on the list.' As she looked at me I felt my body temperature drop even further. 'We obtained the man's telephone number and tried to contact him, but we got no reply.'

'D'you have the man's name?'

'Yes, but we weren't able to reach him.'[5] Miriam paused. 'So when this business with the patriarch came to nothing, we began to attend the sit-in. There we met people who had been in prison in Syria. They were mostly men. They told us that as male prisoners they didn't get to see women prisoners, but that they were sure that there were some women. They had heard the cries of women. They had even heard a woman giving birth.' Miriam broke off, her hand over her mouth. 'It was really horrible. When I heard them talk about how the prisoners had suffered, I found myself hoping that Florence was dead, not alive. Rather than endure such horrors for twenty years, it would be better for her to be dead.'

I nodded, for my voice had deserted me.

'There you are. That's the story.' She folded her hands in her lap. 'Somebody told us that it was Jumblatt's Progressive Socialist Party who kidnapped her originally, they passed her to Hizbullah, and Hizbullah then took her to Syria.'

'Do you think that's possible?'

'Yes, due to the nature of the newspaper for which she worked. *Al Sharq al Awsat* supports the Iraqi Ba'ath party.' Prior to the demise of Saddam Hussein, there was a long-standing enmity between the ruling Syrian Ba'athist regime and its counterpart in Iraq. A journalist who wrote for a pro-Iraqi Ba'athist newspaper would be seen by the Syrians as an enemy.

'What about the Israelis?' I thought for a moment as I asked the question. 'But if they had taken her, I think they would have acknowledged it.'

Emile nodded. 'The Israelis provide lists of their prisoners. They do not operate in secrecy, as the Syrians do. We can't be sure, but it seems less likely it was the Israelis.' I remembered something I had been told about the Lebanese prisoners who were still being held in Israeli prisons. They were permitted to organise themselves inside the prison,

---

5   Nizar Nayouf, a well-known Syrian journalist and human rights activist who was imprisoned by the Syrians from 1992–2001, met with Nasrallah Boutros Sfeir, the Maronite patriarch, in Paris on 3 October 2003. He provided Sfeir with a list of names of thirty-two prisoners whom he had seen and identified during his ten-year detention in Syria. Florence Raad was on the list. Report of *Rassemblement Canadien pour le Liban*, 13 October 2003.

and their leader was in regular contact with the Beirut newspapers by telephone.

'Going back to the Syrian ex-prisoner who went to the patriarch in Paris, did he say that the people on his list were still alive?'

'Yes. But we have no way of verifying this information. We tried to contact the man, but we got nowhere.'

'Have you tried going to Paris?'

'We have an uncle there. We tried to make contact with the Syrian ex-prisoner from Beirut, but as I said there was no reply to the number we were given.'

'And you don't know whether the man is still in France or whether he returned to Syria?'

'No idea.'

'I guess he would have been afraid to return to Syria after twenty years in prison there.'

'I don't know.'

'And now the Syrians have left Lebanon, is it possible the Lebanese government will start to ask questions of the Syrians?'

'I don't know. There are 1,700 people who are thought to be in the hands of the Syrians. The situation has snowballed, since this movement began, with many people who have a missing relative joining the protest. And of the people who have been released by the Syrians, some have wished to speak out and others have chosen to remain silent. Even the number of missing people is not precise because there are some families who refuse to come forward.'

'Did *al Sharq al Awsat* newspaper do anything to help Florence?'

'No.'

'Not even back in 1985?'

'No.'

We all fell silent. I turned the story over in my mind, searching for angles we had not covered. It was appalling to imagine that Florence might still be in a prison in Syria, now, at this moment, twenty-one years after her disappearance. If she were, she would be sixty-three years old. My mind baulked at imagining what state of health she might be in. I knew for a fact that the Syrians were in the habit of holding some prisoners for lengthy periods of time, but in Florence's case I didn't want to believe it.

'Surely the Syrians wouldn't want to feed her for twenty odd years?' I addressed my question to Emile.

'Why not?' He clearly thought the question naïve. 'The food they provide in the prisons is cheap! And they would have a strong motive for holding her: if they let her go, she could cause them a lot of trouble by what she might say.'

I was surprised by this. I doubted that a regime like the Syrian one cared about its human rights record. Florence was well-connected, it was true, but I didn't think anything she might say or write about life in a Syrian prison would differ greatly from material already published by Amnesty International.

'So probably the best hope for Florence is a change of regime in Syria.' I spoke my thought aloud, remembering the moving stories I had read in the press in 1991 about Iraqi prisoners escaping from gaol during the uprising against Saddam which followed the 1991 Gulf war. I still held in my mind images of white-haired men with beards that fell to their knees and fingernails like talons, staggering out into the sunlight after twenty years in underground cells.

But the family misunderstood me, thinking I was referring to the American and British invasion of Iraq in 2003. In Iraq, they retorted, one generation of prisoners had been released from Saddam's prisons, only for a fresh lot of prisoners to be abused by the Americans in Abu Ghraib. I let the subject go, privately thinking that I was right. By change of regime I didn't mean a Western-led attack on Syria, but an uprising by the Syrian people against the forty-odd-year dictatorship by the al-Assad family. At that point, the doors of the prisons might be expected to open.

I took a deep breath. 'So how do you feel about Florence, now, after twenty-one years?' My gaze fell first on Miriam, then on Emile.

Emile shifted in his chair, interlacing his fingers once again. 'We feel guilty.' He looked at me. 'For example, when Florence's brothers and sisters count themselves as a family, should they say "We are six"; or "we are seven"? There is never an answer to this question. If they say "We are six", it is as if they are deciding she is dead. But they don't know this. And if they say "We are seven", then they feel that they must find her. But how?'

Miriam began to speak. 'During the war, life was so difficult that in a way it was easier not to think of her than it is now. We lived from day to day, doing our best to survive, struggling to raise our children.' She paused. 'Now that peace has returned, and life is easier, I find myself thinking of her more often.'

'Her legal status is a problem, too,' Emile added. 'Should she be treated as someone who is dead or as someone who is alive?'

'Does she own property?'

'She had a rented apartment in Paris. Her things were sold and the apartment was returned to the owner. But still, it would be easier if her status were clear.'

Georgette shifted in her seat beside me and I turned towards her. 'What we want, is either to know that she is dead; or to have her back with us, safe and sound.'

'Of course you do.' I met her eye, trying to express my sympathy. The words 'safe and sound' had a dreadful ring, for I couldn't see how a woman who had spent twenty-one years in a Syrian prison could possibly emerge with their physical or mental health in tact.

The maid was circulating again with more coffee. I had no more questions, and thanked the family for sharing Florence's story with me. Separate conversations sprang up among the relatives and the tension in the room began to disperse. Georgette edged closer to me on the sofa and asked what I thought of Lebanon. I told her that I liked it – it would have been impolite to say otherwise – but that I was shocked by the extent to which the shadow of the war still hung over people's lives.

She wrinkled up her nose. 'We don't feel secure. Look, take my situation. Both my children live in France, and I am always asking myself if I should leave and go to join them.'

'On a permanent basis?'

She nodded. 'On one level it would be very sad to leave Lebanon. I was born here and I've lived here all my life. But I don't feel safe. It's very hard to know what to do.'

The family called a taxi to take me back to Barbir in West Beirut, where I had arranged to stay the night with my friend Zeinab. I sat very still on the back seat in the darkness, my arms wrapped tightly around the bag in which I kept my books and my tape recorder. As we approached Barbir a wave of panic passed through me. The streets were poorly-lit and deserted, so that the area looked different from how it appeared during the day. What if I couldn't find my way to Zeinab's apartment? I asked the driver to drop me by the gate of the old hospital, reminding myself that I had found my way to Zeinab's from that landmark only a few days earlier. I paid, got out, and walked as fast as I could past the shuttered shops. If a car pulled up now and I was dragged inside, no-one would have any idea what had happened to me. Zeinab would wonder why I hadn't turned up, Hiba would worry the next day when I didn't reappear, but neither of them would have the first idea of how to find me.

By the time I had finished running through these dark scenarios, I was at the door to Zeinab's building.

I slept badly that night, too disturbed by Florence's story to let myself go into restful sleep. Although the room was warm and I had a pair of thick blankets over me, my body felt chilled. In the morning I got up early with Zeinab and her little girls and took a lift with them to Achraffiyeh, where the girls' school stood in the same street as the university where Zeinab lectured. At a little after eight, I left Zeinab's office and set off in search of a café in which to have breakfast. It was drizzling and, although I no longer felt cold, I was grateful for my thick coat.

After wandering through the streets for a quarter of an hour, I found a deserted restaurant where an old man agreed to make me tea. The floor, tables and chairs were dark brown and the stale air was thick with the previous night's cigarette smoke. But I was tired of walking in the rain and wanted to sit and write my journal.

Weary from my wakeful night, I stirred sugar into my tea and swallowed some crumbly biscuits which the old man brought me. When I picked up my pen, a new set of thoughts about Florence flooded my mind. What if the family were wrong, and she hadn't been kidnapped at all? I imagined her setting off from the bridge at Joun in the morning sun, observed by her brother. He would have seen her car climbing up the mountain road, until it rounded the first hairpin and was gone from his sight. What if, ten miles down the road, the car had been hi-jacked, and Florence had been killed? It would have been easy to dispose of her body in the mountains, without leaving a trace. The country was in such turmoil at that time that there would have been no risk of a search party coming to look for her. And then the hi-jacker could have changed the number plates on her car and driven it away. I half wanted to call the family and ask if they had considered my hypothesis. But it didn't explain how the Syrian ex-prisoner had given Florence's name to the Maronite patriarch in Paris as recently as 2003. The hypothesis was a fantasy, produced by my mind to alleviate the sense of horror which Florence's story had instilled in me.

21

HIZBULLAH

Dahyya, southern Beirut, April 2006

✧

The *servees* took twenty minutes to reach Dahyya in the lunchtime traffic. On the way I called Hanan – not to inform her that I was off to meet a representative of Hizbullah, which might have worried her – but to enquire after her cousin.

'The Gendarmerie released him this morning.'

'And is he okay?'

There was a pause. 'I don't know. My aunt Nahla looked very shaken when she passed by to tell us he was out. I didn't like to ask her too many questions. We're just relieved he's been released.' I said goodbye and put the phone in my bag, wondering if the men in white from the Ahbash had been released, too.

I was starting to feel anxious now about my meeting with Hizbullah. Perhaps I had been influenced by the US and Israeli categorisation of Hizbullah as a 'terrorist' organisation, although I didn't agree with it. In my view, whatever dubious tactics Hizbullah and its External Security Organisation had adopted over the years (and there had certainly been some which it was impossible to stomach), their own characterisation of themselves as a 'resistance' organisation was accurate. Hizbullah had played a major role in getting the Israelis to abandon their long, illegal occupation of Lebanon. But I was nervous, nonetheless.

As I got out of the *servees* and walked towards Hizbullah's offices, I took a careful look at the neighbourhood, to see how it compared to Muna's description. Four- and five-storey apartment buildings lined the street, the striped awnings of their balconies billowing in a light breeze. At ground level, shops opened onto a wide, dusty pavement. I saw no signs of acute poverty; if anything, the area appeared more affluent than the district of Tariq al Jaddideh where Hanan's family lived.

When I reached Hizbullah's building, I asked an old man standing in the entrance whether I was in the right place. He stepped aside and waved me up a flight of filthy concrete steps. Halfway up, a broken window gave onto a piece of derelict ground at the rear of the building. This was more squalid than the street at the front, but I was not going to be put off. I continued climbing in the semi darkness, until I reached the second floor, where a glass door led into a suite of brightly-lit offices. The words 'Hizbullah – Foreign Relations' were displayed in English on the wall above the reception desk.

The man on the desk showed me into a waiting room and closed the door behind me. I stood for a moment examining a pair of portrait posters on the wall, showing senior Shi'a clerics with thick grey beards, before sitting down on one of the wood-framed sofas that lined the walls. How long I would have to wait? Behind an identical sofa opposite, the wall was clad from floor to ceiling with mirror glass, cut into the shape of a pair of double doors.

Fifteen minutes went by and I began to feel jumpy. But at last the door opened and a smiling man in his early thirties stepped into the room. He greeted me in English with an energetic air, introduced himself as Hajj Hussein Nabulsi and ushered me down a long corridor to a small office. Here, he waved me to a swivel chair and took his seat behind the desk.

I asked if he would mind my recording our conversation.

'No, go ahead,' he nodded with a trace of impatience, as if all his visitors made the same request. As I took the tape recorder out of my bag and placed it on the desk he raised his eyebrows. 'Oh,' he said, 'it's very old.'

'But it works!' I inserted a fresh cassette and placed the microphone on the desk. He was accustomed, I told myself, to speaking to foreign correspondents with state of the art equipment. But surely I was less likely to be a spy if my equipment was rudimentary? I sensed him waiting for me on the far side of the desk, a ball of energy and intelligence. His shoulders were broad and powerful, his face clean-shaven, his sallow skin unblemished.

I began by asking about the size of the Shi'a community in present-day Lebanon.

'Okay,' Hajj Hussein nodded. 'The Shi'a used to be the largest sect, but now the Sunnis number about 100,000 more.'

'And of the Shi'a population, do the majority support Hizbullah?'

Hussein Nabulsi raised his hands so that they hovered a few inches above the desk and drew back his head, apparently wrestling with the best way to express himself to an unknown foreign woman. His forehead furrowed into lines as he raised his eyebrows, and his cheeks bulged. 'I don't know how much you know about the Lebanese political system?'

'I know the basics.'

'Okay, good. Under the Ta'if Agreement, in our parliament there are sixty-four seats for Christian deputies and sixty-four for Moslems. And of the sixty-four Moslem seats, one third, or twenty-one seats, are for the Shi'a.' He grimaced. 'It's a very complex, sectarian system. We have a particular kind of democracy which only exists in Lebanon, called "consensus democracy". But it doesn't function very well.' He hesitated. 'Am I making myself clear?'

'Very clear, your English is excellent.'

'I could express myself better if we spoke in Arabic, but I don't know if you can…'

'No, I'm sorry, your English is much better than my Arabic.' I laughed.

'Okay.' The ice was broken. Hajj Hussein rested his hands on the desk in front of him and I noticed that his fingers were short and fleshy. 'To go back to your question. What we want is to change the electoral system. If we had a system of proportional representation, and if all of Lebanon were one district, then Hizbullah's representation in parliament would be bigger than it is now, that's for sure.' He glanced at me sharply, to check that I was following him. 'But we have a sectarian system, and we are stuck with this quota. Even if the Shi'a were eighty per cent of the population, the quota would still apply.' He drew breath.

'What we want is an electoral system that represents all Lebanese; all strata of society. We want Lebanon to be one electoral district so that for example I can vote for… an MP in Tripoli; and a man in Tripoli can vote for an MP in Sidon or Tyre or wherever. At the moment all you have is two choices of candidate, this person or that person, related to your small local area.'

'Is there some means by which you can bring about this electoral reform?'

Hajj Hussein leaned back in his seat and let out a laugh of despair. 'We can't. First we have to get rid of sectarianism from the hearts and minds of… It's very difficult.

'Now if you ask me whether we represent the majority in our own community,' he went on, 'I will tell you that in the municipal elections in 2004, Hizbullah swept up *all* the seats in the Bekaa; and all those in Dahyya, Ghobeiri and Bourj al Barajneh.' These three districts were all in south Beirut. 'And in south Lebanon, we took sixty-five percent of the seats.'

I noticed that Hajj Hussein did not mention Hizbullah's rival in the Bekaa, former Hizbullah Secretary-General Subhi Tufayli, who left the party in 1992. In 1997–1998, Tufayli had led a populist movement called 'the revolution of the hungry' and had stood in the 1998 municipal elections on a platform which implicitly criticised Hizbullah for failing to attend to the needs of impoverished Bekaa farmers. Tufayli had roused quite a following and captured several seats in the Bekaa, prompting Hizbullah to improve its programme for the Bekaa in the 2004 elections.

The door opened and an old man came in bearing a tray. He placed a tiny cup of strong black coffee in front of me and another in front of Hajj Hussein.

'How about Amal? Where are their seats?'

'Amal took the other thirty-five percent of the Shi'a vote, mainly in the south. They have no real movement in the Bekaa, and no representation there. They are a little bit active in Beirut, but not much.' He wrinkled up his nose. 'In the past, Amal was the *only* Shi'a political movement. I was in the Amal movement… Sheikh Nasrallah himself was in the Amal movement, he was in charge of the Bekaa. But now things have changed, we are in 2006…' Hajj Hussein picked up his cup and took a swig of coffee.

I sat across the desk, wondering what to ask next. Hajj Hussein fascinated me, with his sharp eyes, his brilliant, US-accented English and his brimming energy. I would have loved to ask him about his personal journey from the secular, reformist Amal movement into the upper echelons of Hizbullah. Had he always been a believer, I wondered, or had faith acquired greater significance in his eyes after he had witnessed the failure of Arab secular politics? But I feared such questions might be seen as impertinent. Instead I asked him to tell me about the social welfare aspects of Hizbullah's work.

'Look.' Hajj Hussein fixed me with his eyes. 'We are a unique party in everything, everything. In principles, ideology, system, mentality, way of life, way of thinking: everything is different.'

A car hooted in the street below.

'We provided a unique experience for Lebanon and the Arab world. And now we are considered to be a model for many Arab resistance movements. That was very clear in occupied Palestine, specially after the liberation of south Lebanon.' He paused.

He was referring to the timing of the second Palestinian *intifada,* which began in September 2000, just four months after the Israeli withdrawal from south Lebanon. Many observers had made the point that Hizbullah's success in ousting the Israelis from south Lebanon had played a role in mobilising the Palestinians, as had the propaganda put out by its television station, to which residents of the West Bank and Gaza frequently tuned.

'When I say "unique",' Hajj Hussein went on, 'I really mean it. We started from scratch. Lebanon was in turmoil and in civil war. Israel invaded Lebanon. We created the so-called "Party of God". Our main task and target was Israel: to defend our country and get the Israelis out of Lebanon. Our movement began to grow bigger and bigger and there was at that time a great need for welfare services. We had martyrs and we needed to take care of the families of the martyrs. We established an association called "The Martyrs' Association." We began to see wounded people and so we created the "War Wounded Association."'

Hajj Hussein raised his hands again above the desk. 'You know, the process was gradual and sometimes it was not really planned. The welfare organisations grew in response to urgent need. For example, we didn't have any hospitals. From Dahyya, sick people had to be sent to West Beirut in order to be hospitalised. So we built hospitals. We built clinics. Now we have two, three, four hospitals in Dahyya. We also built schools. So this is how we began the gradual development of our infrastructure.' Hajj Hussein rubbed his right hand over his forehead. 'And now we have everything, we don't need anything any more.' His tone conveyed confidence and pride.

'So you don't really need the Lebanese state?' I was beginning to understand what people meant when they said that Hizbullah operated as a state within a state.

But Hajj Hussein wouldn't have this. 'No,' he replied firmly. 'No, no. The Lebanese state is something which has to do with your existence. You can't get out of belonging to your country.' He smiled. 'This is, at the end, your country. You've done all what you've done for this country.' He began to gesticulate again, and it suddenly struck me that his right hand was larger than his left. 'I mean, *why* did we decide to provide all these services? If I was living in Denmark, or if I was living in Canada, I would not have to do that, because the government would provide everything. But this is not the case in Lebanon.

'Because Lebanon was sectarian,' he paused for emphasis, 'and because all the privileges were given to the Christians,' he paused again, 'and the Christians had everything, all the privileges, and the Moslems, *especially* the Shi'a, were deprived; that is why Imam Musa Sadr created the Amal movement. In Arabic it's called *Harakat al Mahrumin*, the Movement of the Deprived.'

Imam Musa Sadr was an extraordinary Iranian cleric who settled in Tyre in south Lebanon in 1960, having been invited by the Shi'a community to replace their deceased *mufti* (chief expounder of religious law). From then until his mysterious disappearance in Libya in 1978, he played a pivotal role in the development and politicisation of the Shi'a community.

'In the past,' Hajj Hussein went on, 'all our grandfathers were peasants. If you compare how things were for us in the past and how they are now, you will see how effective we have been. The development has been unbelievable.'

I agreed with him. It was impossible not to be impressed by the way Lebanon's Shi'a community had taken control of their own fortunes in the last forty years, creating their own health and social welfare institutions to fulfil needs which had long been neglected by the Lebanese state, and moving away from the political attitude of submission which had characterised the community for so many centuries. Both Amal and Hizbullah had played major parts in this process.

Migration had also been a factor. From the early years of the twentieth century, many sons of impoverished Shi'a families had migrated to West Africa, South America and the Gulf, where they had gradually established successful businesses. Some had later returned to plough their wealth into South Lebanon and the Bekaa.

'Nowadays we have many many doctors, *important* doctors, *important* engineers, *important* lawyers, everything.' Hajj Hussein looked at me intently to check that I was taking in what he was saying. 'That's why, as I told you, we have reached a point where we don't need anything. And we did it because we knew that our community was in urgent need of development.

'I remember during the civil war, we used to collect garbage from the streets and provide drinking water to people. Even now we have associations which are just for the poor and the needy. Without our help, the situation of the Shi'a would still be miserable. We have had to work very hard, you know, to get to where we are now. It has not been easy.' He paused for breath and leant back in his chair, once more resting his hands on the desk, palm down.

'I want to tell you that we sacrificed 1,800 martyrs for the sake of liberating Lebanon. We spilled our blood on Lebanese soil. It was not a picnic. *It was not a picnic!* We paid a price: but we got the result!' Again he drew breath. 'Can I tell you something?' He spoke with such passion that I was swept along in the current. 'What differentiates Hizbullah from others is that, when we do something, we really mean it. We don't do it for political reasons or political gains. We do it for the sake of God! And that's what differentiates us from others. For example, if I want to give you assistance, I don't do it for your sake, and I don't do it to get something in return, to get you to vote for me or to get political support. Do you know, we even support families of those who were in Lahhad's militia.'

I raised my eyebrows in disbelief. Hajj Hussein was referring to the SLA, the militia which the Israelis had set up in 1978 to police Lebanon's southern border. If it were true that Hizbullah had assisted SLA families, that was astonishing. '*Do* you?' I gasped.

'Yeah, yeah, yeah!' Hajj Hussein was pleased with my reaction. 'We have examples of that. And the funny thing is that we support them, we provide them with food, and they *hate* us.' He smirked.

'But they take the food?'

'Yeah, they take it. They take it but they hate us. When we do it, we do it because we know that this family is in need. We do it for the sake of God. We know that if we don't provide food to this family, their situation will be *miserable, miserable*. So we don't do it to get something in return; honest to God, we have never never never done anything for the sake of getting something in return. Never, never, never. Otherwise, we'd be losers.'

Hajj Hussein had lost me now. From my perspective, Hizbullah was a political organisation, albeit perhaps a remarkable one. I simply could not accept that a political organisation could act out of pure altruism.

'And we do believe in that,' Hajj Hussein went on. 'We are faithful. I tell you, we believe that this is our religious duty. We have to do this, because if we don't do it, God will punish us. If we have the capability to do it, we must do it, because God asks us to help the poor. This is a religious obligation. God tells us we must pay twenty per cent of our income to the poor.'

Now I felt I understood. To me, religious duty was something other than altruism, particularly if it was coupled with the threat of punishment.

'Every Shi'a believer should pay twenty per cent of his annual profit to the poor. In fact, this amount of money *must go* to the poor. That's why in our religious system we have no funding problem. Sometimes when they speak of freezing Hizbullah's assets, we just, you know, make fun of it.' He looked amused.

'Because it won't really matter?'

'First of all we have no money in the banks in America. Second thing is that in our religious system, from the very beginning, when the *marja*'s began to take over, the *marja*'s were completely independent financially.'

A *marja'–e taqlid* is a Shi'a religious man, sometimes described as a 'source of emulation' for ordinary Shi'a.

'Look at the history of the Shi'a,' Hajj Hussein went on. 'Not a single *marja*' in the Shi'a world depended on this or that government. Even in Iran – this thought just came to me – the *marja*' doesn't take money from the government, he is always independent. The people give twenty per cent of their money to the *marja*' and the *marja*' gives it to the poor and to the clerics. So they have a real, independent authority.' Hajj Hussein drained his coffee.

To me, his remarks about the *marja*' seemed a little spurious. However independent the Iranian *marja*' might be, there was little doubt but that Hizbullah regularly received substantial funding from the Iranian government. I could understand why Hajj Hussein might wish to divert my attention from this issue, for western observers frequently cited Iran's financial support for Hizbullah as proof that it is an organisation to be regarded with extreme suspicion. For me, however, Iran's financial support for Hizbullah was no more remarkable as a fact of *realpolitik* than America's financial support for Israel.[6]

'Tell me about the south,' I said after a moment, 'where the war damage was so severe. Is Hizbullah involved in reconstruction work?'

'Okay, I'll give you an example. In 1993 Israel launched a large scale attack on the south, causing unbelievable destruction. Houses were damaged, agriculture, everything. Hizbullah took responsibility for *all* the reconstruction of houses. *All* of it. We have an association called "Construction Jihad". This association re-built all the damaged bridges, houses, everything. Then in 1996 there was the Grapes of Wrath, when over one hundred civilians were killed in the UN building and lots of homes were destroyed. Again, Hizbullah took the responsibility and re-built. That time we received some support from other countries, but Hizbullah initiated the rebuilding of the damaged houses.

'This is a very small example. Look, if I want to count the number of associations we have – there are so many. Firstly we have the Martyrs' Association. We pay a monthly salary to the wife of any martyr. We buy her an apartment. She picks the apartment she wants: we just pay. Also if she doesn't have, say, a refrigerator, or a washing machine, we buy her one. On top of that, children of martyrs get free education, either in our schools or in the school they choose. You can't force the family to choose this school or that school. Then, they get healthcare, one hundred per cent.'

'Does that include maternity, hospitalisation, everything?'

---

6   Clearly one cannot draw an exact parallel between one country providing financial support to another, as in the case of America's support for Israel, and a country providing financial support to an armed group belonging to another country, as in the case of Iran's support for Hizbullah. The fact that Iran supports a group within Lebanon rather than the Lebanese government itself reflects the fact that, unlike Israel, Lebanon is still in the process of becoming a single, unified nation. The Lebanese government effectively depends on Hizbullah to defend it against Israel, but cannot take this stance openly, because to do so would risk alienating western governments and some of its own Christian citizens. While western governments refuse to recognise the threat which Israel poses to neighbouring Arab states, governments such as the Lebanese one will be forced to maintain such ambiguous stances and to allow their defence to be partly funded by anti-western states such as Iran.

'Everything. When I tell you "healthcare", some of my colleagues here say "we wish we were like martyrs, because at least our wives and children would get fed."' Hajj Hussein gave a warm, happy chuckle. 'We really take care of the families. Because when someone sacrifices themselves for the country, if then you abandon the family, it's a betrayal! No, no, we need a resistance society and you cannot build that by abandoning the families. At least when someone goes to the front to fight, he knows that someone else is going to take care of his wife and his children.

'Then, we have a special War Wounded Association. We have Construction Jihad, which has a very important agriculture section nowadays. It provides lessons, guidance, seeds to the peasants. And we have many social offices which provide urgent assistance to the poor. For example, someone who has no money needs to be taken to hospital, so they come to us. We either call the hospital or we provide some money.

'The families of martyrs are directly under the auspices of Said Nasrallah, because those people need intensive care. And you know, most of those who work in the Martyrs' Association are women. Men are not allowed to visit martyrs' families: we believe that women best understand the need, the psychological problems. A martyr's wife will be able to talk freely to another woman. We allow men to work in the offices, on the computers, for example, but they aren't allowed to visit.

'We also have five hospitals in Lebanon; between ten and twenty clinics and twelve schools. And a TV station, a radio station and a newspaper.'

I took a deep breath, for I wanted to ask a question which I thought might be tricky.

'What is Hizbullah's current position on seeking to establish an Islamic state?'

Hajj Hussein smiled. 'I'll take you back to the 1980s. When Hizbullah was established, the situation in Lebanon was quite different from what it is now. Lebanon was divided and Israel was in occupation. America was in Lebanon too, as were the French and Italians.

'We were indeed influenced by the Islamic revolution in Iran,' Hajj Hussein went on. 'We, as individuals, would *love* to see an Islamic state here. But this cannot happen at all. Why? First of all, we do believe that a real Islamic system – this is what *we* believe, others do not agree – provides justice, provides security, provides freedom and democracy.

We have an example in the Islamic Republic in Iran.' He paused. 'We do believe that. And it's my democratic right to believe that an Islamic state is good for the country. But, I have to be realistic. First of all, there's a verse in the Koran which says that you can't impose anything by force, especially in terms of religion. It's impossible. We believe that. And anything against the will of the people, anything, will be counter-productive. Example: look what happened in Afghanistan, Pakistan, Taliban. Look at how they live. We as Hizbullah cannot bear such faith and mentality and ideology. We do believe that Islam is complete freedom. Complete freedom. You cannot impose anything. Yes, by dialogue, by discussion, if the people welcome it, that's fine. If not, it's up to them.

'There's another verse in the Koran which says "you have your religion, I have my religion." And we have a saying from the Prophet "It is either your brother in humanity or your brother in religion". So, we believe in that. I'll tell you something. If we in our areas in the south and the Bekaa make any violent practice, any, *any* one, people will directly abandon us. Because, what kind of Islam is this?

'If all of Lebanon were Shi'a, and I wanted an Islamic state, I would have to present my view to the people. If they accepted it, that would be fine. If they didn't, impossible.

'In Iran, when the Islamic revolution broke out in 1979, it was the choice of all the Iranians. But in Iraq not all Iraqis want an Islamic state, so you cannot make one. They need a constitution that suits all the Iraqis. This is the case also in Lebanon. You have a right to believe the way you want, but this is your belief. You can't impose it on others.'

I shifted in my seat. The Islamic revolution in Iran had not been the choice of all Iranians, but I saw little point in arguing. Instead, I said, 'I have one more question. I've been told that, before the war, people from different sects mixed with each other more, whereas nowadays they live separately. Do you agree that there is a need for more education, to help each sect understand the other sects better?'

Hajj Hussein didn't hesitate. 'This is *not* what we need. Personally, I have many Christian friends. We go out, we dine, whatever. The problem is not in the individuals. The problem is in the heads of those communities, in the leaders of the sects. There is no real trust. So this sect, just like before, depends on the Americans; this sect on France, this sect on Syria, this sect on Saudi Arabia, Egypt. There is no trust. And Lebanon is not given primacy: primacy is given to the sect.'

I thought this was a bit rich coming from the representative of a sectarian organisation known to have close affiliations with two foreign powers – Iran and Syria – but I listened in silence.

'The priority should be, must be, Lebanon. Hizbullah was once accused of being sectarian. We proved to all the Lebanese that we are patriots. Who liberated this country from the Israelis? Who spilled his blood in this country?' Hajj Hussein's voice rose. 'Our party is religious? – Yes, it is religious. Sectarian? No. You have secular parties in Lebanon which are sectarian. Hizbullah is religious, but not sectarian. What we need is trust.'

It was true that Hizbullah had served the interests of the Lebanese people as a whole by its contribution to driving the Israelis out of south Lebanon. For this it had gained the respect of a large number of Lebanese, from across the sectarian divide. But to me it did not follow that Hizbullah was not, in essence, a sectarian party.

'So you think the leaders need to trust each other more?'

'Correct.'

'But I also have the impression that the people need to trust each other more.'

'Well, the people are influenced by their leaders. The only solution for Lebanon, the only way, as I told you at the beginning, is this consensus democracy. We have to believe in this consensus democracy and we have to reform the electoral system, so that the strong cannot eat the weak.'

Fourteen years earlier, in 1992, prior to Lebanon's first post-war elections, Hizbullah's leadership had hotly debated whether or not their organisation should engage in the domestic political process. This was a tricky issue because, since its foundation in the early 1980s, Hizbullah had denounced Lebanon's confessional political system as corrupt. There was also the issue of whether it would be legitimate for Hizbullah, as an Islamicist organisation, to participate in a non-Islamic system. While I knew that the pragmatists had won the day, under the leadership of Nasrallah, and the decision had been made to participate, it struck me as ironic that in 2006 Hajj Hussein should be saying that the only way forward for Lebanon was concensus democracy.

'Let me tell you something else,' he went on. 'Just imagine Hizbullah didn't exist: what would happen to Lebanon? I will tell you. You wouldn't see a president. You wouldn't see a prime minister. You wouldn't see a parliament. You wouldn't see an economy, tourism, tourists, security; all of these things happened because of the resistance. If the resistance hadn't existed, *Lebanon now would be under the feet of Israel.* You would see Israeli settlements in Lebanon. This weak country proved to be the strongest in the region and the only country that the Israelis were forced to leave in humiliation and defeat.

'In the past, during the civil war, people used to feel shy, if they went to America or Canada, to say "I am Lebanese". After the liberation, they became proud to say "I am Lebanese". Why? It's because of the resistance. Now, I'll tell you something. If we have a kind of security, or a stable government, it's because of the balance of terror that we have created in south Lebanon. If this balance of terror did not exist, you will see the Israelis come back again. Despite this, some officials here in Lebanon fight each other for everyone to get his own share. They want to take us back to the old days, whereas we in Hizbullah always speak about unity.

'Honest to God, if any leader in Lebanon, whether Christian or Druze or whatever, had the power and the support that Hizbullah has, in what kind of language are they going to speak? Once they feel they have some strength, you can't control them. They think "we can rule, we can do everything." But it is *us* who have the real power. We have everything. We have an army. We have popular support; we have money. And how do we deal with people? We deal with people as Lebanese. We *always* speak about the unity of Lebanon; about national dialogue. We were the ones who called for national dialogue.'

Following the assassination of Hariri, there had been a series of high level meetings between Lebanon's senior politicians, under the slogan "national dialogue".

'We were the ones who said the only solution for Lebanon is to sit at the negotiating table and talk. I think Hizbullah is *the* most important force for the stability of Lebanon.' He paused. 'Even though some believe otherwise. We are popular because of our practice on the ground. Even if we had kicked the Israelis out of Lebanon, if we had a history of violence, no-one would accept us. For example, during the liberation of south Lebanon in 2000, what happened? Did we kill and slaughter? Nothing happened. We just caught the people who had collaborated with Israel and handed them over to Lebanese security. They were really well-treated, despite the fact that these people had killed our own people.

'After the defeat of the Nazis, look what happened: the French resistance killed about 10,000 collaborators. Ours is one of the most important liberations ever in the world, since the early days of Prophet Mohammed till this day. Look what happened in Serbia; in Croatia; in Bosnia-Herzogovina. Look at the suffering over there, and look at what happened in Lebanon. In Lebanon, people were dancing in May 2000. People were throwing rice.' Hajj Hussein fell silent. After a moment he spoke again. 'I'm not telling you this to convince you, by the way. These are the facts. This is how it was on the ground.'

Hajj Hussein was speaking the truth. The Israeli withdrawal in May 2000 had been remarkable for the absence of revenge attacks against those Lebanese who had collaborated with the Israelis. Some collaborators chose to follow their Israeli pay-masters and settle in northern Israel; but those who remained behind were allowed to live in peace.

After I left Hajj Hussein, I took a *servees* to Hamra. The driver wore an orange cotton bomber jacket stretched tight across his shoulders. His head was large and in the mirror his face was angular and ugly. When I got in asking for Hamra he did a U-turn, setting me wondering if we were going the right way. But I need not have worried. Twenty minutes later, we glided into Hamra. Rain began to chuck down and the traffic ground to a walking pace.

'Rain, rain, and more rain,' I remarked.

'Oh yes, lots of rain at the moment.' He turned his head towards me, apparently surprised at the possibility of conversation. After a moment he ventured, 'you're not Lebanese, are you?'

'I'm from Britain.'

'What's the difference between Lebanon and Britain?'

'*Yani*, they are very different.' Where to begin?

'Do you have heavy traffic like this in your country?'

'Easily as bad. Especially in London.'

'As bad as this?'

'For sure.'

The driver clicked his tongue. 'You live in London?'

'No, in a small city outside London. Even there we have too much traffic.'

'I'm from Ba'albek.'

'I went there once. The ruins are very beautiful.'

'Ah, you saw the ruins? Aren't they wonderful?'

I wanted to ask the driver what he thought of Hizbullah. 'D'you live in the town of Ba'albek itself?' I began.

'No, I live here. Well, I live in both. I have a home in Ba'albek and a home in Beirut. It's very cold in Ba'albek at the moment.'

'Rain?'

'Snow.'

'Really?' I found it hard to imagine snow lying on Ba'albek's flat plain.

'In the mountains. Today it snowed. And paraffin is very expensive.' He gestured with his free hand, rubbing his forefingers against his thumb and grimacing. 'Paraffin is very dear, and so is electricity.'

I recalled the poverty I had seen in Ba'albek on a previous visit to Lebanon and imagined the cold closing around people's bones. 'How's life in Ba'albek in other ways?'

'The situation's bad. Economic problem.'

The same story as in Beirut. 'Lots of unemployment?'

'Lots.'

I plucked up my courage. 'You're Shi'a?'

The driver's face broke into a smile. 'I'm a Shi'a from Ba'albek. But I'm not with any party, I just drive a taxi.'

'Aren't Hizbullah active in Ba'albek?'

'They are, but I'm not with them. They're always taking money off people.' He made the same gesture with his fingers and thumb, this time with distaste. 'Only twenty per cent of the people are with Hizbullah.'

'Really? I thought lots of people in Ba'albek supported Hizbullah.'

The driver frowned and shook his head. 'No, no, only twenty per cent. They are bad, they take too much money off people! Soon it will be only ten percent who support them.'

This was getting interesting, but the car had reached the junction of Hamra Street and I had to get out.

22

'SOMETIMES, LIFE IS SO DIFFICULT THAT
THE ONLY THING TO DO IS LAUGH'

Sidon Old Town, April 2006

✧

On Sundays, Hiba's youngest brother drove to Tyre to visit his business partner, and Hiba suggested that he give me a lift to Sidon, which was on the way.

'You should visit the antiquities and the soap museum,' she said, 'and be sure you go to one or two bakeries. The biscuits they make in Sidon are the best in the country!' After nearly a week in the concrete jungle of Beirut, I was longing to see some old buildings, but I was also curious about Sidon because it had a large Palestinian population.

Hiba's brother sat relaxed at the wheel of the Fiat, joking about the inadequacies of Lebanese political leaders as we sped south down the coastal highway.

The weather was grey and overcast, and rain smattered on the windscreen in short bursts. Apartment buildings lined the road, allowing only occasional glimpses of the sea, a quarter of a mile distant across a wasteland of scrub. In less than an hour we were in the old town of Sidon. Hiba's brother dropped me on the Corniche.

'You can walk to everything from here,' he told me, 'the Sea Castle, Khan al Faranj, the *souq*. Hope you enjoy yourself.' He smiled, waved and drove away.

I turned up my coat collar, put up my umbrella and sauntered along the Corniche. To start with I barely noticed my surroundings, because I was going over in my mind the conversation I had had with Dan earlier that morning. Paul had had a job persuading him to come to the phone, and when at last he did his voice was thin and flat.

'How are you, my darling?' I asked, trying to send as much warmth down the line as I could muster.

'Foin.' Dan still spoke with the rural accent he had picked up at nursery school.

'How was the end of term? Are you getting ready to go camping?'

'Don't know.' Dan fell silent, and I felt worried. Usually when we spoke on the phone during Dan's weekends with Paul, he was chatty.

'I think you're going to Cornwall tomorrow,' I volunteered. Paul was taking Dan camping for the first week of the Easter holidays, because we had felt it would help to take his mind off my absence.

After a moment, Dan muttered something about a castle. 'What, darling?' I asked. 'The line's not very good, tell me again.'

'Daddy made me a castle.'

'Did he?'

'But it didn't win the prize.'

'I'm sorry. What does it look like?' Paul was brilliant at making things with Dan.

'It's got four turrets.'

'Has it!' I hesitated. Dan clearly didn't want to chat. 'Shall I send you a hug?' Our usual ritual involved me sending several flying hugs and kisses down the phone, accompanied by rocket noises.

'No, thanks.' His tone was frosty.

'How about a kiss?'

'No thanks.'

I took a deep breath. 'Okay, darling. I'll say goodbye now. Have a lovely time in Cornwall, and I'll phone again soon.'

I felt dreadful when I came off the phone. If I had been alone I would have wanted to curl up under a duvet and sob, but Hiba's brother was arriving and I had to get ready.

Halfway along the Corniche I decided that, in the drizzle, Sidon's sea front was not an appealing sight. The small, concrete buildings looked drab and scruffy, and the fishing harbour was empty of boats. When I came to the ticket booth for the ruined sea castle, I bought a ticket and followed a handful of Lebanese tourists across the narrow stone causeway, gazing down into the dark, salt-smelling water which slapped against it.

The castle had been built by the Crusaders in the twelfth century, on the site of a Phoenician temple. At the end of the causeway, a jumble of broken pillars and eroded walls rose from a flagstoned island. The sandstone was a rich yellow ochre, and in bright sunshine it would have looked beautiful. Today, in the rain, it was hard to see more than dilapidation and neglect. I waited while the Lebanese tourists climbed a flight of stone steps onto a flat roof, overgrown with weeds. Then I crept into a dark hall and found a private place to sit in a niche which had once framed a window. I took out my journal, removed the lid of my pen and wrote the date. But it was useless, for I was feeling much too sad to write anything. A tear rolled off my nose and blotted the page. Why had Dan not wanted a hug? He had never cut me off like this before. Was he trying to punish me for going away? Which would be perfectly understandable, for I had never felt sure it was okay to leave him. Or was it simply his way of coping with my absence? Perhaps his strategy was to put me out of his mind until I reappeared, in which case my phone call had upset and confused him. I pulled a tissue out of my bag and blew my nose, cursing the day that Paul and I had decided to separate. Separation had given me my freedom, but at what a price. I blew my nose a second time and craned my neck through the niche to see what the tourists were doing. They were coming down the steps, their shoulders hunched against the rain. I was getting cold, too. My feet were warm and dry inside my boots, but in the small of my back I could feel the chill rising off the water.

I put away my journal, came out of the hall and stood beside a squat golden column, letting my eyes travel out to sea. The water was a pale milky green, the sky grey with dark, fluffy clouds. Two small red boats and a large tanker drifted on the horizon.

From the sea castle I made my way to Khan al Faranj, a vast sandstone building at the far end of the Corniche. Built by the Emir Fakhr ad Din in the seventeenth century to store goods and accommodate travellers, the *khan* had once housed the French consulate for the city. The entrance was through a pair of grand wooden doors on a side street. I stepped across the threshold, expecting to find a guard or a keeper, but the place was deserted. An enormous gravelled courtyard lay before me, a fountain at its centre. Following the traditional design, the two, cloistered storeys of the *khan* formed the perimeter of the courtyard. I walked slowly to the fountain, but water no longer played over its curves. Under the cloister on the far side of the courtyard I sat down on a bench and looked out between the golden arches at the vast, peaceful space. From somewhere on the roof, a bird cheeped tunelessly; in the far distance I could just make out the rumble of traffic. I laid my umbrella beside me on the floor, its flowery fabric sequinned with raindrops.

It seemed miraculous that the *khan* had escaped damage during the Israeli bombardment of Sidon in 1982. I had read Robert Fisk's descriptions of the devastation Sidon had suffered in the first week of the invasion. In one case, 125 people had died in a shelter beneath a primary school.[7] The worst of the bombing had occurred in the new town, a kilometre inland from where I was; and in the Palestinian refugee camp of Ein al Helweh.

My eyes traced the curves of the cloister opposite, as I counted its seven graceful arches. Above them, at first-floor level, seven smaller arches echoed their shape. A climbing plant clung to the stonework, its green leaves and purple flowers vibrant in the drizzle. After I had been sitting for a few moments, a tabby cat appeared from nowhere, rubbing its shoulder against the pillar closest to me. As I watched the cat I noticed that the surface of the stone had eroded unevenly, so that it had the appearance of sand on which rain is falling.

After I left Khan al Faranj, I took a street which ran inland from the Corniche, where the pavement was crowded with shoppers. It was a short step from here to the narrow alleys of the *souq*. After a few paces I stopped in front of a money changers' stall, for I was running out of lira, and needed to change some cash. I reached inside my coat for my wallet and stepped up to the counter. Four middle-aged men in dark wool overcoats stood crowded together on the inside, smoking, drinking tea and exchanging news with one another.

'*Itfaddali*,' said one, 'how much do you want to change?'

I asked for the exchange rate and gave him a hundred-dollar bill. The other men glanced at me as he counted out my lira. 'German?' asked the first man.

I shook my head. 'English.'

He frowned, and I sensed a ripple of disapproval circulating amongst the whole group. 'Welcome in Lebanon,' said the first man. 'But Tony Blair,' he grimaced, 'is a very bad man.'

'And George Bush, very bad,' added the oldest man in the group, wagging a finger at me. The others growled in sympathy.

'I agree with you, I don't like either of them.' I hesitated, before adding 'Lots of people in Britain don't like Tony Blair.'

---

7   Robert Fisk, *Pity the Nation*, Oxford University Press.

'They don't like him?' The four men watched me from beneath heavy eyebrows, leaving me in no doubt about how deeply Blair's foreign policy had offended them.

'Didn't you see on television the number of people who demonstrated in London against the invasion of Iraq?'

Some of the men nodded.

'None of those people like Tony Blair. But he doesn't take any notice of ordinary people.'

I put away my money, said goodbye and walked on up the street. In a hundred metres I was at the entrance to a covered alleyway, where the old part of the *souq* began. I stepped inside, under a roof of corrugated plastic. Small shoe shops lined the alleyway, and women in headscarves and long *gelabeyyas* mingled with children and young men. Some glanced at me as I passed, but the atmosphere was calm and pleasant. I felt strangely at home, for the small shops and confined space reminded me of the *souq* in the Old City of Jerusalem. At the top of the alley I struggled through a bottleneck where every shop sold underwear and pyjamas, past an old man with a trolley hawking a platter of *ka'ik*, and turned into a long street of sweetmakers' shops. Here, clusters of electric cables drooped like disused washing lines from a solid concrete roof, again reminding me of Jerusalem. The bakers made little attempt to press their wares, regarding me languidly from the doorways of their shops as I passed, evidently accustomed to foreign tourists. I was beginning to feel hungry, and wondering whether I should buy a kilo of biscuits for Hiba, when a man with a moustache beckoned me into his shop. He cut a small slice from a circular platter of sweetmeat, placed it on a square of paper and handed it to me.

I took a bite. It was crumbly, sweet and tasted of almonds.

'You like it?' His smile was professional, but warm.

'It's delicious.' The problem was, it would have tasted much better with a glass of tea.

'Where can I get tea?' I asked.

'In the square. Keep straight for fifty metres, turn left and you'll see it.' He nodded and resumed his station in the doorway.

At the end of the alleyway I found myself back in the open air, in a triangular open space. On one side stood a beautiful stone mosque; on another a café with outdoor tables and chairs and on the third a long, low building that housed a school. A handful of men sat smoking at the tables and a group of boys played football under a tree in the centre. A small girl rode by on an adult-size bicycle. Her headscarf was so white that it dazzled my eyes.

I sat down at a table, feeling happy for the first time that morning. There were no cars, no high-rise buildings, just ordinary people going about their business. It was as if I had closed my eyes and been transported back to Palestine.

I ordered a glass of tea from a tall, lean man who hurried out of the café towards me. When he had established where I was from, he told me he was Palestinian and asked if he could sit down, as he wanted to practise his English. I agreed readily, saying I was interested to know how life was for the Palestinians of Sidon. He sighed and launched into a depressing tale of poverty, unemployment and overcrowded living conditions, both in the Old Town and in Ein al Helweh. Then, suddenly changing the subject, he asked me what I had thought of Princess Diana.

'I liked her so much,' he told me with passion. 'Her death was a tragedy. What did you think of her?'

'I liked her too,' I answered truthfully. 'She was a good woman.'

'Oh, so good, so good. I cannot be friends with anyone who does not like her.'

When I had finished my tea I said goodbye to the man and set off in search of the soap museum. But I had not gone far when I realised that I needed to find a toilet. I was back under the covered alleyways, in a place where most of the shops sold ironmongery and wicker baskets. As I rounded a corner a woman standing in a doorway caught my eye. She wore a *gelabeyya* and a headscarf and her relaxed pose suggested she had finished her morning tasks. I greeted her politely and asked if she knew where I might find a toilet.

The woman looked at me for a moment. She was neither young nor old. 'A toilet?' she repeated in a low voice. '*Ittfaddali.*' Her face softened into a smile. 'Come into my house.' She stepped through the doorway, which opened onto a flight of stairs. I followed, grateful for her kindness and intrigued at the prospect of seeing a home which had been constructed above the tiny claustrophobic alleys I had just been walking through.

At the top of the stairs we came out briefly on a flat roof, and I glimpsed a chaos of TV aerials before we passed through another door into the woman's kitchen. She led me to the adjoining bathroom, showed me how to lock the door, and withdrew.

When I came out she had removed her headscarf and was shaking out her short, greying hair. She held a safety pin between her teeth and gestured to me to be patient with her for a moment. As she folded the scarf and pinned it back in place under her chin, I thanked her warmly and told her how kind she had been.

'No problem!' she cried as soon as she could speak again. 'No problem! You're not from here are you? From where?'

'England.'

'England!' She took a step towards me and scrutinised my face, as if this fact made me more interesting. 'I am from Palestine,' she added.

I smiled.

'Married?' the woman demanded.

'Divorced.'

'Children?'

'Just one.'

'Just one?' Her tone was incredulous. 'Why?' Often I felt irritated when people asked me this question, but the woman exuded such warmth that I began to laugh.

'*Yani*,' I said, raising my hands in a gesture of fatalism, 'I got married late, it took me a while to get pregnant and now I'm too old to have more children.'

'Really?' She looked at me disbelievingly. 'Too old?'

I pursed my lips, raised my eyebrows and nodded. She was so nice that I felt like telling her my whole life story. 'How about you,' I asked, 'how many children do you have?'

'I have twelve,' she replied, looking at me steadily. 'I married when I was twelve years old and now I'm fifty-one.'

'When you were twelve?' Now it was my turn to be incredulous.

The woman pointed to her chest. 'I was so young, I didn't even have breasts.' She burst out laughing. 'Sometimes,' she went on, 'life is so difficult that the only thing to do is to laugh. My husband has been sick for a very long time. He has needed endless medical treatment, which has used up all our money.'

I raised my eyebrows again.

'Oh, we have had too many problems to deal with, too many problems! Between my husband and my children, life has been a night-mare. The children couldn't stay in school, because there was no-one to support them. All of them, from the ages of twelve or thirteen, went out to work. It's been a nightmare, and sometimes I think the only way to avoid going mad, is to laugh.' She beamed. 'Where are you going now?'

I explained that I was hoping to get to the soap museum before it closed.

'The soap museum? It's just round the corner. Come back downstairs and I'll point it out to you.'

I followed the woman back out of the kitchen onto the roof. To one side was a broken wall and a pile of rubble. Beyond the TV aerials, the rain fell in slanting lines over the sea.

'Is this from the war?' I asked, gesturing at the remains of the wall.

'The Israelis,' she replied. 'We don't have money to fix it. But never mind!' She laughed again, and led me down the stairs. At the bottom she pointed up the alleyway.

'Go straight for twenty metres, then take the turning to the right. You'll see the museum on your left.'

I thanked her, squeezed her hand, and said goodbye.

In the immaculately laid out soap museum, I spent half an hour examining the wooden moulds and other tools which until recently had been used in the relatively simple process of turning olive oil into soap. When hunger overcame me, I left and found a café serving *hummous* and *foules mesdames* with bunches of mint and cubes of bright pink pickle. I sat writing my journal and doing my best not to let the stares of the boys behind the counter bother me. Afterwards, I wandered back to the Corniche, looking for a shop which sold bottled water. Half-way along I came upon a building like a small warehouse, with bare concrete walls, open to the street. The dusty shelves were thinly stacked, with an improbable collection of items that included packets of cigarettes, tablets of soap and custard cream biscuits. I found a bottle of water and went to pay the shopkeeper, who sat hunched behind an old wooden desk in a corner of the warehouse. He was a small man and wore a navy blue anorak and a wool hat pulled down over his ears.

'Where are you from?' he asked as he passed me my change.

'From Britain.' Curious as ever, I hovered.

'Welcome.' His skin was dark brown and when he smiled, creases appeared at the corners of his eyes.

'Are you from Sidon?' I asked.

'*Yani*, I'm Palestinian, but I've lived here all my life. *Ittfaddali*, have a seat.' He gestured to a dirty plastic chair which stood on my side of the desk.

'My family's from the Galilee,' he said as I sat down 'They came to Lebanon in '48, and I was born a year later.'

'So you've never seen your homeland?'

The man shook his head. 'Some of the Palestinians I know still have the keys to their houses in Palestine, but we can't go there.'

'I was hoping to visit Ein al Helweh,' I said after a pause. I wanted to see what conditions were like there.

The man frowned. 'There's a check point at the entrance,' he told me. 'It's not easy for foreigners to get in. Unless you know someone, that is. If you know someone who lives there and they take you in, then it's okay.' He gazed at me steadily. There was warmth in his eyes, but his expression was very sad. 'Life's very difficult.' He cleared his throat and I asked him what he meant.

'We Palestinians are very highly-educated people,' he began, 'among the best educated in the world. We have doctors, lawyers, engineers... you name it, we have it. But the Lebanese don't allow our professionals to work. Take my family, for instance. I have a brother who is a doctor, another who is a computer engineer and a sister who is a teacher. My two brothers are not allowed work at their professions. So what are they supposed to do? Work with their hands or do nothing.'

'I've heard that some Palestinian children go out to work,' I ventured. 'Sometimes as young as twelve or thirteen...'

'Younger!' The man opened his eyes wide. 'Here in the Old Town, lots of young boys work. Why the garage next door employs several boys, I know them well.' He stared at me for a moment. 'If you don't believe me,' he went on, 'I'll show you.'

'Yes, please,' I replied. 'I do believe you, but I'd be interested to meet them.'

'Okay, I'll take you now.' He pushed back his chair and stood up slowly, as if his joints were stiff. 'Come, this way.'

[205]

I followed him across the shop, wondering if he was going to lock it up. But he stopped in the doorway and shouted to a boy who stood on the edge of the pavement, beside the front wheel of an articulated lorry.

'Mohammed, come here! I've a foreigner who wants to meet you.'

The boy stopped what he was doing and stared at the shopkeeper. His face and clothes were covered in grease and he held a monkey wrench in one hand. When I looked down I saw that he was in the process of removing the wheel.

'What?' he called, 'Why?' When he caught sight of me, an expression of disbelief spread across his face, as if he were wondering what a foreign woman could possibly want with him.

The shopkeeper glanced up the street, took a quick glance at his abandoned desk and walked towards the boy, gesturing to me to follow him. 'Mohammed,' he repeated when we were standing in front of him, 'I told this woman that you gave up school to work in the garage, but she didn't believe me.'

'I do believe him,' I protested, 'but I wanted to meet you.' I smiled at Mohammed.

'Do you mind if I ask how old you are?'

Mohammed gazed at me, almost tongue-tied. 'Sixteen.'

I was surprised. He was stocky, but little over five feet tall. 'And how long have you been working here?'

'Since I was ten.'

'Do you go to school?'

'I went till I was ten, and then I started work.'

'You see?' The shopkeeper looked at me. 'His father's been out of work all this time, so he has no choice but to do what he can to help his mother.'

23

BOURJ AL BARAJNEH REFUGEE CAMP

Beirut, April 2006

I hovered in the entrance to Abu Basem's nut shop, eating giant peanuts from a little paper bag. I had bought two hundred grams from the avuncular Abu Basem, partly to kill time, partly because I felt less conspicuous on the threshold of his shop than standing on the street. A hundred yards away, a slow stream of overloaded cars, motorbikes and men came and went through the entrance to Bourj al Barajneh refugee camp. Opposite the entrance, on the far side of the street, a high wall only half-concealed the debris of a vast car breaker's yard. Old tyres were piled to a height of twelve feet, dwarfing the slightly built boys who walked along the pavement in ragged clothes.

I took a step backwards, anxious not to attract attention. A Palestinian NGO had assured me that in Bourj al Barajneh I had nothing to fear as a foreign visitor, but I was jumpy; and the dearth of women on the streets set me doubting whether the Palestinian with whom I had spoken by phone that morning could really be on her way to meet me.

Behind me, Abu Basem was sweeping the floor. Business was slow, despite the astonishing array of nuts and seeds arranged in open metal drums around the walls.

'I'm sorry,' I began, 'my friend said she would meet me in your shop.'

'No problem, no problem,' Abu Basem smiled. He was in his forties, with wiry hair and gold fillings in his teeth. His accent reminded me of the way people spoke in East Jerusalem. 'Would you like a glass of tea?'

'Thank you, I'd love one!' I wasn't sure if I had time for tea, but his generosity touched me. He produced a rush-seated stool and called through the back door to a young boy.

I ate another nut, savouring the strong salty flavour and the rough texture of the dusty pink husk. I felt safe, now, for in an exchange of eleven words I had become the guest of Abu Basem. When the boy brought the tea, I watched from the stool as my host served a couple of teenagers. I found a curious satisfaction in the way he thrust his curved steel shovel into the drum of nuts, tipped it backwards then poured the nuts into the gusseted paper bag, holding it over the scales as a precaution but not losing a single nut. I even liked the simplicity of the paper bags, printed with the name of the shop and a picture of a peanut. I took a sip of tea.

An old man was buying *bizer*, dried sunflower seeds in their husks. I had just raised my glass to take another sip when a hand touched me lightly on the shoulder and a woman's voice said 'Teresa'. A small figure stood beside me, neat in a jacket and trousers but more than a little out of breath. 'I was waiting for you by Haifa hospital,' she explained. 'You were meant to call me when you reached the camp.'

I put my hand over my face. 'I'm so sorry! You're right, I completely forgot!'

Kholood laughed. 'At least it wasn't me who forgot! And Abu Basem gave you tea.' She nodded at the shopkeeper. 'Come, first I'll take you home and later we'll make a tour of the camp.'

As we walked slowly in the dirt from Abu Basem's towards the camp entrance, Kholood told me about her work as an interpreter and translator. She had taught herself English by listening to the BBC and nowadays she earned her living interpreting for visiting NGOs and translating documents for foreign researchers working in the camp.

'So plenty of foreigners still come to Bourj al Barajneh?' Years ago, I had read Pauline Cutting's harrowing book, *Children of the Siege*, about her work as a surgeon in the hospital here during the Camp Wars, when Bourj al Barajneh was under siege by the Shi'a gunmen of Amal. From 1985 to 1987, Amal had attacked Bourj and other Palestinian camps with the backing of Syria, in an attempt to prevent the PLO from re-establishing itself in Lebanon following its forced exodus in 1982. Hundreds of Bourj's inhabitants had been killed and wounded, and eventually thousands had come close to dying of starvation. Pauline Cutting had worked alongside Palestinian doctors and a small group of western medical volunteers.

'*Yani*, not so many as before, but enough to keep me busy. We have a Swedish man working with the youth; a Dutch girl in the hospital and a couple of German PhD students who come and go.'

Inside the camp entrance we passed through a small open area where the cars which I had seen earlier dropped their passengers, turned and drove out again. Beyond, the alleyways were too narrow to allow the passage of vehicles. Kholood led me down a lane which led into the heart of the camp. To begin with, it was a couple of metres wide and we were able to walk side by side, but when the lane changed direction it narrowed to little over a metre. The concrete floor sloped down in the centre, forming an open drain, and every few metres a breezeblock doorstep jutted out from a doorway. On some, young men sat watching the world go by, while toddlers played on the ground beside them.

The confined space would have been claustrophobic, but for the fact that few of the buildings were more than two storeys tall. By Beirut standards one did not have to raise one's eyes very high to be gazing into the pale blue sky; and, as the alleyway twisted and turned, in between patches of shadow there was always a whitewashed wall drenched in light. At first I wondered why the place felt familiar, but it didn't take me long to work out that the intimate conduits and small buildings reminded me of the Arab quarter in Jerusalem's Old City.

Kholood greeted everyone we met. Once a woman called out to her from an upstairs window. As I stood half-listening to their snatched conversation, I noticed that, far from being built in neat, straight lines, the upper walls of the houses jutted this way and that at bizarre angles, as if the men who had constructed them had been prepared to defy gravity in order to create sufficient space for their large families. In some places an upper window on one side of the alley projected to within a few inches of the building opposite.

The other thing I couldn't fail to notice was the giant tangle of electric cables that hung only two or three feet above my head. Thin red wires, fat black ones, white, more black. In some places they were bunched together, in others they separated and drooped anarchically.

'*Yalla*, bye,' Kholood cried to the woman and we walked on, until the sound of an approaching engine broke the quiet, sending me into a panic which again I remembered from the Old City. Ten feet ahead of us, the alley twisted to the right, making a blind corner.

'Careful!' Kholood flattened herself against the wall and gestured to me to do the same, as a moped appeared around the corner, its driver a teenage boy. Almost expressionless, he glanced from me to Kholood and back again, murmuring to the lad who rode pillion behind him.

We walked on a few paces, passing the open doorway of a tiny shop, but another moped was on its way, driven by another youngster. Kholood took my hand and pulled me into a recess in the wall, letting him pass before attempting to move on. The second bike bothered me less than the first, but the youth of the drivers left me uneasy. It was from young men more than anyone else that I anticipated hostility. It would be so easy for a youngster on a bike, in an angry mood, to round a bend, spot a westerner and decide to vent his feelings there and then.

'You speak some Arabic?' Kholood regarded me with curiosity.

'Not as well as you speak English!' I replied, switching language to show willing.

'Where did you learn?'

'In Palestine.' I looked at Kholood, wondering how she would take this information. 'I lived there for a year in 1990.'

'Whereabouts?' To my relief, her expression brightened. 'Come, this is my house, up these stairs.' We turned into a side alley and climbed a flight of outdoor steps.

'First in Ramallah, then in the Old City of Jerusalem, in the Armenian quarter.' I had lived with a friend in a one-room stone apartment, which like Kholood's home was reached by a flight of outdoor steps. We used to wake in the mornings to the sound of the Italian monks in the neighbouring apartment singing their matins chants. Later we walked to work through the narrow covered alleys of the Moslem *souq*.

'You speak with a Palestinian accent!' Kholood was beaming as we reached the top step. She pushed open the door, and ushered me ahead of her into a small, square living room. 'Dima!' she cried, addressing a young woman who sat cross-legged on a sofa in a T-shirt and cut-off jeans, fiddling with the television remote control. 'Meet Teresa! She speaks Palestinian Arabic, and she used to live in Ramallah!'

Dima untangled her legs and stood up, stretching out her hand. She wore her dark, curly hair cut in Affro style around her head and gazed at me with remarkable self-possession. 'Good to meet you,' she said. 'Mum didn't tell me she had a visitor coming.'

[210]

'Have a seat, *habibti*.' Kholood waved me to a chair. 'I'll make tea in a minute. Tell us about Ramallah, when were you there and what were you doing exactly?'

'It was a long time ago,' I began, unzipping my boots and adding them to the pile of shoes stacked against the wall inside the door. 'I did a piece of research with Palestinian women ex-detainees, about the interrogation methods used by the Israelis.' I felt unexpectedly at home in the company of Kholood and her daughter and it made me happy to remember my time in Palestine. In those days, life in the West Bank and East Jerusalem had still been pleasant in some respects. The Palestinians had had a sense of pride in the *intifada* and hope for the future. For me as a foreigner it had been a rich and interesting life. The complexity and beauty of the Arabic language fascinated me, the Palestinian landscape and light provided an unending feast for my eyes and although Israeli treatment of the Palestinians made me very angry, I liked having a clear role as a foreign 'witness'.

I had a connection to Judaism, though not to Israel, through my paternal grandfather, who was German Jewish. According to Jewish law I was a gentile, but that didn't prevent me from feeling a sense of shame at the way the Israelis abused the Palestinians.

'So you're interested in women's issues,' Kholood concluded when I had finished describing my research with Palestinian women detainees. 'Me too, I like this subject very much. You know, many of the NGOs which are working now in the camp focus on the needs of women and girls. There's a project to provide work for camp women and one for girls who were not able to complete their education. These girls are given work in the kindergarten. It's not a big salary, but at least they are employed.' She paused. 'You know, sometimes the fact the women are working causes problems with their husbands, because in our society the men are expected to provide for their families. There is no work for the men, so they can't provide, but they find it very difficult.'

'Lazy louts!' Dima exclaimed. 'Men who stay at home while their wives go out to work should do the housework!' She threw her mother a meaningful look.

'And do they?'

Kholood shook her head. 'Many of these young women, when they come in from work, still have to take care of the house, the children, the husband, everything. Often the men are too depressed to help them.

And most think it's too humiliating for a man to do housework.' She sighed, adding, 'We understand. They feel it should be their responsibility to work and support their families and they can't do that, so they feel very bad.' Her tone was one of indulgence, but I thought I detected a trace of sarcasm.

'How many men are unemployed?'

'About eighty percent. You'll see as we walk round, most of the men are sitting outside, smoking cigarettes or hubbly bubbly; doing nothing.' She paused. 'I expect you know that Palestinians with professional qualifications are not allowed to practise their profession outside the camps? So if you're a doctor, a lawyer, or an engineer, you can only work in the camps. With the doctors it's controlled through membership of the doctors' professional association. As a Palestinian doctor you can work, for example, at Haifa hospital here in the camp, because it's run by the Palestine Red Crescent Society and they do not require you to be a member of the doctors' association. Or you can work for the United Nations Relief and Works Agency (UNRWA). But you can't work in a Lebanese hospital, unless you pay something like 15,000 US dollars to join the Lebanese doctors' association; and no one from the camps has that kind of money.'

'What if you're an engineer?'

'In theory you can work in the camp, but in reality we have no need for engineers because there's no space to build. You can see how close the houses are to each other, so that we feel as if we are living with our neighbours.' She gestured at the open door, through which I saw a tangle of TV aerials, water tanks and washing hanging out to dry on roofs. The neighbour's satellite dish virtually touched Kholood's outdoor steps.

'Is there a restriction on the height of the buildings?'

'No, there are no rules, but we can't build higher than four or five storeys because the foundations are not that sound. Most families prefer to stop at two or three, although if they have a lot of children, they have to go higher. If a family has four sons, when they grow up and get married where are they going to find a house? The family is obliged to build a couple of new storeys onto their existing house.

'Is there anything to stop Palestinians living outside the camp?'

'There is no law requiring us to live here. But outside the camp we're banned from owning property. The ban applies to property bought a long time ago, as well as to property bought now. When you die the government takes the property back.' She paused. 'And of course if you live outside the camp you face racism all the time, as a Palestinian. I lived outside the camp for five years, and I suffered so much abuse it was intolerable.' She grimaced. 'The Lebanese constantly say bad things about us. I have many foreign friends. They come to the camp by taxi. When they tell the driver they want Bourj al Barajneh, sometimes the driver advises them not to come here.'

I thought of Muna and Ruhiyya and nodded. 'Some of my Sunni friends were pretty negative about the camps.'

'Oh, the Sunnis are the worst. They hate the Palestinians.'

'I was a bit shocked, because I had imagined that, of all the Lebanese, the Sunnis would support you the most.'

A look of bitterness crossed Kholood's face. 'In this country you can't trust anyone. They love you today, they hate you tomorrow. This is the rule in Lebanon.'

'Everyone is very suspicious of everyone else?'

'Yes. There's no trust. The Lebanese don't even like *each other*, so what will they feel about us Palestinians?' She looked at me unhappily. 'We're human beings and it's not nice to be on the receiving end of racism. I once worked with an Australian film maker. He was making a movie about Palestinian life here in the camp and we went to show it in Hamra. After the showing a woman stood up and made a comment about how the Palestinians are not educated people and how in her opinion we are ignorant and we live like shit... So I asked her if she had ever been to one of the camps. "Have you seen how many educated people there are among us?" I asked. "It's because your government doesn't allow our professionals to work that you think we're ignorant; but we're not. You should come to the camp and see how many of us have diplomas hanging on our walls." She couldn't answer that.'

'The ban on work must make people feel so frustrated.'

'It does, of course. And it creates problems for young people growing up. Now I am facing a big dilemma about my daughter.' She jutted her chin towards Dima. 'Because I have a lot of friends abroad, she has the opportunity to go abroad for her university education.' Dima was listening intently, waiting to see what her mother was about to say. 'We discuss this constantly. I have said that it's okay with me, she can go if she wants to; but in reality I will find life very difficult without her.'

[213]

Dima breathed in noisily and drew herself upright, so that she was sitting in a half lotus position on the couch. 'And anyway, what's the point of getting a degree abroad,' she remarked, 'because I won't be able to work when I come home?'

'You see?' Kholood responded. 'Dima's eighteen and she understands the situation we are in.' I sensed that both women were brimming with anger. 'It's so frustrating,' Kholood went on. 'I wasn't able to finish my education because of the Camp Wars, when Amal attacked us in 1985. Twenty years later, my children have the opportunity to complete their education, but even if they do they will be unable to work.'

'Unless they take jobs abroad,' I murmured, 'but that would be awful for you.'

'Exactly.' Kholood raised her eyebrows and shrugged her shoulders in a gesture of despair. After a few moments she went on, 'Of course, with *wasta*, then perhaps you can get a job here.' *Wasta* meant connections with influential people. 'But not a job as a professional, even with *wasta* Palestinians are not allowed to work as doctors, engineers, lawyers and journalists.'

A tortoiseshell cat appeared in the doorway, rubbing its back legs against the door jamb. Kholood reached out her hand and called it to her. 'I feed this cat every day, even though she's not mine.' I remembered the hoards of mangey cats that had lived as strays in the Old City, feeding out of rubbish bags. By comparison this one looked relatively healthy. 'Even to be hired by UNRWA, you need good *wasta*,' Kholood went on as she bent down to tickle the cat behind the ear. 'Just to get a job as a garbage collector, a Palestinian needs *wasta*.'

I was beginning to feel depressed. It was no wonder that the camps were seen as dangerous places, if their able-bodied inhabitants were trapped in poverty and inactivity. 'Was it any better during the war?'

Kholood nodded. 'During the war, it was completely different. At the time of the Palestinian Revolution, we worked in every field you can think of and our financial situation was very good, much better than it is now.' By the 'Palestinian Revolution' she meant the period when the PLO was in control of a large section of West Beirut, in the years leading to 1982. 'But nowadays so much has changed.' The bitter expression appeared on her face again. 'People became sick of the Revolution because they discovered that it was useless. They have seen that, no matter what they do, the will of the Israelis and the Americans always prevails. So it's pointless to struggle. This is why Palestinians no longer think of revolution.'

Although I understood it, I found the anger and despair in Kholood's voice deeply disturbing. These were the emotions which, 150 miles to the south in Gaza and the West Bank, had led a generation of young Palestinians to volunteer as suicide bombers.

'Let's be honest,' Kholood went on. 'No matter what we do, no matter how much we protest, or go out on the streets, or refuse or deny, or object to this or that UN resolution, it makes no difference: if the Israelis and the Americans want it, they get it.'

'Has the election of Hamas made things more difficult for Palestinians in the camps here in Lebanon?' Hamas was a Sunni Islamic fundamentalist organisation. After it had won the elections to the Palestinian Authority (PA) in January 2006, Israel and the United States had refused to recognise it as the legitimate Palestinian government, thereby depriving the PA of access to funds on which it and hundreds of thousands of Palestinians depended.

Kholood thought for a moment. 'Even what happens in Palestine doesn't make any difference to our situation. Whether Hamas or Fatah gets elected is irrelevant. Our situation never alters.'

Through the open door, the sky was changing colour. We heard a distant rumble of thunder, followed by a smattering of rain. Kholood stood up and closed the door. 'Sorry, Teresa,' she began, 'I have to go to the kitchen for a few moments. My husband will be home soon and I have to start the dinner. If you like you can come with me and we can continue talking.'

I followed her through a doorway into the kitchen, leaving Dima to watch TV. The kitchen was small and had no window, but it was well-equipped with units and work tops, a large refrigerator and a full-size gas cooker. Kholood filled a *briq* with water and set it to boil for tea.

'My husband's a carpenter,' she announced with pride. 'He built the kitchen.' She tipped a bag of potatoes into a plastic bowl. 'You're very welcome to eat with us. I am making something simple, meat with potatoes and a tomato salad.' She washed the potatoes under the tap and started to chop them into small cubes, as another clap of thunder sounded close by. 'Oh my god, this is going to be a big storm.'

Rain was drumming on the roof above the kitchen. It was already six o'clock, and would be dark in an hour. 'Kholood,' I said, 'I'm not too keen to be leaving the camp after nightfall.'

'Don't worry, I'll walk with you to the road and help you find a *servees*. Now, what else would you like to know?'

'Tell me more about how the camps are run. Who is responsible for law and order?'

'Okay. The camps are run by us, the Palestinians. We have a Popular Committee and a Security Committee. If for example there is a murder, and a camp resident is wanted by the Lebanese state, the Lebanese Gendarmerie come and arrest him through the Committee, because the Gendarmerie are not allowed to come into the camp.' She tipped the pile of chopped potatoes into a large frying pan and lit the gas.

'Is it true that there are lots of weapons in the camps?'

Kholood looked at me with a slight air of exasperation, as if she had been asked this question too many times by too many foreign visitors. 'Let's be honest. It is not a matter of heavy weapons.' She began to push the potatoes around the pan. 'We have the ordinary guns which we fought with during the sieges; but those who say we took the Syrians' weapons are telling a big lie. We don't have the space for heavy weapons!' She raised her eyebrows and pulled a face, as if to imply that this should be obvious. 'There's barely enough space for us to live in this camp, there's nowhere for our children to play, so where would we put heavy weapons? Ordinary guns, yes. Because of the Revolution everyone in the camp has ordinary guns.'

'I've heard that all Lebanese have ordinary guns!'

'They do!' Kholood became animated. 'Whenever something goes wrong between two Lebanese, and you might think they would go to the police, instead they just take out their guns and shoot each other! This is a fact of life in Lebanon.'

'So nothing's changed, really?'

'It's a big lie, to say it's changed. Because if the Lebanese had changed, they would show respect for their state and they would respect their president and their ministers and follow their orders, but they don't!'

'Quite a few people have told me that the government has no real control.'

'Of course they don't. None at all.' She seemed rather pleased with this state of affairs, and from her point of view I could see why. She felt it was hypocritical for the Lebanese to complain that the Palestinians operated with autonomy from the government when that was precisely what the Lebanese did, too.

'Another thing I don't understand,' I began again, 'is how camp dwellers survive economically, given there is 80 per cent unemployment among the men. How can people afford to eat?'

Kholood's mood became more sombre. 'Mostly each family has someone living abroad, who sends them money. Not always that much money, but it helps. After the sieges in 1985–7 a large number of people emigrated, especially the young. Now they are settled abroad and are able to help their families.' She gave the potatoes one last stir, put the wooden spoon on the counter and turned the gas very low. 'We can go and sit down. Come into the back room, then we won't be disturbed by the television.'

I followed her through the living room to a small adjoining room, with a low divan and a computer. 'This is my work room, where I do my translations.'

I sat down beside her. 'Is there one Lebanese community with whom you feel more comfortable than with the others?'

'*Yani...* I suppose it would have to be the Sunnis. I know the Sunnis hate us, but I still prefer them to the Shi'a, after what I went through in the Camp Wars. But I don't really like the Sunnis. They are so snobbish, and they think everyone else is shit and that they are the best thing in the world. You know,' she went on, 'I like the Lebanese, but they're stupid. All they care about is fashion and movies and dancing... They have no idea about politics. They follow the politicians without knowing what they mean. They don't know what is best for their country. Sometimes I think they actually want foreign powers to interfere and solve their problems for them because they can't be bothered to do it themselves. All they care about is having a good time, a nice life...

'You know, the Lebanese are superficial. They don't care about the truth. They don't care, for example, about who assassinated Hariri. And they don't have any kind of respect, they don't even respect each other.'

It was clear that Kholood felt wholly negative towards Amal. What, I wondered, did she feel about Hizbullah?

Kholood looked me in the eye. 'I know I told you that I don't like any of the Shi'a, but I have a lot of respect for Hizbullah, because they care about their country. Hizbullah never took up arms against any of their countrymen. And, let's be honest, after the assassination of Hariri, who prevented civil war breaking out again between the Lebanese? Hizbullah. They refused to engage with people who tried to cause trouble by saying bad things. They were so patient and they did everything they could to maintain calm. They, more than any other group, showed an understanding of what could happen if calm was not maintained. And even though the military criticised them a lot, it was Hizbullah who stopped the situation from getting out of hand. Really, they were good.' She paused. 'I already told you I don't trust any Lebanese. But, let's be honest, Hizbullah were good. And when you look back over the history of Hizbullah, they *never* shot *any* Lebanese or Palestinian. None.'

We sat in silence for a moment while I mulled over her words. I recalled Pauline Cutting's description of Hizbullah's attempts to help the Palestinians of Bourj al Barajneh during the siege in 1986–7. Hizbullah had been opposed to the brutal violence visited on the camp inhabitants by their rival organisation, Amal.

But Kholood's claim was not entirely accurate. I had read claims that Hizbullah had slaughtered many Lebanese Communists during the civil war. And in 1988–1989, there had been vicious fighting between Hizbullah and Amal in the south and in Beirut, in which many civilians had lost their lives.

'Is your view of Hizbullah common among camp Palestinians?'

'For sure. People have a real respect for them. Because Hizbullah deserve it, they *are* respectable. They don't like to treat you in a bad way, and they prefer to talk about problems. Which is good, the Lebanese need people like that. They need them badly.'

There were of course aditional reasons why many Palestinians liked Hizbullah. Following the Israeli withdrawal from the south in 2000 and Hizbullah's decision to continue to participate in the Arab-Israeli conflict, it had forged strong links with Hamas, despite the fact that the latter was a Sunni organisation.

A teenage boy stood in the doorway. 'Mum,' he said, 'Dad's home.'

'Ok, *habibi*, I'm coming.' Kholood stood up. 'This is my son, Basil. He's fourteen. Teresa, have something to eat with us and then I'll take you for a tour of the camp.'

Behind Basil, in the living room, a man dressed in rough work clothes lounged on the couch where previously Dima had sat. As I followed Kholood out of her work room the man glanced at me, grunted in response to Kholood's introduction and returned his eyes to the televison. Even by English standards his behaviour would have been rude, and by Palestinian standards it was appalling. I glanced at Kholood, wanting to communicate my sympathy for the embarassment her husband was causing her. She raised her eyebrows with an air of weariness and disappeared into the kitchen. Dima stood at the stove, stirring small pieces of meat into the potatoes.

A few minutes later Kholood carried a plate of sliced tomatoes into the living room and drew a tiny table up to the couch. Dima brought the dish of fried potatoes and a pile of flat breads. Basil drew up stools, the husband dragged himself into a vertical position and the meal began. Kholood herself declined to eat, but urged me to do so.

'*Kulli*, Teresa, *kulli*,' she kept saying, (eat, Teresa, eat), tearing a portion of bread from a large round and passing it to me. I was hungry and the potatoes and meat were deliciously saturated with garlic, so I ate with enthusiasm. It bothered me, though, that my hostess wasn't eating.

When the plates were empty, Basil went to the fridge and came back with a large bottle of coca cola and a couple of glasses. The husband downed a glassful and lay down again on the couch, his eyes fixed on the television screen.

Kholood opened the door and peered at the sky, which by now was almost dark. 'Okay,' she said, 'the rain is stopping, are you ready for a tour of the camp?'

I could barely see to pick my way down the outdoor steps. At the bottom a dim light burned on the wall of one of the neighbour's houses, powered by a lead connected to the Medusa's rope of electric cables. I stayed as close as I could to Kholood and kept my eyes on the ground.

'I'm going to take you to the hospital,' she began, 'but first we'll do a little tour of the streets. Mind out, there's a big puddle here.' She turned into the alleyway we had walked along earlier, taking me by the arm and steering me away from the open drain. 'When it rains, the houses become damp inside, which causes health problems. The underground sewers fill up with water, and then they overflow.'

'And does the rain sometimes go on for days?' I recalled Pauline Cutting describing how the floors of Haifa hospital had run with water, and her feet were never dry.

'Two or three days. Sometimes the water reaches this high' – she held her hand a foot above the ground – 'and sewage gets mixed in with the water.' She wrinkled up her nose. 'They say this doesn't cause diseases, but I'm sure it does.'

'With little children running round in it...'

'And we have this bad problem with rats. Huge rats.'

I winced.

Kholood glanced at me. 'Funnily, I don't care. I don't feel scared of rats.'

'But they carry diseases, don't they?'

'We never had diseases from them. Because they don't go into the houses, they're always in the sewers or in the streets. Sometimes as you're walking along you may step on one, or hear them. In fact, my neighbour got bitten by a rat, but they cured her straightaway.'

Rain was spitting again as we made our way towards the hospital. The alleyways were empty now, although at one corner I glimpsed a couple of teenage girls sitting behind the counter of a simple shop, waiting for custom by the light of an electric bulb.

'Are there lots of health problems associated with overcrowding?'

'Sure there are. I worked as a translator on a study of the most common diseases in the camp. From the damp, we have problems with respiratory diseases. And there is a lot of depression. Diabetes and hypertension, too, these are very common; and of course depression is linked to diabetes.'

I had not heard this before.

'Of course! If you're depressed all the time, and sad, thinking of your family and thinking of... many things.' Kholood hesitated and I assumed she was referring to the appalling personal losses that many camp dwellers had suffered during the war years and afterwards. 'If you're feeling like that all the time, it makes the blood sugar in your body go up! We did a medical study of the causes of diabetes.' She paused. 'Also we have a lot of heart attacks, and a lot of cancer, because you know during the war people were exposed to bombs and radiation… A lot of people died from cancer in the last ten years.'

'Can Haifa hospital deal with cancer?' We had just emerged in the open area near the camp entrance and were walking towards it.

'They can't do anything. The problem with our hospital is that we don't have big equipment. I wish we could get it, because if anyone in the camp has a big heart attack we can't treat them here, we have to send them out. The Lebanese hospitals charge at least 1,500 dollars just to admit the patient, and if you can't pay, you die.

'They charge that just for one night?'

'Just for one night. This rule applies to everyone. And if you can't pay, they won't treat you. In Lebanon this is a huge problem with the medical system, it's not something against the Palestinians. Anyone who does not have either money, or medical insurance, is refused treatment.'

At the entrance to the hospital, Kholood pushed open a swing door and greeted a man sitting behind a desk. 'Everyone knows me here,' she explained, ' so I can take you upstairs without getting special permission.'

I followed her along a dimly lit corridor and waited while she called the lift. Given my vivid memories of Pauline Cutting's descriptions of the hospital, I found it faintly astonishing to see that the linoleum covered floors were dry and clean, and that the walls were not dripping with moisture and laced with green mould. In the middle and latter days of the 1986–1987 siege, the upper floors had been destroyed by shelling, the corridors were flooded and the ground-floor windows sealed with sandbags. All operations were carried out in the basement and the highest floor where patients could be accommodated was the first. Much of the time the hospital had been in darkness, due to a shortage of fuel to run the generators.

'Also open heart surgery,' Kholood went on, 'that's another thing which can't be dealt with here, because we don't have the equipment.' She spoke as if she were a member of the hospital staff. 'Only small operations are done at Haifa. Anything big, and you have to go out.' The situation had been the same in Cutting's day, but during the sieges (when it was impossible for anyone to leave the camp) she had been obliged to perform numerous operations, including brain surgery and amputations, using the meagre equipment available.

[221]

We took the lift to the fourth floor. 'Doesn't UNRWA help, when people have to go to hospitals outside the camp?'

'If you have surgery, they cover you for four or five days, maximum. Also it depends on the kind of surgery; and you have to buy your own medicines. The UNRWA covers just the bed and the operation.'

We walked along another corridor and stopped at a small booth where two nurses in headscarves were loading up a steriliser with instruments. They looked up as we approached and greeted Kholood with affection.

'Nursing is also a big problem for us,' she went on as we continued down the corridor. 'For the whole of the surgery department, there are only two nurses. The salary is very low and people don't want to work here. When a lot of patients undergo surgery at one time, two nurses are simply not enough. So the patient's parents have to stay with him in the hospital to take care of him, because the nurses simply can't do it.'

Kholood opened a door onto a flight of stairs and we began to descend. As we passed the entrance to the third floor, a young man in green overalls burst through the swing doors and greeted her. She introduced him as Khalil, the newly-wed husband of her cousin's daughter. 'Khalil works in the pharmacy,' she told me. 'And he's a great joker.' Khalil made a quip which I couldn't follow, and Kholood burst out laughing. She smacked him gently on the cheek, and we continued down the stairs.

'So our medical system is not good, but we survive,' she went on. 'Even our primary health care is expensive. We pay about seven dollars to see the doctor, and if we need an X-ray or blood test we pay for it on top.'

I couldn't see how people experiencing eighty per cent unemployment could possibly pay for medical care.

'Presumably some people who have no work just can't pay?' I was trying to imagine what it would feel like to be unable to obtain medical treatment for a sick child.

'That's the problem. Sometimes we have fights at the hospital because people don't have the money to pay and UNRWA refuses to help them.'

We had reached the ground floor and Kholood pulled open the door of a ward. Most of the beds were empty, except for two elderly-looking patients who dozed in beds in the far corner. The ward appeared clean and orderly, if a little spartan. 'Okay, that's everything I can show you,' Kholood announced. 'Let's go back to my house.'

When we opened the main door of the hospital, the rain was torrential. Kholood took my hand and we made a dash across the open ground. When we reached the first alleyway, a stream of water several inches deep was coursing down the middle of it. Drenched and breathless, we stopped for a few seconds under the shelter of a balcony. As we huddled together against the wall of someone's house, gazing upwards through a morass of electric cable, a flash of lightning lit the sky, followed immediately by a loud clap of thunder. Kholood seized my hand again and I followed her through the twisting arteries, as the rain soaked my hair and ran down my face. In three minutes we were at the foot of her outdoor steps, cold and wet but relieved to be close to shelter.

'You can't leave while it's raining like this,' she told me when we stood inside her front door, the drips from our clothes forming a puddle on the floor. 'I'm going to lend you some clothes, and I think you should consider staying the night.' She led me to a large room behind the kitchen, which was empty of furniture apart from a big, built-in wardrobe. We were laughing about the fact that she was nine inches shorter than me, when Dima appeared in the doorway holding a pair of tracksuit bottoms.

'These'll fit you,' she said, holding them out. 'Maybe a bit big round the waist but they'll do, won't they?' She smiled her cool, ironic smile and I took the trousers and thanked her. 'You can come in here to get changed,' she went on, ushering me into a room with two single beds and another large wardrobe.

After I had changed we sat on the beds and talked. Dima wanted to know how many children I had, so I got out my pictures of Dan and showed them to her. She was intrigued by his long fair hair, and liked the shots of him and his friends tobogganing in Wales on his birthday.

'Are you still at school?' I asked Dima when she passed the photos to her mother.

'This is my last year. I have to take the baccalaureate this summer, then I'm done.'

'And then..?'

Dima glanced at her mother. 'Then... we'll see.' She gazed at me with a certain intensity, and I divined that she would prefer me not to ask about her future plans.

'Is it an UNRWA school you go to?' I asked breezily. Dima nodded. 'What's it like?'

'It's… pretty crap I'd say. I'm very bored with it, Basil's very bored with it' – she glanced at her brother, who was pouring over the photo of Dan and his mate Pete on a toboggan. 'There's only one UNRWA high school for the whole of Beirut, so it's very overcrowded. If you fail a year, they chuck you out, because they don't have the space to let you repeat.' She gazed at me, wrinkling up her nose. She was a well-built, attractive girl, but the quality she radiated most was a powerful intelligence. 'And they beat a lot of the kids, on a daily basis.'

'What? The UNRWA teachers beat the kids?'

Kholood looked up, regarding me as if I were hopelessly naïve. 'They have sticks, *habibti*. They beat the kids all the time. I have this argument again and again with the teachers. Last time I went to see Basil's teacher he said, "Ok, I'll hit your son in front of the whole school." I told him, "If you dare to even touch my son, you'll be sorry." I know there is a rule which says that UNRWA is against any kind of violence or beating of school students, but they do it just the same. In fact they do everything they can to make their students hate going to school. You ask the students. Many of them will say, "We don't like school because our teachers say bad things, they hit us and they treat us badly." Also now some of the younger students have back problems because of the weight of the books they have to carry to and fro every day.'

Dima got up off the bed, left the room and returned with a massive holdall full of books.

Kholood went on, 'My niece is nine years old and her spine is no longer straight, because of the weight she is forced to carry.'

'Why does she have to bring her books home?'

Dima stared at me. 'You're not allowed to leave them at school. And if you forget one book the next day, the teacher will beat you…'

Kholood sighed. 'As a parent, what can you do? You need your child to be educated, and yet the school is causing them a lot of problems. Most of the students don't even want to finish their education, because they hate school so much.'

This was a bleak picture. But there was something I didn't understand. 'How come so many students go on to get good degrees?'

Kholood thought for a moment. 'Some students stop going to school. Others are made to go by their parents. Generally, the students who get to the high school have hopes and aims for their future and want to have better jobs and better lives than their parents had, so they keep on going. We have some very smart students. You won't believe this: in the government exams, the UNRWA students get the highest marks.'

'And the girls are smarter than the boys!' Dima added, a hint of smugness in her smile. 'In my brother's school a maximum of forty per cent pass their final exams, whereas in the girls' school, eighty to eighty-five per cent pass.'

'Because the girls study more than the boys,' Kholood added, glancing at Basil. He lay back on the bed, still studying the last of the photos.

It was gone eight-thirty by the time the rain stopped. Kholood reiterated her invitation to stay the night, but Hiba was expecting me and I felt I ought to go. I bade farewell to Dima and Basil, thanked Kholood for her hospitality and accepted her offer to help me find a *servees*.

24

'ALL LEBANESE ARE BITTER'

Hiba's home, near Beirut, April 2006

✧

I had just finished breakfast and was preparing to go into Beirut when Hiba arrived back from the school run.

'No electricity, again!' she panted as she opened the door. 'And I have a huge pile of washing waiting for me.'

'You walked up the stairs?'

'Never mind,' she smiled. 'It helps to burn up the calories..!' She looked at me. 'Are you going this very minute, or do you have time for a quick cup of tea?'

I was in no great hurry.

'I bought us a little treat at the bakery on the way back from school, I hope you're going to like it!'

I had barely seen Hiba the night before, so while she removed her coat and shoes I went into the kitchen and put a *briq* of water on the stove. A moment later she followed me, clutching a paper bag. She smiled at me guiltily, tore open the bag and revealed two balls of puff pastry filled with a type of crème patisserie.

'This is a local delicacy, Teresa, and I do believe you should try everything once while you're with us in Lebanon. Now, how was your visit to Bourj al Barajneh?'

As I made the tea I described my impressions of the camp and the warm welcome I had received from Kholood and her children. 'She was lovely,' I said, 'but I did find her bitterness quite disturbing.'

Hiba tipped the cream buns onto a plate. 'Yes,' she replied, 'and all Lebanese are bitter. It's the legacy of the war. I have noticed that a lot since we came back here to live. I see it as almost a kind of jealousy: people don't wish to help others to have the things they don't have.' She picked up a bun in her fingers and pushed the plate towards me. 'Let me give you an example. You know, when we first rented this apartment we had almost no furniture, so when the children started school I was running this way and that trying to buy things. I bought some bunk beds and a chest of drawers for the boys from a shop in town. They arrived flat-packed but the shop sent some men to assemble them.' She took a bite of bun and wiped her mouth with a tissue. 'These men went at the new beds and the chest of drawers so aggressively that they damaged the wood. They drove the screws too far in! I was very annoyed. So I called the shop and complained. They sent the men again, the same men, and they did the same thing! I was watching them and when I saw what they were doing, I asked them to be more careful.'

'Did they take any notice?'

Hiba rolled her eyes. 'They told me, "Don't worry, madam, we know what we are doing…" So all my new furniture got spoiled.' She paused, smiling. 'What d'you think of the pastry?'

'Delicious.'

She winked at me. 'Good, eh? And very fattening, but you will get away with it! Okay, here's another example of this kind of bitterness I see in the Lebanese. I go shopping. Let us say I am in a food shop, one of the small neighbourhood shops near where my parents live, in the centre of town. Long queue for the till. So I stand at the back, three or four people in front of me, I wait my turn. Fine. Then, just as I get to the front, one of these fancily made-up French-speaking women barges in front of me and insists on being served first. *And the shop keeper serves her!* This sort of thing has happened to me a number of times since we came back from England. I feel that with all that make-up and those fancy clothes these women should know better, but they don't seem to…'

'Do you complain?'

'No, I don't want to get into an argument, with everybody shouting… But you see, I think the underlying attitude of these women is the same as with the furniture men. They cannot bear to see another person have something which they don't have themselves. I see it when I'm driving, too.' Hiba swallowed her last mouthful of bun, stood up and rinsed her fingers at the sink. 'Yesterday I was sitting in a traffic jam and the person in the lane beside me couldn't move because his lane had come to a halt. Now, just as my lane started to move, so that I could go forwards, what did he do? He shot across my bonnet, blocking my way. So both of us were trapped. And this was what he wanted: he gained nothing for himself, but he stopped me from gaining anything.'

25

IN THE DRUZE MOUNTAIN

Aley and Baysour, Mount Lebanon, April 2006

✧

In the dark interior of an ironmonger's shop, a pair of elderly men with fine moustaches and white knitted skullcaps stood chatting together. The crotches of their baggy black trousers hung level with their knees. This was the traditional garb of the Druze, which I had first seen in villages in the Golan sixteen years before. Another man in similar attire moved slowly across the road in the drizzle, in front of a waiting pick-up truck. As he walked he raised his arm to wave at a shopkeeper who stood under the awning of a vegetable shop.

I was loitering at the window of a children's clothing store, pretending to scrutinise a set of baby bootees, when a feminine figure robed in black darted past me. Turning, I saw a young woman, barely out of girlhood, disappearing into the next-door shop. Her hair and most of her face were draped in a long white scarf which covered her mouth and trailed down her back, so that only her forehead, eyes and nose were showing. She was gone in a couple of seconds, but I saw that her skin was pale and clean of make-up. I strolled on along the road, wondering what sort of life such a girl must lead, when another black-robed figure ran in front of me, crossed the road and disappeared through a doorway. She looked very similar to the first girl – slight in figure, pale-skinned and similarly veiled – and the speed and lightness of foot with which she moved suggested that she was not really permitted to be out in public at all.

Today, most of Lebanon's Druze live in the villages surrounding Aley, where I was, and in the Shouf, twenty or thirty kilometres to the south east. They number no more than five per cent of the total Lebanese population. A strong and cohesive community, by and large the Druze remain rooted in a traditional, agriculture-based lifestyle.

As to their identity and history, the Druze derive from a schism in Shi'a Islam. They broke away from mainstream Shi'ism in the twelfth century and went on to develop highly esoteric religious practises. For a long period, external political factors obliged the Druze to lie low and practise their religion in secret. Then, from the sixteenth to the eighteenth centuries, two Druze clans, the Ma'ans and the Shihabs, came to dominate the Mountain. This period ended with the rise of Maronite power in the nineteenth century and the serious conflicts which erupted between Druze and Christians in 1841 and 1860, in which eleven thousand Christians were killed.

I crossed the street to look in the window of the ironmonger's. In amongst a muddle of electric cable, hubbly bubbly pipes, brass jugs and sets of matching enamelled saucepans, I saw a coil of yellow nylon string. Dan, I thought immediately. For all his access to sophisticated toys, he often amused himself for hours with string, and he would like the colour. I had had a text from Paul that morning, telling me that the sun was shining in Cornwall and all was well with him and Dan. I pushed open the door of the shop.

Behind the counter, the two elderly men whom I had spotted from the street sat drinking coffee from tiny cups. One rose to his feet and greeted me warmly, selling me the string for a couple of hundred lira.

'Anything else?' he asked as I tucked the yellow coil into my bag.

I hesitated, running my fingers over a bunch of hubbly bubbly pipes made from corrugated paper which hung from a nail beside the counter. Dan would love one of those.

'I'll take a pipe, please.'

The old man nodded, detached the pipe, wrapped it in a scrap of newspaper and handed it to me. 'Five hundred lira,' he said. That was the equivalent of twenty pence.

It was nearly one o'clock, time to call Rashid, my one and only Druze contact. I found a café, sat down in a window seat and dialled his number, watching the rain fall in slanting lines on the roofs of the parked cars. Rashid answered on the first ring and said he would be with me shortly. In less than three minutes, the door swung open and a short, middle-aged man in a grey suit walked towards me, holding out his hand.

'Teresa?' He smiled with warmth. 'I was just round the corner.' He pulled out a chair, sat down and called to the waiter for a coffee.

I had been given Rashid's phone number by an acquaintance in England who had known him when they were both working for a NGO in Beirut some years back. Rashid was an elected member of his local village council, a leftist and a strong supporter of the Palestinians. He spoke fluent English.

I explained what I was doing in Lebanon and that I would like to meet some Druze families. When he had finished his coffee, Rashid pushed back his chair.

'Ok, Teresa. I'll take you to my village. It's about twenty minutes from here. We can have lunch at my house and then I'll take you to meet some people.'

'Do you think they'll be willing to see me?'

'I think so. The people I'm thinking of suffered a great deal in the war, so it may be painful for them to talk about their memories, but we can try.'

We drove slowly down the narrow shopping street and out of Aley. On the outskirts of the town, small, grey apartment blocks were scattered across the hillsides under low, white cloud. After ten minutes, Rashid turned onto a single-track country road and headed down into a steep-sided valley. Soon the view was obscured by high banks, dense with bamboo and cow parsley.

'What do people grow?' I asked.

'Olives, figs, fruit… Some keep goats.'

The car was struggling now as we climbed up out of a dip in the land. 'In a minute,' Rashid began, 'you'll see the old Damascus road.'

As we rounded a bend at the top of the hill I could see into the next valley, at the bottom of which a pale brown road twisted like a muddy river in a series of meanders.

Rashid made a broad gesture at the landscape. 'Traditionally this area was mixed Druze and Christian. But after the fighting which began in 1983, many of the Christian families left.'

'Where did they go?'

'To East Beirut, mostly. In some of the villages Druze and Christians had lived side by side for generations, even as next-door neighbours.'

We coasted along the top of the hill and started to descend into the next valley. 'Down there, for instance,' Rashid went on, gesturing at a group of roof tops I could just see at the bottom, 'that village was mixed Druze and Christian before the war.'

'And now?'

'The Christian families left during the fighting. A few have come back, but not many.' He frowned. 'It needs time for people to begin to trust each other again.'

During the Israeli invasion of Lebanon in 1982, the Druze had refrained from engaging in the fighting, even when the Israelis took control of Druze towns and villages in Aley and the Shouf. After the Israelis began to pull out of these areas in 1983, the Lebanese Forces had rushed in, hoping to take the place of the Israelis. Their campaign was ill-thought out, however, and met with forceful opposition from the Druze militias. After the Lebanese Forces had retreated from the area, a terrible revenge for their actions was wreaked on the Christian populations of Aley and the Shouf.

'Is your village mixed?'

'No, Baysour is unusual. It's a large village, with twelve thousand inhabitants, and it's all Druze.'

We were climbing again. At the bend of each zig-zag we passed a small house, a patch of cultivated land, a parked car or pick-up truck. The rain had stopped and a brighter light pushed its way through the clouds. At last we came out on the ridge and drove in a straight line towards a house constructed on stilts over the valley.

'Our house was destroyed in the war, so my brother and I built this one,' Rashid explained as we got out of the car. 'My family are on the top floor, he is below.'

Rashid's wife Fatin met us at the front door, a pretty woman dressed in a grey tracksuit with long black hair which she wore uncovered. She seemed pleased to see me, and after kissing me on both cheeks ushered me down a long corridor to the kitchen where she was cooking. I felt the warmth of the room as soon as we entered. In the centre of the floor stood a small cast iron stove, with a chimney rising to the ceiling.

This was a far cry from Beirut, and I was beginning to feel at home.

'What do you burn?' I asked as I sat down on the divan built into the walls around the stove.

'Paraffin.' Rashid opened the stove door and showed me a row of blue flames.

'I guess it's very cold up here in the winter?'

Rashid held out his right arm and flicked his wrist in a gesture of affirmation. 'Two weeks ago we had a foot of snow. We are high up here, and unprotected from the weather. Come and see the view.'

I followed him out of the kitchen and across a sitting room at the back of the house, to a pair of French windows which opened onto a balcony. As we stepped into the fresh, damp air, I caught my breath. Less than a kilometre away a ridge rose even higher than the one on which Rashid's house was built. The valley between the two ridges was so deep that I couldn't see the bottom. I stood drinking in the rich dark green, dappled here and there with the pale shapes of small houses. By focussing on the top of the far ridge I could just make out the pale silhouette of the ridge behind it, and above that the one behind, drifting into the distance with the promise of real mountains.

When we returned to the kitchen a short, squat man was standing beside the stove, warming his hands. He wore an old-fashioned wool jacket and trousers and regarded me with ill-disguised interest. Rashid introduced him as Shakeeb, a fellow member of Baysour town council and a family friend.

As we sat down to lunch with Rashid's teenage sons who had just arrived from school, Shakeeb apologised for the weakness of his English and launched into a monologue in French.

'I am pro-Syrian,' he announced as dishes of *hommous*, rice, salad, olives and chips were passed around. 'In this respect I am not in agreement with Rashid,' Shakeeb added, shooting a glance of affection mixed with disapproval towards his friend.

For some reason which was not immediately clear to me, Rashid's sons found the spectacle of Shakeeb holding forth in French acutely comic. They doubled up over their plates convulsed with laughter, making feeble attempts to cover their faces with their hands. The table was small and Fatin quietly took her plate of food to the divan, while her giggling boys squirted large quantities of ketchup onto their chips.

I too found it difficult to take Shakeeb too seriously. It appeared that, by launching into French, he hoped to exclude Rashid and his family from our conversation.

'Why do you like the Syrians?' I thought the best way to find out why the boys were giggling was to engage with Shakeeb.

He leaned forwards across the table. 'We need the Syrians,' he disclosed, 'to protect us from the Americans and the British.' He shot me a kindly smile, which seemed intended to reassure me that his distrust of the British did not extend to individual females.

I was taken aback. 'You think the Americans and the British are planning to intervene in Lebanon again?'

Shakeeb smiled enigmatically. 'They are always here.' He met my gaze, apparently searching for some sign that I accepted the truth of what he was saying. 'They always have spies here, always.' He took an olive and spat the stone into his hand. 'But, above all, we need the Syrians to protect us from the Israelis.' Pleased with his political analysis, he turned to Rashid and repeated it in Arabic.

Rashid groaned and switched into English. 'Shakeeb is always saying this, but I don't buy it myself. The Syrians caused a lot of trouble in Lebanon and we are better off without them.' He reached for the salad. 'Have some more chips, Teresa. Oh, you don't like them? Have some rice.'

'George Bush is a very bad man,' Shakeeb began again. 'His policies have brought disaster to the Middle East.'

'Sure.' This was easier ground.

'And your Tony Blair, we don't like him either. What is he doing supporting the Americans in everything they do? Why did he have to go into Iraq?'

I tried to explain that I felt Blair had made huge mistakes, avoiding going into detail as to what, precisely, I felt he had done wrong. As Fatin cleared away the plates and put coffee on to boil, I trotted out my usual, rather misleading line, that most of the British people had opposed the invasion of Iraq. (Personally, I had not opposed the invasion at the time, because many of the Iraqi Kurds I knew felt that it was justified as the only way to rid their country of Saddam Hussein. I had changed my view some months later, when it became apparent that proper plans had not been made to secure the country and facilitate the transition to self-government.)

'We know, we know.' Shakeeb nodded with avuncular kindness. We saw the demonstrations on the television. More than one million, wasn't it, on the streets of London?'

'More than a million, but Blair didn't take the slightest bit of notice. That's our democracy for you. He had a large majority in parliament and could afford to ignore the views of ordinary people.'

Salma sat on the edge of the sofa, her back very straight, her expression strained. We had been introduced by Rashid on the threshold of her home only five minutes earlier, and now I faced the delicate task of persuading her to tell me about the tragic events that had shaped her life. As we walked up the flight of new concrete steps that led to her home, Rashid had told me simply that she had lost more than one member of her family during the fighting between the Druze and the Christians in 1983. She had greeted us at the door, surrounded by a crowd of relatives, most of whom followed when we were ushered into a small sitting room at the front of the house. As we waited for everyone to settle in their seats, I took in a large television and a glass coffee table spread with crocheted doilies. The room was light, airy and spotlessly clean.

Salma was twenty-four, an English literature graduate and a new mother. She had wide cheek bones, large eyes and curly brown hair which fell to her shoulders. Dressed in jeans and a jersey, she sat with her hands folded in her lap, watching her tall, bulky husband stoop over a Moses basket to pick up the baby. Judging by the slow manner in which he moved and the kind, rather sad expression on his face, I decided he was probably a good few years her senior.

Beside Salma sat a woman in her late forties. Her face was lined and her hair cut short. This was Nada, Salma's mother.

'Okay,' Salma cleared her throat and turned to face me with a polite smile. 'I will tell you my family's story.' Her English was perfect but she held herself stiffly and I anticipated she would tell me just the bare bones of the story, with all emotion removed.

'Thank you,' I nodded and smiled.

'My mother married my father during the war, in 1981. My father was killed in fighting in 1983, when I was one, and then in 1984 my mother married my uncle, my father's brother.' Salma paused, and after a moment I saw that she was weeping. She reached for a tissue, wiped her eyes and sat very still. I stared at the carpet, shocked to discover how wrong I had been.

'When my mother re-married she had my two brothers with my uncle. And then my uncle was killed, too, in the war against General Aoun. My youngest brother was only nine months old.'

I put my hand over my mouth.

'In 1983,' Salma went on, dabbing at her nose with the tissue, 'my father was fighting with Walid Jumblatt's Progressive Socialist Party against the Lebanese Forces, here in Baysour. My mother had gone away to another village because of the fighting, taking me with her. We were with my grandmother and my aunt.' She looked at me, uncertain of whether she was telling me what I wanted to know.

'Could you explain what the fighting was about?' I asked gently.

Salma leaned forward. 'All the Druze martyrs who died here were defending their land. It was not as though they left here and went to fight somewhere else.' I heard an urgency in her voice, as if it mattered to her very much that I should understand what she was saying. 'It was their own land they were defending.' She looked at me. 'It was not our choice, to go to war. We fought in order to defend ourselves.'

'Was this after the Israelis left the area?'

'Yes.' Salma glanced at her husband, who sat rocking the baby in an armchair on the far side of the room. He said something which I didn't catch. 'When the Israelis left,' she went on, 'they handed their military positions to the Lebanese Forces, leaving us little choice but to fight.'

I turned to Salma's mother, who up till now had sat very still, apparently content for her daughter to do the talking. 'How do you feel now,' I asked her in Arabic, 'about the Christians who killed your first husband?'

Nada gazed at me with small, dark eyes. 'I try to forget about the past,' she said softly. 'I have forgiven the Christians.' She paused. 'Now that my children are grown up, I am happy with my life and I can forgive and live peacefully in Lebanon with Christians and Moslems.' She sighed and glanced at Salma. 'At least, I try hard to overcome my bad feelings towards the Christians. Mostly I'm successful. Even though it's very difficult, it's better to forget what happened and live peacefully, than to dwell on a bad experience. And nowadays I can see that we were forced into going to war.'

'By the Israelis?' I looked from Nada to Salma.

'Maybe not only the Israelis,' Salma replied. 'But my mother doesn't mean that she has forgotten my father, or that it would not have been better if he had not been killed. Of course it would be better if both my father and my uncle were still here beside us. What she means is that she tries not to dwell on their deaths.'

'Of course.' I hesitated. 'How about you, do you remember your father at all?'

Salma turned her large eyes on me. 'I have no memories of my real father, because I was one year old when he died. But I have lots of memories of my uncle. He was the person I saw as a father.'

I turned back to Nada. 'Was it very difficult to manage financially as a mother on your own?' I was sure I knew the answer, but I wanted to see how she would put it.

Nada looked down at her hands, which were clasped in her lap. 'It was very difficult, but I had to do it. I found a job as a teacher.' I glanced at the shadows under her eyes.

Salma butted in. 'She's still working as a teacher now. As her daughter, I can tell you that we did not want for anything. My mother managed to provide us with everything we needed. We didn't feel there was any difference between us and other children.'

'Did your mother's parents help?'

Salma looked uneasy. 'Not really. They loved us and were kind, but my mother managed on her own, without help from anyone. It was very difficult, but she's very strong.'

I was touched by the pride in Salma's voice. As the daughter of a lone mother myself, I could imagine how protective Salma felt towards Nada.

'Do you have memories of the war?'

'The first thing I remember is the war with Aoun.' Salma hesitatated, looking down. 'I remember my uncle's death. We were here in the village when he died. I was seven. We were sitting...' Her voice tailed off and she began to weep again, soundlessly. After a few moments she went on. 'We were sitting having lunch when they came to the house.' She glanced at her mother. 'My mother didn't tell me at first that he was dead, she told me later.' Her voice dwindled to a whisper.

I waited for a few moments. 'How has your uncle's death left you feeling about the Christians?' I addressed my question to Salma but Nada answered, looking at her daughter.

'I still hate Aoun. I cannot forgive him.'

Salma returned her mother's gaze, as if expecting her to say more, but Nada fell silent.

'Okay, my mother hates Aoun, but we have no problems with anyone. We have to live peacefully with others. We have to accept them and they have to accept us, it's the only solution.'

I looked at her. 'To me, it always seems amazing how people here manage to move on. It's very impressive.'

Salma nodded. 'Perhaps we carry on because we understand what were the real reasons for the war. You see, we were pushed into it, not only by the Israelis but also by the Syrians. The war was part of a plan, to prevent this country from continuing to develop. Knowing this helps us to overcome our bad experiences.'

'Do you feel the Palestinians bear some responsibility, too?'

'The Palestinians were another reason for the war. But we have to accept them, and help them.' She spoke without feeling, as if her words did not quite tally with her real views.

I looked at Nada again. 'Has your life changed since the war?'

Nada stirred in her seat. I couldn't tell whether her air of reserve was due to shyness or whether she felt suspicious of me as a stranger.

'My life was easier before the war. And during the war. Since it finished in 1990 I have had a lot of responsibilities. My two sons are still dependent on me; and the economic situation is not good.' She sighed. 'It's hard for me as a woman to be head of the family, because as a woman I have limited abilities. I do not have the same abilities as a man, there are lots of things which I can't do. Life would be easier if I had a man beside me.'

I glanced at Salma.

'These are my mother's views, not mine.' Salma smiled. 'In my view, men and women are equal.' She paused. 'But I think things are easier for my mother now that we're grown up. Soon my brothers will be able to work and help her. Before, it was very tough. She had to work hard for a low salary, and there were a lot of financial demands on her. Everything here is expensive and salaries are very low.'

'What about the effect of the war on her health?'

'It had a big effect on her nerves and on her health generally. She suffers with anxiety and she has hormonal problems. Her periods stopped when she was only thirty-six, from shock.'

'Is she on medication?'

'She used to take sleeping pills, but not now.' Salma brightened. 'Now her life is busy with my brothers and me and my daughter and my husband...'

'What about you? How were you affected by your experiences in the war?'

'My brothers and I were affected in lots of ways. Sometimes when the fighting got very heavy we had to leave the village, although we never went very far because we had nowhere to go, and the men had to stay here to defend our land. At other times we stayed in the house, but we couldn't go to school.'

'Did the fighting frighten you?'

'Of course! When bombs fell, I was always frightened. I remember once I was sitting at home with my parents and suddenly the window shattered and fell on our heads. It was terrifying. And then my uncle wanted to go outside to see what had happened, and I didn't want him to, because I was afraid for him.'

'Do these experiences still affect you now?'

'When I remember them, yes, but life is full and sometimes I'm able to forget. When I remember, I feel really frightened. I hope that time will never come again. If I see a war scene on TV, or if I walk past a damaged building, I start to remember. You see, the war happened very close to where we live. It was in Souq al Gharb right here beside us and there are still a lot of destroyed places close to our village. Many of the locations used by the fighters are very near here. Some of them are still being opened up, and that reminds us of the war.' She stopped speaking for a moment. 'And of course the other thing which was very hard for me and my brothers during the war,' she dropped her voice to a whisper 'was to see other children growing up with their fathers, when we had to go on without one.' She shot a glance at Nada and spoke in her usual voice again. 'Of course our mother helped us with this, she was our mother and our father; she tried her best not to let us think about it too much. We had also lost our grandfather during the war.'

'Your mother's father?'

'No, my father's father. My grandfather was killed in fighting after my father was killed.' Salma looked at me steadily. 'In six years we had three martyrs from our household.'

I shook my head in sympathy. 'Is your father's mother still alive?'

'My grandmother is seventy-six and still working.' Salma smiled proudly. 'She makes things by hand.' She picked up a crocheted doily from the coffee table in the centre of the room. 'She made this – and she sells the things she makes. She is a strong woman. She lost her two sons and her husband and then she helped my mother to take care of me and my brothers. We lived with her when we were growing up. We love her a lot, a lot.'

'Did your grandmother have other children?'

'Only girls. Four girls.' Salma gestured at a young woman sitting on the far side of the room. 'Nadia, my cousin, is the daughter of one of my grandmother's daughters.'

I smiled at Nadia. I had been dimly aware of her throughout the conversation, listening intently as Salma told her story. She had long, very straight, reddish blond hair and was dressed in similar style to Salma.

Salma looked at me. 'My mother has to leave shortly. Is there anything else you wish to ask her?'

'I don't think so, I'd just like to thank her very much for talking to me.' Nada and I both stood up. We shook hands and I thanked her again. As she left the room, Salma's husband and three of the in-laws followed her into the hall, leaving the room feeling less crowded. I asked Salma if she agreed with her mother's view that life was more difficult now than during the war.

'I do think it's more difficult, especially since the death of Hariri. We aren't able to live as citizens in other countries live, we're still suffering a lot, we're still afraid every day, not knowing what will happen.' Salma was more relaxed now, leaning back into the cushions of the sofa, facing towards me; but I could see the worry in her face. 'We wake up every morning and think "maybe there'll be a bomb today, maybe someone will be killed today".'

'Is it because of the tension between the people who like Syria and the ones who don't?'

Salma nodded. 'We're afraid things may get worse. I don't think there'll be war again, but it's not an easy situation. It's having a bad effect on us as young people. We need to work and get on with our lives, but you feel that everything is connected with the political situation, which is very uncertain. Something is threatening our lives. We have to find a solution… but I don't think we will be able to.'

She was alluding to the power struggle between the people of March 8 and the people of March 14. In the past year, a number of prominent individual supporters of the latter grouping had been assassinated, almost certainly by Syria.

'Has the situation got worse since the death of Hariri and the investigation into who killed him?' I asked.

'The death of Hariri is one of the issues, but there are many others. The Syrian influence, the Israelis… everything has its effects. And I think that we as Druze living here in the Mountain, feel the effect more than the Christians or the Moslems. Life in the city is easier. Most Christians and Moslems live in the cities, where there's more possibility of finding work. Here in the Mountain there's no work at all.' She hesitated. 'But nearly all Lebanese are suffering economically. The big majority of people are suffering.' She lifted her long, slim hands from her lap and opened them in a gesture of uncertainty. 'Sometimes we feel pessimistic, sometimes optimistic. We are afraid that if things go on like this...' She gestured at her daughter, sleeping now in the Moses basket. 'I have a little baby. What will happen for her? We work hard and there are no great results. Life is very difficult, especially economically. And everything is related to the political situation, in Lebanon, in the region as a whole, with the Palestinians...' She fell silent.

26

DEATH AND REINCARNATION

Baysour, April 2006

It was late afternoon and the streets were empty. In the middle of the village, close to the town hall, Rashid stopped the car at the window of a falafel shop. An old man dressed in baggy trousers and a white skullcap looked up and uttered a string of welcomes. Rashid climbed out of the car and soon the two were laughing out loud.

'Teresa, this is Sheikh Wisam,' Rashid turned to me as I followed him. Without thinking I stretched out my hand, only remembering when it was too late that this might not be acceptable. To my relief the old man shook my hand with vigour. 'And this is his wife,' Rashid gestured at an old woman who stood at a table inside the shop, chopping tomatoes. She beamed at us, wiped her hands on her apron and hurried outside. She was dressed in a long black dress and white headscarf, and her chuckles suggested that she shared her husband's sense of humour.

'Have a *sandweech*!' the old man cried to me. 'Our falafel's the best in town!'

He went into the shop, turned up the gas flame beneath the falafel pan, and dropped some balls of ground chick pea into the simmering oil.

After I had finished my *sandweech* we drove a few hundred yards through the village and pulled up at the bottom of another flight of outdoor stairs.

'We have to walk up,' Rashid was still grinning from his conversation with the sheikh.

'Is this a Druze thing,' I asked, 'to laugh a lot?'

'Sure, we like to laugh as much as possible. It's good for the health.' He beamed at me, then checked himself. 'I'm taking you now to see a lady who has suffered a great deal. We will see what she tells you.'

A gentle breeze stirred the leaves of the dusty plants that stood in pots on either side of the concrete steps. I walked up slowly, turning half-way to look at the view. On the far side of the street the land dropped sharply into the valley. Beyond, line after line of hills receded into the distance.

Two women came to greet us at the top of the steps. Both were clad in full-length black dresses, their heads swathed in white scarves that covered their foreheads and mouths. The younger of the two was called Sana. She ushered me into a large living room where a young man lounged on a sofa. Rashid stayed for long enough to establish that Sana spoke good English, then left me alone to talk with her.

Sana was slightly built with very pale skin and small, delicate features. When she sat down beside me I formed the impression of a woman in her twenties, but gradually I realised that she was much older than she looked. Her manner was cool at first, and formal. She answered my questions with brevity and precision, giving me the facts without the feelings, in a voice so soft that I could barely hear her. I felt disappointed, for I was much more interested in how she felt than in the details of what had happened; but I respected her reluctance to show a stranger the depth of what she had suffered.

Sana had a daughter of twenty-five and a son of twenty-two – the young man on the sofa. In 1983, when the son was a baby of three and a half months, her husband had been killed in the fighting in Baysour between the Druze and the Lebanese Forces. Sana, her husband and the children had been staying in another village, but the husband's brother was in Baysour with the Druze fighters. One night the husband had decided to go to Baysour to check on his brother, leaving Sana and the children with his mother. The husband and brother were caught in an ambush, and never returned. The two men were buried quickly by their fellow fighters, following tradition, which meant that Sana and her mother-in-law did not get the opportunity to see them. Some time later, Sana herself was seriously injured by a piece of shrapnel from a shell.

I asked Sana what it was like for her immediately after her husband was killed.

'It was very difficult!' She spoke in a near whisper, but I could tell she thought my question stupid. 'No money, we were not in our own house, not in our own village.' She paused, pulling her headscarf tightly aross her mouth. 'We had no idea what our future would be like. My baby son became sick, we didn't know what to do... it was a miserable time.'

'Was your daughter sick, too?'

'No, she was okay. When my son was born, the fighting was very heavy and we had to spend most of our time in the shelter beneath our house. It was dirty and airless and crowded with people, very unhealthy, and that is why he got sick.' She tugged at the scarf again. It was made of fine lawn and the tighter she pulled it, the more clearly I could see the shape of her lips and the line of her chin.

'Did you have food?'

'Food was not a problem, this is an agricultural area and the villages were full of food. We always had clean water and paraffin, too. The problem was how to avoid getting caught up in the fighting: that is why we had to spend so much time in the shelter.'

'How do you feel now about the people who killed your husband?'

She dropped her voice to a whisper, but her features betrayed no emotion. 'It was God's wish. He was going to die. Then, or at a later date, it was God's wish. He could have died in an accident.' Her eyes were on mine. 'I accepted it. If I didn't accept it I would have become... crazy. It was God's wish.'

'Do you have Christian neighbours now, and Christian friends?'

'Yes, we have Christian friends, they are so good to us.'

'So you don't hold a bad feeling towards the Christians?'

'No, not all Christians, not all Christians, no. Every religion has good people and bad people.' Sana spoke with simplicity and directness and I felt no doubt but that she meant exactly what she said.

'Tell me about your injury.'

'It happened when we were living in a village called Sharou, near Chtaura. One day shells started to land near our home and we had to run for safety. My mother was carrying my small daughter, my sister was carrying my son and I was running beside them. Suddenly I felt something happen to me but I didn't know what it was. I fell over and could not get up. My mother was shouting 'Stand up! Stand up!' I replied that I could not. My mother said 'Nothing's happened to you, has it?'

THE CURTAIN MAKER OF BEIRUT

I knew something had hit me, but no-one else had seen it. A piece of shrapnel had pierced my back and lodged in my stomach.

'I was taken to Chtaura, and spent twenty-two days in hospital. They operated on me to remove the shrapnel.' Sana paused for breath and pulled the scarf over her mouth. 'When I came out, I had to rest. We left Sharou and went to Syria. We didn't have relatives there so we rented a house for a few months. Luckily, my husband's sisters were still unmarried then, so they were able to help me with the children.'

'Do you still get pain from the injury?'

Sana frowned. 'Not in my stomach; sometimes in my leg. But not all the time.'

I shook my head, thinking Sana lucky to able to walk. 'What about the children?' I asked. 'How did the war affect them?'

She looked at me in surprise. 'It didn't affect them; never. Not even my small daughter.'

I found this hard to believe. 'Not even when there was shelling?'

Sana clicked her tongue. '*I* was the one who was frightened. My daughter used to like to watch the shells landing! My son was not as keen as she was, but he was not afraid, probably because his aunts were not afraid. I was the only one who felt frightened, maybe because of what happened to my husband, and to me.'

'Has the war had a long-term effect on your health?'

'Yes.' Again Sana spoke very softly, but her tone expressed a certainty which was close to anger. 'It's affected my sleep; and it's affected me... how do you say it? Psychologically. It's made me very anxious.' She sucked her teeth. 'Sorry, I have forgotten a lot of English words.'

'But your English is excellent!'

Sana smiled with real warmth for the first time. 'I was a student in an English school in Egypt, so I should speak better.'

'I wish my Arabic was as good as your English.'

'Thanks.' She giggled, obviously pleased. I studied Sana's face. It was slowly dawning on me that she had the same complexion and shape of mouth and chin as a girl I had known at my comprehensive school in Sussex many years before. I could almost, but not quite, remember the girl's name.

'During the first war in 1975, I spent a year and a half in Egypt with my family,' she went on.

I sat back on the sofa. 'How do you feel about the political situation since the death of Hariri?'

A look of anxiety passed across her face. 'I don't know what's going to happen. I am particularly worried because I have a son. I don't want him to go to war.' She looked over at the young man who still lounged on the sofa opposite, listening without saying a word. 'When your children are small you can put them in front of you and give them something to play with, but once they are big, you can't control what they do.'

I hesitated, wondering how far to push Sana on the subject of her worries. 'Are you really afraid there could be another war?'

'Yes.'

'Between whom?'

Sana tugged at her headscarf and gave a small, embarassed laugh. 'This time it will be between the Druze and the Shi'a.'

'Because of the Shi'a's support for Syria?'

'Yes! The Shi'a get weapons from Syria, that's why they support Syria.' I assumed she was referring to Hizbullah.

'Do the Druze like Hariri?' I knew that the Druze as a political bloc were aligned with the Sunnis and the anti-Syrian Christians; but I wanted to see what she would say.

'Some do, some don't. My son doesn't like him. *I* don't like him, but I want the Syrians to stay out of Lebanon.' She paused and looked at me. 'I'm afraid that the Shi'a may come and fight us, but it's *war itself* that frightens me, I am not afraid of the Shi'a as people.'

'Did you have this fear before the death of Hariri?'

'No.' She paused. 'I often think about war. If I hear a gun go off, I feel so afraid, even if I know it's someone shooting at an animal.' She glanced at her son. 'I don't even like my son to shoot wild birds.' She looked down at her hands. 'Fireworks, too, upset me.' She looked up again. 'But in many ways, life was better during the war than it is now. In the war, everything was cheap. Now, everything's expensive. Also, in those days you spent your time indoors, in the house, hiding. Now we don't do that, so life is more expensive; and yet there's no money, because there's no work.'

I looked at Sana's son. 'How do *you* feel about life in Lebanon?'

'I don't like living here,' he replied. 'I'd like to go and live abroad. Australia is where I'd choose, if I could go somewhere.'

'Do you have a job?'

He shrugged his shoulders with an air of disgust. 'I studied mechanics, but I can't find a job as a mechanic. I drive a tractor in the village. I'm fed up with Lebanon because I can't make money here.'

'Are you worried about the political situation?'

'Not really, no.'

Sana glanced at me with a look of frustration. 'Sometimes he says he wishes there would be war. He doesn't understand. He thinks it is like it is when you see it on the TV.' Suddenly she untied her headscarf, removed it and laid it across her knees, revealing short brown hair. Now she reminded me more than ever of the girl at school.

'Is there any special help available to you as a family with a martyr?'

'No, no, there's no special help.'

'Or special respect for you as the widow of a martyr?' I told her about my conversation with Hajj Nabulsi.

'Hizbullah has money to look after the families of martyrs, because they get lots of support from Iran.'

'And from Syria.'

'No, Syria doesn't give them anything. All Syria does is *take* everything. I don't like Syria.'

'I thought it was well-known that Syria gives weapons to Hizbullah?'

'Weapons, yes. But Syria would even give weapons to *us* if we needed them, just to get us fighting each other.'

'Really?'

'I think so.'

'I'd like to ask you something else,' I said to Sana. I felt close to her now, and that made me bolder. 'Do the Christians and Moslems hold any sort of prejudice against the Druze?'

'In some cases. It's not widespread. It's a question of how people raise their children. If a child is raised to hate the Druze, they will hate them.' She looked at me. 'The Shi'a don't like anybody except the Shi'a.'

'And the Sunnis?'

She thought for a moment. 'Possibly. But the Shi'a more. Because they don't accept us as being within Islam. The Christians have many different divisions, the Moslems have many different divisions, but we are seen as *so* different.'

'But surely you are within Islam?'

'We consider ourselves to be within Islam. But we have a lot of traditions that are different from Sunni and Shi'a traditions: we don't go to Mecca, we don't do Ramadan, we don't say the same prayers that they say. We pray in our homes, not in the mosque; and we don't talk much about our religion.'

When Sana fell silent, I asked her about reincarnation. This was a central tenet of Druze philosophy.

'Of course.' Her tone disclosed a measure of surprise, as if reincarnation were more a fact of life than a belief. 'You don't believe in it?'

I hesitated, for the truth was that I had an open mind. 'I don't *not* believe in it,' I began; 'I simply don't know. In many ways I think it makes a lot of sense.'

Sana looked at me with a patient smile, as if she thought me a little slow. 'We see it all the time, here in the village. A person dies, and the soul is re-born in the body of a baby. Sometimes after only a few days, or even a few minutes…'

'My grandmother believed in it,' I remarked. 'When she first saw my sister, just after she was born, she said "she's an old soul", meaning she had been here before.'

'Of course! Sometimes a small baby smiles or laughs for no reason to do with what is happening around them. When this happens, we say the child is remembering something from the life they lived before. And sometimes a child may cry, for no reason that you can tell. Why? Because they are remembering something bad which happened to them in their past life.'

To me this was a startling idea, but I liked it because it seemed respectful of children's feelings.

'You know, when my son was six weeks old, my cousin was holding him in her arms, and he cried "Omma!" which means "mother". At six weeks he could not have learned that word in this life. He was *in the past*! We were so astonished…' Sana smiled with delight at the memory. 'And again when my son was one or two, he used a word which we do not use in Lebanon. We say "*biddi atlak*," to mean "I want to kill you", but he said "*biddi atuhak*" – which is the way they say it in Palestine. One of my neighbours has a son who was born in the war from 1975–1976. He always used to say to his mother "There's blood here," when she couldn't see any. Then when he was older he told his mother "I was doing such and such when I was killed here." So we know that that boy has the soul of a boy who was killed.'

'When an old soul is reborn, is it reborn into the same family as before?'

'No, never in the same family!' Sana appeared shocked by the idea. 'I have a brother who went to America to study, and died there. He was born again in a Lebanese Druze family living in Spain.'

'How did you know that?'

'When he was born, he told his new family, "I am…" many things. But they didn't want him to talk, so we don't know the situation precisely. His grandmother told me, "my son's son has your dead brother's soul".'

I was fascinated.

'That helps us,' she went on, 'that helps us. Sometimes a baby is born and lives two or three days, then dies'. She was speaking in a soft, breathy whisper, which conjured for me the idea of the baby's spirit. 'So where does its soul go?'

I shook my head to indicate I didn't know. 'Can it be quite quick that they're born again?'

'Yes! We say that when you breathe out then breathe in' – she demonstrated with a sharp exhalation followed by an inhalation – 'in that small amount of time, the soul is re-born.'

'When do you say that the soul enters the body? When the baby is conceived, or when it is born?'

Sana answered without hesitating. 'At birth, when the baby takes its first breath. Sometimes you have to hit the baby to make it cry so that it breathes, and that's when the soul enters the body. You hit the baby to make the soul come in. There's also the blood soul. This is when the mother miscarries the baby and he moves but he does not appear.'

'So does he have a soul?'

'No. The soul comes in when he breathes. And when a person dies, the soul leaves the body as they breathe their last breath.'

'And that soul can then…' I searched for the right word '… jump into a baby?'

'Yes.' Sana smiled at me.

'It's a beautiful idea, I like it.'

'In England you can research it more. You have many big libraries there. You know, *I* know about it from *feeling* it.' She laughed and for the first time I noticed fine lines at the outer corners of her eyes. I still found it hard to believe she was in her forties.

'Sana,' I began, 'are you happy for me to write about what you've told me about reincarnation?' I knew the Druze liked to keep their religious ideas secret.

'Of course! You write about it!' She fell silent for a moment, then went on. 'You know the Alawites? The people of Bashar al Assad?'

I nodded. The Alawites were a small Shi'a sect who had ruled Syria for a number of decades.

'They believe that when a good person dies, he will be born again as a good person; but a bad person will be born again as a dog or a cat.' She picked up her headscarf. '*We* say, when someone is born with bad health or very poor, that we don't know what he was in his past life; maybe he was a wealthy man, but probably he did not use his wealth to help other people much.' She lifted the scarf over her head and prepared to tie it under her chin.

'Do your beliefs make it easier for you to accept death?'

'Yes, of course. When you believe these things, the death of someone you love is less painful. It is still painful, of course, but... believing in God's wishes helps. It helps a lot.' Sana finished tying the scarf and looked at me. 'My mother-in-law lost two sons, two *boys* and she didn't even get to see them after they were killed. If she had not believed in reincarnation, she would have gone crazy!' Sana's voice faded to a whisper. 'Believing in God helps...'

It was time to go. I thanked Sana and commented again on the fluency of her English. How did she keep it up, I asked, when she didn't often get to use it?

Sana's smile was radiant. 'I always liked the British!' she exclaimed. 'And I read a lot of books in English.'

'What do you read?'

'Barbara Cartland, Mills and Boon; these are my favourites.'

Sana came with me to the top of the outdoor steps. 'Next time you're in Lebanon,' she said, gesturing at the living room we had just left 'please, this is your house. You'll be welcome to stay with us.'

Night had fallen while I was talking with Sana and Rashid was waiting for me at the bottom of the steps. As we got into the car I asked him what he thought about reincarnation. As a secular leftist I thought he would probably dismiss the idea.

But I was wrong.

'I believe in it. Of course! In Baysour there are so many stories, it's impossible not to believe in it.' He turned on the headlights and started the engine. 'If you're interested to hear about reincarnation I'll take you to speak with Sheikh Wisam's wife. Hers is an extraordinary story.' He drove through the village and pulled up at the falafel shop where, to my surprise, the old man still stood in the window, launching little balls of chick pea paste into the sizzling oil by the light of a single bulb. The old woman stood beside him, regaling us with a string of welcomes.

'Teresa is interested in reincarnation,' Rashid explained to the old woman. 'She would like to hear your story.'

The old woman threw her headscarf across her mouth and smiled at me with her eyes. 'Alright,' she said, 'I am happy to tell you, but wouldn't you like a *sandweech*?' She gestured at the pan of oil.

'Yes please, I would.' I wasn't really hungry, but the Sheikh's falafel was particularly delicious and I didn't want to hurt her feelings.

'Good,' the old woman replied. 'The Sheikh will make you a *sandweech* and we'll go and sit down.' She led me to a couple of low stools on the far side of the yard and we sat down side by side in the dark. 'In a past life,' she began, 'I was married to a very cruel man. I did my best to be a good wife, but nothing I did made any difference to his behaviour. Whenever he lost his temper, he would beat me.' She wrinkled up her nose in distaste at the memory, and I clicked my tongue in sympathy. 'Yes,' she went on, 'this man was very, very nasty. One day Sheikh Wisam,' – she gestured at her husband – 'who was just a boy then, aged about seven, saw my husband beating me. You can ask him if you like, he still remembers it. Anyway, on that day my husband beat me more severely than before.' She swept her hand down the right side of her body. 'He kicked me here, maybe ten or twenty times. My ribs were all broken and I must have had internal injuries, because I passed away.'

The light from the shop barely penetrated into the corner where we sat and I could only just make out the old woman's face.

'I was born again to a family who lived on the far side of the village.' She pointed over my shoulder. 'Down there. When I grew up and was ready to marry, Sheikh Wisam became my husband.' The Sheikh was walking towards us, holding my *sandeech* wrapped in paper. 'He's a much better husband than the evil man I was married to before,' the old woman announced with a smile. 'Aren't you, Sheikh Wisam?' She laughed aloud.

I took the *sandweech* and thanked the Sheikh. 'And what happened to the violent husband? Is he still alive?'

The laughter vanished from the old woman's face. 'He's living in Syria, married to another woman. He has four children. Sometimes he comes to Lebanon and occasionally I see him in the village. I feel very frightened, and I try to hide.'

'What an astonishing story,' I said, looking at her. 'It must be so strange to remember the trauma you went through when you were somebody else...'

'But it's not just the things which happened that I remember,' the old woman replied. 'I remember my *thoughts* from that lifetime. Yes. I can actually remember what I thought.'

Rashid was hovering close to where we sat and I sensed his impatience to leave.

'There's just one more woman whom I want you to meet,' he said as we drove away. 'The mother-in-law of Sana.'

I was tired now, but I felt it was out of the question to refuse. We drove a short distance and climbed another flight of outdoor steps to the entrance to a large house which overlooked the main street. An elderly woman in traditional dress greeted us at the door. She was thin and wrinkled and her face was full of sweetness. She showed us into a large salon with faded sofas and a large grey rug which had seen better days. A couple of younger women joined us, and Shakeeb reappeared from nowhere. He sat on the far side of the room from me, smiling his avuncular smile as he fingered a set of worry beads and listened to the conversation.

The old lady spoke with a strong local accent, so I asked Rashid to translate for me. When he asked about the loss of her two sons, she spoke for a long time in a thin, fragile voice. Rashid re-told the story.

'The fighting was very heavy at the time and she had left the village and was staying in another village with her husband, who had been injured the day before. Her youngest son had been fighting on the front line in Baysour and had gone thirty-four hours without sleep. So when it grew dark the oldest son, who was Sana's husband, went to check on the youngest and to tell him that their father had been injured. He took a group of five friends with him. He found his brother and then the whole group decided to go to the house to collect some things which the family needed.

'They reached the house safely, which was quite something because the front line was right here.' Rashid pointed to the window on the street side of the living room. 'The Lebanese Forces were literally 1,000 metres across the valley from this window, and there was nothing between them and the house. Come, I'll show you.'

He got up and I followed him to the open window. A balcony ran the length of the house, looking over the street. On the far side, I saw a gap of twenty feet between the buildings. In the darkness it was impossible to tell what lay beyond.

'The Lebanese Forces' position was on the far hillside, through that gap. If they fired in a straight line, the first thing they would hit, literally, was this house. So the boys came into the house and started to check that everything was okay. At first they moved around in the dark, not to attract attention. Then one of the boys made a fatal mistake. He switched on a light. Immediately the Lebanese Forces started shelling, and one of the shells landed in the house. The two brothers were killed and their five friends seriously injured. 'And because the old lady was away in the other village, she didn't get to see her sons before they were buried. That was very upsetting for her.'

We sat in silence as I took in what had happened.

After a while, I asked Rashid to ask the old lady how she felt now about the Lebanese Forces.

The old lady replied without hesitating.

'She says that, to be honest, she doesn't like them,' Rashid went on. 'They destroyed her future and killed her children. She cannot love them, even if now their leaders and our leaders are on good terms with one another.' Rashid looked at me. 'I think you should ask her what she feels about the Christians, not the Lebanese Forces,' he murmured.

'You're right,' I said, 'please ask her that.'

I watched the old lady's face as he put the question to her. She was seated close to me and I could see her clearly by the light of the bulb that hung from the ceiling.

Again she responded without a second's hesitation.

'She says that all her life she has lived with Christians and she can still live with them. Not all Christians killed Druze families and destroyed their homes.' He cleared his throat. 'I'm happy to hear her say this,' he added in a low voice.

The old lady was speaking again, in response to a question from Shakeeb. 'She says the house was hit sixteen times in the course of the fighting. They used to have three shops downstairs, and a mini-market full of goods. The basement was hit four times and the shops were burnt out, so they lost all their capital. After the war was over she and her husband had to sell several pieces of land to raise the money to repair the house.'

Shakeeb butted in. 'Some people got a lot of money from the government to re-build their houses, from the Ministry of the Displaced. A lot of Christian families got the equivalent of 20,000 dollars per house.'

'No,' Rashid interrupted, 'more than that. Twenty thousand dollars for each male member of the family. The father and each of the sons received that amount.' He glanced at me, adding, 'This is the way it is done in the East. The money goes to the menfolk.'

The door opened and a younger woman walked in, carrying a tray of pastries. The old lady smiled at me. 'My daughter,' she said. 'She's been baking.'

'Her husband got only 4,000 dollars from the Ministry,' Rashid continued, 'just enough to re-build one room and a small piece of the balcony. She's angry because others got 20,000 dollars, to repair houses a quarter of the size of this one.'

'Why did she get so little?' The pastries were a kind of miniature pancake, folded in half and filled with a fluffy white cream and honey. It was a long time since I had tasted anything quite so delicious.

'Because this village is exclusively Druze. More money was made available in the villages which are mixed Christian and Druze.'

The old lady got to her feet and beckoned me. 'Come with me, some of the damage to our house is still visible, because we can't afford to repair it.'

I swallowed the last mouthful of pancake and followed her through a door into the adjoining room. On the far side, she lifted a large curtain to reveal a missing wall where a rocket had torn into the house. 'You see? This is one of the places where the Lebanese Forces hit us. And look,' she pointed to the far end of the balcony, visible through the gap. There was a crater in the tiled floor and part of the stone balustrade was missing. 'We would need 10,000 dollars to put the house back to how it was before.'

[255]

27

MIRIAM

Beirut, April 2006

'If we Christians had behaved like true Christians, there would not have been a civil war.' Miriam looked at me across the café table. She had just come from school, where she had been teaching classes from eight a.m. to ten, and wore a black wool coat over her black clothes. 'But we didn't behave like Christians.' Her fair hair was scraped back from her face in a bun, as when I had met her the previous week with her cousins, Emile and Georgette. 'We descended from civilisation to the depths of depravity…'

We were sitting in the Café Najjar in Jal al Deeb, at the point where the coastal highway roared out of east Beirut towards Jounieh. Small, circular tables were arranged against the plate-glass windows, and black waist-coated waiters operated cappucino machines behind a large, stainless steel bar.

'Are you a practising Christian?' I asked her.

She nodded. 'As I have grown older, my religion has become very important to me. I go to mass every morning, on my way to work.' She picked up her coffee cup and nursed it in her hands. 'Before the war, religion meant nothing to me, but nowadays it gives me tremendous strength.' She spoke in a calm, unaffected manner and her voice had a deep timbre, which I liked a lot. 'I try to be a true Christian. I hate nobody, and I'm afraid of nobody.'

'And do you genuinely think that if the Lebanese Christians had behaved better, the war could have been avoided?'

Miriam put down her cup and leaned towards me. 'I think of Gandhi. He fought against the biggest world power of his time, England, in order to liberate his country, without taking up arms. I think that all disputes should be conducted like that, in a pacifist manner. In any case we have had proof of this in Lebanon. We got the Syrians to leave peacefully.'

It was true that the Syrians had pulled out their troops without bloodshed, but Syria continued to exert a strong influence in Lebanon.

'When in 1975 they said that the Palestinians were going to take over our country, if we had made a peaceful protest, and said that we didn't want to fight, would we not have succeeded equally well? And wouldn't we be doing better now than we are? I think we'd be in a much better situation.' She paused. 'For me, the Lebanese war, from the beginning, was like a masquerade. There was a decision to go to war, a decision in which we were not involved.'

'Who made this decision?'

'I honestly don't know. I haven't analysed the problem. For example, the house where you visited us last week, that's where the first frontier was, at the beginning of the war, between the Christians and the Palestinians. I used to live there with my parents and I saw that, during the night, there were battles; but during the day nothing happened. We led a normal life. We went to school. We went to the market.

'At that time the Palestinians were much, much better armed than the Christians. They had weapons which the government allowed them to have and they did some stupid things with them, this was undoubtedly why the war broke out. But the interesting thing was that, at the beginning, all the fighting happened at night and during the day there was nothing. So what prevented the Palestinians from coming and taking all the land during the day, for example? For me, it was a decision, a decision to make war from a distance, to put the country into a state of war, without really wanting to take control of the land. It was like a comedy.'

'Was it the Palestinians alone who chose to do it like that, or was it the Christians as well?'

'The Christians didn't have the means to sustain a non-stop war, because the number of their people involved in the fighting was limited. They couldn't make war day and night; whereas the Palestinians could. The Palestinians had many more arms, there were many more of them and they had had the training; none of which was the case with the young Christians at that time. All the young Christians had was a feeling that they must defend their presence as a community in Lebanon. And their attempt to follow that idea without really seeing what was going on, blinded them. They didn't pose the question to themselves in the way that I posed it. They didn't ask themselves why there was no war during the day time, or why when a foreign emissary visited there was no shooting, and everyone waited for him to leave before starting up again. It was a farce! After that, lots of people aligned themselves with one faction or another, for example the Arabs didn't want to help the Christians, so the Christians asked for support from Israel, which was a mistake in my opinion. They asked Israel to supply them with weapons, and they became allies of Israel; whereas before the war, the most ardent enemies of Israel were the Christians.'

'Really?'

'Yes! Before the war, most of the political writing pointing out the dangers that Israel posed to us was written by Lebanese Christians.' She looked at me, to check I had taken this in. 'I can't be categorical, but among those who campaigned against Israel, there were a lot of Christians, of that I'm sure. The point is, it was not in our nature to be allied to Israel, it happened by force of circumstance, because the others had turned against us and we had no support from the outside world. You see, when you push someone into a corner, he will cling onto anybody who's available.'

Miriam stood up, took off her coat and signalled to the waiter to bring fresh coffee and tea.

'I found your aunt's story very upsetting,' I said when she sat down. 'I lay awake most of the night thinking about her.'

Miriam grimaced. 'You see? And so many Lebanese suffered in the same way that she did.'

'What about the Christians?' I asked. 'Did they kidnap their opponents?'

'Everyone is to blame on this issue, the Christians as much as the others.' Miriam's expression was grave.

'What did the Christians do with the people they kidnapped?'

'They killed them.' I heard a tinge of shame in her voice.

'Was there a Christian prison?'

She thought for a moment. 'There was a prison at Dowra. But I don't know if anyone survived in that prison. Most of the people who were kidnapped were executed immediately. These were not kid-nappings with the goal of gaining something in exchange for the release of the prisoner. They were reactive kidnappings: 'you've done that to us, so we'll do the same thing to you'. Really, man became an animal in Lebanon.'

'I find the idea of all the kidnappings quite terrifying.'

'Why?'

'I have too much imagination.'

'Yes, of course. It was atrocious, it was beyond imagination. In those days we spent most of our lives in the shelters... It wasn't easy, it was difficult, very difficult. And also it was absurd. What could be achieved by so much destruction?' She looked at me. 'What happened in Lebanon was abominable.'

If I hadn't been a parent, I might not have found the idea of kidnapping so disturbing. But a parent I was and frequently during the last twelve days, when I'd thought of Dan, I'd had to wrestle with a sense of unease about my being in Lebanon at all. This would be my last visit, I'd decided, despite the fact that I hadn't yet seen all I wanted to see.

I had tried in vain to figure out whether my unease resulted solely from my focus on the dark days of the civil war; or whether I was picking up on Lebanon's present day instability. In reality, there was no real risk that I would be kidnapped as a foreigner going about asking questions in 2006. Nevertheless, I knew that I would feel a sense of relief when I checked in at the airport to fly home in two days' time. And the thought of what had happened to Florence Raad would bother me for many years to come.

I looked at Miriam. 'Do you find it difficult to live with the memory of what happened?'

She thought for a moment. 'We've forgotten it, and for a single reason. This is that we're clear in our minds that it was not the Lebanese Moslems themselves who waged war against us, it was the Palestinians, and the Palestinian fighters have left. In our heart of hearts, our grievance is not against the Lebanese Moslems. Indeed, perhaps the Lebanese Moslems have a greater grievance against the Christians, because, unlike the Moslems, the Christians waged war with their own hands, they didn't use someone else's army. Thus the Moslems' grievance against us is more personal than is ours against them. So you see I go to west Beirut quite happily, without any fear. I know that it was not the Moslems who waged the war and I don't feel anxious. Perhaps *we* inspire more fear in *them*: we Christians who appear so civilised, so educated, but who, once cornered, turned into savages. I understand their fear of us. But I'm not afraid of them.

'Also, it's sixteen years since the war ended. The political situation has moved on. People forget, particularly those who are not nursing personal grievances. *I* know it wasn't the Moslems. Their sin was to remain silent about the Palestinians' behaviour; but it wasn't them who made war against us. Now, if my neighbour had done harm to my son, that is something I might not forget for as long as I lived. But since I know that it wasn't them, it was a foreigner who was staying with them who caused the problem, I can forget it.'

'But when you see walls pockmarked with bullet holes, don't you feel depressed?'

'Yes, sights like that remind me of the war, of course, and I wouldn't wish to re-live that experience for anything in the world. My generation suffered greatly as a result of the war, we lost out on our entire youth. We spent fifteen years from the ages of twenty to thirty-five, the so-called "best years" of our lives, in underground shelters. I wouldn't wish that on anyone.' She sighed. 'But you know, despite the fact that the Palestinians caused a lot of harm in Lebanon, I can't deny that their cause is a just one and that they're given a rough ride by the Israelis. I can't avoid coming to that conclusion.'

'Do you think they're well treated by the Lebanese?'

'The way they're treated now is a function of a joint decision made by the Palestinians and the Lebanese. The Palestinians didn't want to live outside the camps. Because if they'd moved out of the camps and become settled in Lebanon, they would no longer have had a cause. They would have become dispersed. There are a lot of Palestinians who have integrated into Lebanese life and who have had Lebanese nationality since 1948. Those people will never go back to Palestine, for they're well off here. The same thing happens to Lebanese who leave Lebanon and go to live in the United States, they do well and they don't look back. When people are well off economically, they lose interest in what was once their cause. So you see it was a joint Palestinian-Lebanese decision to keep the Palestinians in the camps and not to give them all their rights. They don't have passports, they can't travel, they can't buy a house... this is the price they pay for keeping their cause alive.'

'Who amongst the Palestinians made this decision? Was it the PLO?'

Miriam shook her head. 'The Palestinian people made it. Now where we Lebanese have let them down, is by not helping them as fellow human beings. For example, not helping them when they're ill; not improving the living conditions inside the camps, not providing sewers… We've fallen down in that respect.'

I told Miriam about my visit to Bourj al Barajneh and how Kholood had complained bitterly about the way the Palestinians were treated by the Lebanese and how she had railed against the legal restrictions on Palestinians.

'That is all true, but it's their choice. And as far as living conditions in the camps are concerned, the Lebanese should only shoulder part of the responsibility. The Palestinians' leaders received a lot of material aid, which should have been used to provide better living conditions, but it was not put to good use. Some of the money was embezzled by the leaders. They got money from all the Arab countries, whereas the Lebanese at that time, during the war, only received the remittances that their children living abroad were able to send them. The Palestinians also got money from UNRWA. What has happened to all that money? The Palestinian leaders themselves hold some responsibility for the failure to improve living conditions in the camps.'

'Do you feel they shouldn't complain, having made the decision to remain in the camps?'

'No, they shouldn't complain. In my opinion, they shouldn't.' She paused, gazing at me. 'But if I see someone in need of help, I should help them. If I don't do it, that is my responsibility. We should also remember that the Palestinians fled their country as a result of an international decision. That is a fact, and one which I cannot deny. They have done me harm, but I cannot deny that they have a legitimate grievance.'

'Do you think your attitude to the Palestinians is different from that of the majority of Christians?'

'Families who were obliged to flee – like some members of my family were – and who had to leave everything behind, house, money, everything, so that if they had not had children living abroad, they would have become beggars; people like that, who received no assistance at all, do not have the same attitude as me. They still hold a grievance against the Palestinians who forced them to flee. Some of these people go to extremes. Some say "Who cares about the Palestinians? They behaved badly, so let Israel do what she wants to them." That sentiment exists. And people like me exist. You have a whole range of opinion, between these two extremes. It all depends on how a person was affected by the war personally. It also depends on how deeply you think about religion. If I want to be a true Christian, I can't say "Who cares about the Palestinians?"'

I drained the teapot into my cup. 'The Palestinian woman I met spoke with bitterness about the Lebanese in general. She said they harbour racism towards the Palestinians. She told me that she lived in Raouche for five years during the war and that she was treated very badly by Lebanese Moslems there. I felt she had a real hatred towards the Lebanese.'

'I don't know. I never had the impression that the Lebanese Moslems had ever maltreated the Palestinians. Now, if this woman came into contact with a person who got hurt by the Palestinians, sure she would sense hatred. But it's a limited, personal hatred. It wouldn't be a generalised hatred. I come back to my main point, which is that the Lebanese Moslems were not really Lebanese before the war. They always had alliances with external powers. If they had been truly Lebanese, they would have helped the Christians to bring the Palestinians to heel. But they didn't do that.'

I thought of Hanan's grandfather's friend Mohammed and how he had complained of the behaviour of the Palestinians in Dikweni prior to the war. I told Miriam what he had said.

'Yes, well it's true, they did behave like that. So I ask myself why the Moslems remained silent. Why did they prevent the army from doing its job? Because if at that time the Lebanese army had brought the Palestinians to heel – not killed them and evacuated them, but told them "look, this is your limit, do not over-step it; you are not going to use your weapons against the Lebanese, you have no right to commit offences against the Lebanese," then things might have turned out very differently. The Palestinians behaved appallingly towards the Lebanese: they arrested them, they took them hostage, they extorted money from them, they took their houses, and the Moslems remained silent. If the army had been told firmly to put a stop to it, the Christian militias would not have had to become embroiled in fighting the Palestinians. It should have been the job of the army to keep the peace throughout the country, and then we would not have had all this problem. So why did the Moslems remain silent, if they felt the Palestinians had behaved so badly towards them, too?'

[263]

'Perhaps the Sunnis' resentment towards the Palestinians has come with hindsight.' But I was not convinced by my own words. A more plausible explanation, I suspected, lay in the entrenched Arab ethos of hospitality towards visitors – especially members of one's own tribe – which would have made it very difficult for the Sunnis openly to criticise the Palestinians, or voice opposition to their presence in Lebanon.

'You know,' Miriam went on, 'at the beginning of the war, the young Christians resisted that accepting attitude towards the Palestinians. Theirs was a true resistance, like Hizbullah's resistance against the Israelis; in my opinion it was the same thing. Later it degenerated into politics, but at the beginning, it was a resistance to the Palestinian invasion.'

I was glad Miriam had mentioned Hizbullah. I asked her what she thought of them.

She hesitated for a moment. 'In some ways, I like them. Among Lebanese political parties, they're probably the least corrupt. But having said that, I don't altogether trust them.'

'In what ways?'

'For example, they claim not to want to establish an Islamic state in Lebanon, but it's not true. In reality, an Islamic state is what they want. Then again, I have heard them say that they would be happy for Christians to join them in the resistance against Israel; and that's not true either. Why would they call it the *Islamic* resistance, if they wanted Christians to join them? I don't know. In some ways I respect them, but I don't believe that they put Lebanon first.' She paused. 'The same was true of the Sunnis, of course, until the death of al Hariri. Before his death, the Sunnis saw themselves as Sunnis first, Lebanese second. And in those days they supported Syria: it's only since al Hariri was killed that they withdrew their support for Syria.'

When the waiter passed again, Miriam signalled to him to bring the bill. As we waited, I asked her what she did in her spare time.

'I read.'

'What sort of thing?'

'Whatever I can get hold of. Novels, books, newspapers, anything that comes my way. During the war, the thing that enabled me to concentrate and stopped me losing my mind, was crosswords. Doing crosswords even took my mind off the noise of the bombs, I concentrated so hard. And I played with the children. We would concentrate on the game and forget what was happening outside.' She smiled.

'How old are your children now?'

'The oldest boy is 25, the girl is 21 and my youngest boy is 15.'

'What do they do?'

'The oldest one works in business computers, the girl is doing a Masters in nutrition and the youngest is still at school. And yours? How old are they?'

'I've just got one, a little boy of six.' I was counting the hours till Sunday, when I would get to hold him in my arms again.

'Oh, he's very small. It's hard to leave them when they are that small…'

I winced. 'I've hated being away from him. But I didn't feel I could bring him with me.'

'It would have been difficult for you to do your research if you'd brought him. Is he with his father?'

'He's with his father and they're on holiday at the seaside.' The text I had received that morning said that they had spent the whole of the previous day on the beach.

28

HOMEWARD JOURNEY

April 2006

At one thirty a.m., barely awake, I wheeled my bag to the door of the apartment and turned to embrace Hiba. She stood in her dressing gown, smiling with sleepy eyes, sisterly and kind to the last. When the buzzer sounded she pushed me through the door.

'She's just coming,' she whispered through the entry phone to the taxi driver who was waiting in the street below. 'A tall foreign woman in a brown coat, you'll see her coming out of the building in a minute.'

I dragged my bag across the lobby into the lift, turned and blew Hiba a last kiss. I had no idea when I would see her again, and that made me sad. Her boys were coming to England for a holiday in July, but she was not planning to accompany them.

At the foot of the building, a white Mercedes stood waiting in the street, its boot open. The driver greeted me politely, stowed my bag and helped me into the passenger seat. As we swung onto the coastal highway, I studied his profile, thinking he looked incongruously smart for the late hour. He wore black trousers and a black lambswool jersey over a shirt with a stiff collar, and he was clean-shaven save for a neatly-trimmed moustache.

'From which country you are?' he asked me in English. When I told him, he smiled with an air of satisfaction, announcing that he was an admirer of everything British.

'Have you been to Britain?' I asked wearily. I had slept for only three hours and, although I was looking forward to going home, the prospect of sitting upright in planes and airport seats for the next nine hours was unappealing. I had to change planes in Milan.

The driver sucked his teeth. A moment later he declared, 'Britain very strong. *Great* Britain. No one messes with British passport, eh?'

'True.' I wondered where the conversation was heading.

'Married to a Lebanese?'

'No. My husband's English.' I thought of Paul with gratitude. Late at night in situations like this it was always wise to claim the existence of a husband, even if he were an ex.

The driver fell silent for a few moments. Then, as we left the highway and turned into the airport, he spoke again.

'Blair goo-od, mm?'

I didn't hesitate. 'I don't like Blair.'

But the driver remained undaunted. 'Blair good, Bush good. The Moslems don't like them, but *we* do.' He turned to me with a self-satisfied smile, implying that he and I belonged to the same tribe, even if I were loath to admit it. 'I'm a Maronite,' he added.

By the time my plane took off at five past four, my thoughts were focussed exclusively on the hazards I was about to face. With motherhood I had acquired a fear of flying which had never troubled me in my childless days, so that although I had now left Lebanon safely, my chances of making it to London seemed shockingly low.

I glanced at the man sitting next to me, wondering if my fear were very obvious, but he was absorbed in an Arabic-language newspaper.

In my mind I held Dan and Paul at a distance. To think of them would be pointless, given the uncertainty that I would ever walk on solid ground again. They were travelling back from Cornwall later this morning, and were due to reach home a couple of hours before me. But this was highly abstract, for my survival was in the balance. I shut my eyes, pressed my folded arms against my rib cage and focussed on the terrible roaring of the propellers. To try to shut out the sound would only make the fear more intense. I let the roaring fill me as the plane taxied along the runway and rose into the air. Opening my eyes briefly I saw the lights of Beirut in sharp white points below, but in a matter of seconds the plane veered to the west and out over the sea. I pressed my eyelids back together, sickened by the thought of all the water that lay below.

Five minutes later, when the cabin lights came back on and the roaring dropped to a soft hum, I noted with astonishment that the plane had made it safely into the sky. As my fear subsided, I felt an unexpected pang for the country I was leaving behind.

It was a fascinating place, however uneasy it had made me on this last visit, and however ugly and polluted the urban jungle that was Beirut. I would miss Lebanon, and all the people I had met there. And it would always bug me that I hadn't managed to explore the rural south.

I pulled out my journal and for the next hour sat writing, keen to record every last detail of the previous few days. Eventually I put the journal away, tilted back my seat and dozed off to sleep.

When I woke, a soft light filled the cabin. Leaning across my sleeping neighbour, I saw a pale blue sky streaked with pink and, down below, green fields and rivers. My eyes smarted at the corners. This was Italy, and the plane was starting to descend.

In the café at Malpensa airport I watched my fellow travellers – some Italian, some British – drinking coffee, eating pastrami baguettes and arguing with each other, with a sense of gratitude and affection. God, I muttered to myself, I'm back in Europe. These are my people, *my* people. No longer was I too tall, too pale skinned, too red-headed to belong.

By the time I boarded the flight to London my mood was upbeat. If I had made it this far, perhaps I would make it all the way home. And now that Lebanon was receding behind me, I began to re-assess my decision not to visit again. It would be a shame, having made so many contacts, not to go back. I wouldn't go alone again; perhaps, if the situation remained reasonably stable, I could take Dan with me? He would have a lot of fun with Hiba's children. And maybe I could leave him with Hiba for a day and go to explore the south?

This time, when the plane took off, I focussed my thoughts exclusively on Dan. My eyes kept filling with tears as I imagined how it would be when I got off the airport bus in our home town. I would abandon my bags and scoop him up in my arms, that was for sure. I would squeeze him and hold him for as long as he would let me.

✧

In the queue for the carousel at Heathrow I took out my phone and dialled Paul's number. It was eleven thirty a.m., and he and Dan would be somewhere on the road.

'Hello?' said a small, familiar voice.

'Hello darling,' I replied, 'It's mummy.'

'Hello, mummy.' Dan sounded just a teensy bit pleased to hear my voice. I turned round and beamed at all the strangers in the queue behind me.

'Whereabouts are you, lovely?'

'I don't know, mummy, shall I ask daddy?'

I heard Paul's voice.

'Daddy says we've just passed Exeter, and we'll be home in about an hour. Do you know, mummy, I found a fossil on the beach at Housel Bay?'

29

THE JULY WAR

In July 2006, Hizbullah captured two Israeli soldiers in a major cross border raid and shot dead a further five. That night, the Israeli air force destroyed three runways at Beirut airport while Israeli warships established a blockade of Lebanese sea ports. Bombs were dropped on villages, army bases and bridges, severing the main road from Beirut to Damascus and killing fifty Lebanese.

I was at home in the UK, listening to the radio. An Israeli general had announced his intention to 'bomb Lebanon back twenty years' if the two captured soldiers were not released. Meanwhile, Hizbullah had fired rockets into Israel, killing a woman.

Within a few days, several hundred Lebanese had been killed and the country's infrastructure had been severely damaged. Israeli planes were dropping leaflets on Dahyya, warning residents to leave and hinting that Nasrallah (who lived there) might be a target for an attack.

In a TV interview, Nasrallah seemed genuinely shocked by the ferocity of the Israeli assault on his country. If he had known the Israelis would respond in this way, he said, he would not have ordered the capture of the soldiers.

The following day I saw on the TV news in graphic detail what the Israelis were doing to Dahyya. The camera panned what remained of a group of apartment buildings close to the offices where I had met Hussein Nabulsi. The apartment buildings were reduced to a mountain of rubble, at the back of which buckled steel girders barely held up the frames of eight-storey blocks which had lost their walls and balconies.

Over the next days and weeks, Israel flattened entire villages in south Lebanon, destroyed dozens of apartment blocks in Dahyya and bombed the Bekaa valley, sending some 900,000 mainly Shi'a civilians into flight – a full quarter of the Lebanese population. Some families were killed on the roads, when the Israelis bombed civilian vehicles. In at least one incident, a convoy of clearly marked ambulances carrying wounded people was hit.

The Israelis claimed that they were obliged to bomb civilian areas because Hizbullah were deliberately firing their rockets from populated positions, but Hizbullah denied this. Whatever the truth, Israel could not explain why, after warning Lebanese civilians to vacate the border areas in the south, it had then bombed the roads on which they were fleeing. Some observers suggested that the Israeli Air Force were deliberately targeting civilians. It was an obvious strategy for Israel to adopt: create maximum suffering among Lebanon's Shi'a, in the hope of turning them against Nasrallah and Hizbullah.

Most of the civilians who died were Shi'a, but the bombing of roads, bridges and factories affected Sunni, Druze and Christian areas as well as Shi'a ones.

I found it ironic, that, as the days went by, media reports suggested not only that Israel's strategy wasn't working, but that Lebanese with no natural allegiance to Hizbullah were beginning to support them. I read anecdotes about Lebanese Christians saying that, whereas they had used to hate Hizbullah, they now felt impressed by the courage and skill the party was showing in defending the country. I found myself wondering what Miriam thought about it all.

To many observers, as well as to ordinary Arabs, the Israeli campaign appeared to be one of vengeance, aimed at making the whole population suffer for the government's failure to disarm Hizbullah in accordance with Resolution 1559.

A high proportion of the casualties were children. Every day, the newspapers carried a fresh picture of a small body lying unnaturally still in the arms of a distraught rescuer, the smooth, statue-like face coated in a layer of grey dust. These photographs made my stomach churn with shame and shock. I imagined being in Lebanon now. What could be said to comfort the mother or father of such a child?

I wanted to know what Hizbullah had hoped to achieve in their cross border raid on July 12 and I managed to establish the following. Since the unilateral Israeli withdrawal from south Lebanon in May 2000, although confrontations between the Israelis and Hizbullah had continued, their frequency and intensity had reduced dramatically. In January 2004, Hizbullah had succeeded in negotiating a prisoner exchange with Israel, in which 423 Lebanese and Palestinian live prisoners were returned to Lebanon, together with the remains of nearly 60 dead fighters, in exchange for the release of one live Israeli hostage and the bodies of three soldiers. The deal had enhanced Hizbullah's prestige in Lebanon and convinced the organisation's leaders that the best way to obtain the release of the few remaining Lebanese and Palestinian prisoners held in Israel would be to exchange them for new Israeli hostages. The cross-border raid on 12 July had been launched for this purpose.

It had probably been deliberately timed to coincide with a massive Israeli incursion into the Gaza Strip, which had begun on 28 June, in response to the capture of an Israeli soldier there by Palestinian militants. Hizbullah was claiming that it could bring about the release of this soldier, as well as that of the two it had seized in northern Israel, in exchange for the Arab prisoners it wanted.

Notwithstanding the above, some commentators claimed that Israel had been planning a military campaign against Hizbullah for many months, with the approval of the USA, and had seized on the capture of the two soldiers as a convenient pretext. It was not difficult to see that, to the Bush administration, such a campaign would appeal as an indirect way of confronting Iran.

Whatever Hizbullah's leaders had been expecting by way of response to their July 12 operation, its fighters put up a vigorous fight against Israel. On most of the thirty-three days that the conflict lasted, Hizbullah fired at least 150 rockets across the southern border, hitting civilian as well as military targets and even killing civilians in Arab-Israeli villages. On one occasion, eight civilians were killed in Haifa. I found it distressing and disappointing that Hizbullah felt it necessary to target Israeli civilians, and when I met a Jewish woman on an anti-war vigil in the city where I lived, I shared her anxiety for her grandchildren who were in Israel on holiday. But it was clear from the start that the number of casualties inflicted by Hizbullah was small compared to the number inflicted by Israel. Besides, Jewish Israelis had access to well-equipped underground bomb shelters, whereas the Lebanese Shi'a had little to protect them. By the war's end on August

14, only forty-three Israeli civilians had been killed, compared to 1,109 Lebanese.

For me, one of the most shocking aspects of the war was the snail-like response of the international community. I would not have expected an appropriate response from the Bush-led US administration, whose failure to urge restraint on Israel was facilitated by the condemnations of Hizbullah's action issued by a number of Arab governments. But the hands-off attitude adopted by the British government filled me with shame.

By now the EU had sent envoys to the region, criticising Hizbullah as irresponsible but declaring that the sea and air blockade were unjustified and deploring Israel's disproportionate use of force and the resulting loss of civilian life. By contrast, Tony Blair and foreign secretary Margaret Beckett flatly refused to call for a ceasefire or to condemn the Israeli action. Instead, Downing Street adopted the US position of giving Israel time to reduce Hizbullah's military capacity, as if it accepted Israel's attempts to portray Hizbullah as a terrorist group on a par with al-Qaida.

I followed this in anger, for I found the ignorance, hypocrisy and inhumanity of the Blair government appalling. They seemed unable to appreciate that Hizbullah were a legitimate Lebanese political party with at least one well-founded present grievance against Israel (the continuing Israeli occupation of the Shebaa farms) and a host of well-founded historical grievances (relating to Israel's twenty-two year occupation of south Lebanon). To me, Hizbullah's support for the Palestinian Islamicist organisation Hamas was a legitimate political stance within the context of the Arab-Israeli conflict and should not be used as an excuse to destroy them, however uncomfortable it was for Israel and the West.

I was also baffled by the sheer stupidity of the government's position; for what could anger young British Moslems more than the spectacle of their government sitting idly by while Israel smashed the lives and homes of Lebanese Moslems, using military equipment some of which had been manufactured in the UK and sold to Israel under government license? As I watched each bulletin, I found myself wondering how many young British men were at that moment sitting in their living rooms in cities around the country, making the decision to volunteer for jihad.

With every day that the Americans and British 'looked the other way', more atrocities were committed by Israel.

On Sunday 30 July, amid rising international concern about the numbers of Lebanese children losing their lives in the conflict, Israel perpetrated a massacre of civilians at Qana. Qana was the ancient village in south Lebanon where, in 1996, the Israelis had killed 106 civilians sheltering in the UN base from its 'Grapes of Wrath' campaign.

This time Israeli bombers struck a house in which two extended families, the Shalhoubs and the Hashems, had taken refuge. Journalists later reported that these families had been unable to afford the extortionate taxi fares required to get them to relative safety in Tyre and had hoped that the walls of the house would protect them. Members of the two families were crouched together on the ground floor when two bombs hit the house just after one a.m. By the end of the day, the Lebanese authorities reported that more than sixty bodies had been pulled from the rubble, thirty-four of which were the bodies of children.

A few days later came the assault on Bint al Jbeil, the border village which the Israelis had been trying to capture since the beginning of the war. By now all the able-bodied inhabitants had left, leaving only a handful of elderly who were too weak or sick to flee. When the place had been levelled to the ground, the journalists filmed an old woman who had crawled out of a basement, begging for water. She was so weak that she could not stand.

Of all the stories I read in the press in the course of the war, one lodged in my mind as epitomising Lebanon's pain. This was the story of a man from a village outside Tyre. Up until July 12 the man had run a shop selling chocolates, opposite the house where he lived with his wife and two small daughters. On July 17, a few minutes after he stepped out of the house, a bomb landed on it, crushing his loved ones in a chaos of fragmented concrete.

Homeless and bereaved, the man had taken refuge in a nearby hospital, where he spent his days in a state of dislocated grief, watching the dead and wounded being carried in through the gates. The doctors understood his anguish and allowed him to camp out in the cardiology ward where he played solitaire on the hospital computer. When the bulldozers came to pull the bodies of the wife and little daughters out of the rubble, the chocolate seller stayed away. And when his parents asked him to join them in Beirut, he refused.

It was the massacre at Qana that finally prompted Arab governments to condemn Israel. Most had now been convinced by demonstrations in their own capitals that to continue to look the other way might lead to domestic unrest, for there was huge popular support for Hizbullah. This in turn pushed the US to seek a UN formula for bringing the war to an end.

Resolution 1701, passed by the Security Council on 11 August, provided for the enhancement of UNIFIL, the existing UN force in south Lebanon, by the addition to its numbers of troops from various European countries up to a maximum strength of 15,000. Resolution 1702 provided, in addition, for the deployment of up to 15,000 troops of the Lebanese army to the area south of the Litani river. It was under these two resolutions that a ceasefire was finally declared on August 14.

From Israel's point of view, their campaign had failed abjectly to destroy Hizbullah. Although the organisation had suffered the loss of approximately 200 fighters, its prestige among Shi'a Moslems emerged as greater, if anything, than before the war; and its popularity across the Arab world was now inestimable. Compounding Israel's failure was the fact that the prospects for Hizbullah being disarmed by the Lebanese government seemed more remote after the war than they had before. In the course of the ceasefire negotiations, Hizbullah had agreed that its fighters could be stopped if seen carrying arms in the area of UNIFIL's deployment, between the Israeli border and the Litani river; but UNIFIL was expressly prohibited from taking any action to disarm the organisation without the prior agreement of the Lebanese government. As for the Lebanese army, half of whose rank and file were Shi'a, it soon made clear that it saw its new role in the south as one of working in co-operation with Hizbullah.

EPILOGUE – JULY 2010

The sense of unity which brought the Lebanese together during the July war was short-lived. From the ceasefire in August 2006 until the autumn of 2009, Lebanon was riven by an ever more vigorous power struggle between the 'people of May 14', lead by Saad Hariri, and the 'people of March 8', led by Hizbullah. This came to a head in May 2008, when the nation teetered on the brink of renewed civil war. But in the wake of the June 2009 elections, in which Hizbullah failed to achieve a widely predicted victory, hope was expressed for a new era of national reconciliation. Relations between Lebanon and Syria were beginning to thaw, and by the summer of 2010 a new stability graced Lebanon.

By the early autumn of 2006, Hizbullah was not only claiming victory against the Israelis in parades through Beirut, but also trying to use its new-found prestige to bring down the western-leaning government of Fouad Siniora. After investing an impressive amount of money and expertise in works of reconstruction and help for those dispossessed by the summer's war, Hizbullah withdrew its two ministers from the government, claiming that the current parliament had been elected under unjust laws devised by the Syrians. It argued that new elections should be held after a process of electoral reform.

While there was some accuracy in Hizbullah's criticism of the electoral laws, the underlying bone of contention between Hizbullah and its allies, on the one hand, and the government, on the other, was the continuing UN investigation into the assassination of Rafiq Hariri. Siniora's government supported the setting up of a tribunal, with UN support, to try the suspects; whereas Hizbullah, as close allies of Syria, were determined to frustrate the process. By withdrawing the two ministers and thereby making the government inquorate, it succeeded in creating an impasse.

Since 2005, there had been a series of assassinations of anti-Syrian public figures in Lebanon, presumed by many to be the work of Syrian agents. In late November 2006, following the assassination of Pierre Gemmayel (grandson of the former leader of the Lebanese Phalange party and a minister in the government), Hizbullah supporters established a sit-in outside the parliament building in downtown Beirut, demanding the resignation of the government. This was followed in January 2007 by a strike, in the course of which Hizbullah supporters and their opponents threw stones at each other and four people died.

There were further confrontations on the second anniversary of Hariri's death, on 15 February, in the course of which Shi'a and Sunnis turned against each other on the streets.

As I followed the news and read emails from Hiba, I was reminded again and again of the sense of forboding expressed to me by Salma and Sana. At the time I hadn't fully understood what they were saying, but now it was clear that their political instincts had been sharp ones.

In May 2007, as pressure mounted for the Lebanese government to agree to the setting up of the tribunal to try Hariri's alleged assassins, a new dispute erupted between the Lebanese army and a group calling themselves Fatah al-Islam. The latter claimed to be inspired by the ideas of al-Qaida and had secretly established themselves in the Palestinian refugee camp of Nahr al Bared, near Tripoli, where they now sought to use Palestinian civilians as human shields. Under cover of the security vacuum in the camps, and quite probably with the connivance of the Syrians, they had acquired sophisticated weapons and built up a fighting force of several hundred.

Lebanese troops surrounded the camp but were initially unable to subdue the fighters, despite clashes which constituted the most serious internal violence since the end of the civil war. Siniora sought help from the US government, which hastened to airlift in military hardware, against a backdrop of warnings from Hizbullah that Lebanon should not allow itself to be drawn into the US 'War on Terror'.

The conflict lasted throughout the summer. When it ended, on 2 September 2007, 460 were dead. These included sixty-four civilians, mostly Palestinian refugees; 170 Lebanese soldiers and 226 members of Fatah al-Islam.

Another serious crisis came in November 2007, when there was failure to reach agreement as to who should become president when the term of the incumbent, Emile Lahoud, came to an end. The two main political blocs were by now so polarised that any candidate put forward by either of them was unacceptable to the other. The only candidate perceived as independent, yet trusted by both blocs, was Michel Suleiman, then commander of the Lebanese Army. He could not however be elected until two fundamental disagreements between the two blocs had been resolved. The first was whether there was a need for a government of national unity and the second was the content of new electoral laws for the parliamentary elections due in 2009. (A commission set up by Siniora had made recommendations for reform of the electoral laws in May 2006, but the July war had derailed debate about its proposals.)

While these issues remained unresolved, parliament entered a period of paralysis which lasted for eighteen months and led to acute unease throughout the country. Matters came to a head in early May 2008, when Fouad Siniora's government made two decisions which outraged Hizbullah. The first was to 're-assign' the chief of security of Beirut airport, a Hizbullah supporter, on the basis of an allegation that Hizbullah spy cameras had been set up to overlook the main runway; the second was to close down Hizbullah's independent telephone network. Nasrallah called the second move tantamount to a 'declaration of war'. In response, he sent Hizbullah's and Amal's militiamen into West Beirut, where they attacked Sunni newspaper offices, television and radio stations and the office of Saad Hariri. Soon the whole of West Beirut was under the control of the militiamen, in the worst internal violence in Beirut since the civil war. By 9 May, eleven were dead and scores were injured; Beirut's port was forced to close and the airport virtually ceased to function.

On 11 May, Hizbullah pounded the hills of south east Beirut until Walid Jumblatt made clear that the Druze were not prepared to fight.

Prior to May 2008, Nasrallah had always maintained that Hizbullah would never turn its guns on its fellow Lebanese – as Hussein Nabulsi had been at pains to tell me. The new, gloves-off approach created waves of fear and shock, particularly among Sunni Moslems and Druze, who bore the brunt of the violence. (Aoun was careful to remain aloof from the fighting, and the impact on Lebanon's Christians was less.)

A major concern was that, if asked to confront the militiamen, the Lebanese army might fragment into its sectarian components. In any event, the army was known to be a much less effective fighting force than

Hizbullah's militia. Before the unthinkable could happen, the government, effectively brought to its knees by Hizbullah, opted to rescind the two decisions which had triggered the violence. Hizbullah then withdrew. Shortly thereafter, from 17–20 May 2008, negotiations were held in Doha, Qatar, attended by senior representatives of all the major political parties. Agreement was reached that Michel Suleiman would be the preferred candidate for the presidential election, and on 25 May, back in Lebanon, the Lebanese parliament elected him in its first session for 18 months. An additional, and crucial, agreement reached in Doha, was that the Hizbullah-led opposition would have a right of veto over all cabinet decisions. This in effect meant that although the March 14 bloc officially ran the government, they could not put into effect decisions which were disliked by their rivals.

Once elected, Suleiman put forward a list of priorities which included national reconciliation; the protection of Lebanon's independence; creating conditions for economic and social growth; fighting terrorism and opposition to permanent settlement for Palestinian refugees.

Meanwhile, after a productive period in 2006, the UN-backed investigation into the murder of Rafiq Hariri had lost momentum. During the period from 2007 to 2009, in the climate of fear created by the series of assassinations of anti-Syrian political figures and journalists, the UN's International Independent Investigation Commission (IIIC) found it increasingly difficult to gather testimony. Witnesses suffered sudden bouts of amnesia, or went to ground altogether. Despite this, in June 2007, the scope of the IIIC's work was widened, in response to a request by the Lebanese government, to include investigations into other assassinations and terrorist attacks committed in Lebanon since October 2004.

On 1 March 2009, the UN Special Tribunal for Lebanon (STL) opened in The Hague, pursuant to an agreement previously entered into by the Lebanese government to defer jurisdiction over the Hariri case to it, on the basis that the STL apply Lebanese substantive law rather than international law. One of the first acts of the STL was the release, on 29 April 2009, of four pro-Syrian Lebanese generals who had been detained by the investigating team since 2005–6. The tribunal said that it was releasing the men due to an insufficiency of evidence to convict them. It is believed that a key witness had retracted their evidence prior to the release of the four.

The four generals were the only people to have been held in custody in relation to the Hariri investigation.

In May 2010 the head of the STL announced that he hoped to be in a position to file charges by the end of the year, but this remains to be seen.

In September 2008, parliament had reached agreement on a new electoral law for the 2009 parliamentary elections. This amounted only to a partial reform of the existing law, and preserved in tact the existing system of confessionalism. In the run up to the elections, in the spring of 2009, it was thought that the March 8 bloc had a good chance of winning an overall majority. But in the event, after an exceptionally high turnout by the electorate, and polls which were declared by international observers to be free and fair, the March 14 bloc headed by Saad Hariri achieved seventy-one seats, as against fifty-seven for the March 8 bloc. Hizbullah immediately accepted the results.

At the end of June 2009, Saad Hariri was named as the new prime minister by Suleiman, with the backing of 87 of the country's 128 parliamentary deputies. He announced his intention to form a government of national unity, which would very likely include members of Hizbullah.

It took Saad Hariri more than four months of difficult negotiations to establish agreement about who would take which cabinet posts in the new government. In the uncertainty of that period, many Lebanese feared renewed instability. But internationally, the arrival of Barack Obama in the White House in January 2009 heralded a period of optimism. Mindful of its strategic aims of withdrawing from Iraq and containing Iran, the new US administration soon sought improved relations with Syria. This in turn lead to a thaw between Syria and the US-allied Saudi Arabia, which had cut diplomatic ties with Syria after the murder of Hariri, the king's protégé and friend. It was in this context that Saad Hariri and Walid Jumblatt, both of whom had publicly blamed Syria for the murder of Hariri, and both of whom had strong personal reasons to loathe the Assad dynasty, decided to swallow their pride and seek a measure of reconciliation with Syria. Jumblatt held a meeting with Nasrallah, signalling that the people of March 8 and March 14 were now willing to cooperate; and Saad Hariri visited Damascus. As a symbol of the new relationship, the two countries exchanged ambassadors for the first time ever.

[281]

Following his visit to Damascus, in November 2009, Saad succeeded in forming a government of national unity with his pro-Syrian rivals. According to the agreement reached, fifteen ministers were appointed by the March 14 bloc, with Hizbullah appointing two and another eight going to Shi'a Amal and Aoun's bloc. The remaining five ministers were to be appointed by President Suleiman. In effect, these five hold the balance of power and enable the March 14 bloc to gain a simple majority.

In the months which have elapsed, Saad Hariri has been relatively moderate in his change of tone towards Syria, but Walid Jumblatt has gone much further. After delivering what amounted to an apology to Syria, on the symbolic date of March 14, 2010, Jumblatt made a speech offering to 'forgive and forget'. He has since withdrawn from the March 14 bloc.

Thus far, the political and economic reward for the public stance of 'forgiving and forgetting' has been generous. In 2009, Lebanon experienced its biggest tourist season ever. Money has flowed into the country, leading to a fresh boom in construction. Tensions remain along the UNIFIL-monitored border with Israel, and between Lebanese villagers and UNIFIL, but to date matters have not escalated out of control.

Some fear that Lebanon's new stability could easily be de-railed by the indicting of Syrian or pro-Syrian individuals by the Special Tribunal at the end of this year. While that is a real possibility, it is also possible that the STL will succumb to political pressure to duck the issue, finding an inconclusive or uncontroversial way to close the case.

It goes without saying that the accommodation between Lebanon and Syria reached in the last year is a story of *realpolitik*, not to be read as representing a real change of heart on the part of the people of March 14. For those Lebanese who have suffered at the hands of the Syrians over the last thirty-five years will never be able, in their hearts, to forgive and forget; particularly those who still suffer the pain of not knowing the fate of their disappeared loved ones.

TT
July 2010

CHRONOLOGY

1841	Conflict between Druze and Christians in Mount Lebanon.
1860	Druze massacre Christians in Mount Lebanon; 11,000 dead.
1861	Mount Lebanon becomes a *mutasarifiyya* or special governorate within the Ottoman Empire, under a Christian governor elected by the European powers.
1861–1915	The 'long peace' in Mount Lebanon.
1914–1918	First World War.
1920	San Remo conference of war victors gives northern parts of Greater Syria to the French; Iraq, Transjordan and Palestine to the British.
1920	'Grand Liban' created by the French by annexing to Mount Lebanon the cities of Beirut, Tripoli, Tyre and Sidon, their hinterlands and the Bekaa valley.
1926	Grand Liban becomes the Lebanese Republic.
1939–1945	Second World War.
1943	The unwritten National Pact enshrines the confessional political system whereby the president is a Maronite, the prime minister a Sunni and the speaker a Shi'a. Parliamentary representation is to be in a fixed ratio of 6 Christians to every 5 Moslems, with the same ration applied to the distribution of civil service posts. Lebanon becomes independent from France.
1948	Creation of the state of Israel; first Arab-Israeli war. 150,000 Palestinian refugees arrive in Lebanon.

1958   Brief civil war, quickly suppressed.

1964   Foundation of the Palestinian Liberation Organisation (PLO).

1967   The Six Days' War (Arab-Israeli) in which the West Bank, Gaza and Golan are occupied by Israel. Arabs left with major sense of defeat and humiliation.

1973   The October War (Arab-Israeli).

1975   Outbreak of Lebanese civil war; Green line divides Beirut.

1976   Syria sends troops into Lebanon; country split into Syrian and Israeli zones of influence.

1978   Israel invades south Lebanon up to Litani river; UN force 'UNIFIL' sent in to keep peace; Israel sets up proxy militia in occupation zone north of its border with Lebanon.

            Camp David Accords under which Egypt makes peace with Israel unilaterally; Sadat visits Jerusalem.

1982   Israel invades Lebanon and besieges West Beirut; after a 3-month siege of the city, the PLO fighters are evacuated under American safe conduct; Sabra and Shatila massacres follow.

            Bashir Gemmayel elected president but assassinated after 18 days; Amin Gemmayel replaces him.

1985   Israel withdraws, leaving SLA to operate in 'security zone'.

1983–1988   Increased activity by Shi'i and fundamentalist groups; kidnapping of western hostages.

1988   General Aoun 'appointed' Prime Minister.

1989   Ta'if Agreement ratified by National Assembly, modifying the National Pact of 1943.

1990   Saddam Hussein invades Kuwait; America gathers international coalition to expel him.

1991   Syria blockades Aoun and drives him into exile, and Ta'if
            Agreement comes into effect. Civil war ends.

1992   Rafiq Hariri appointed Prime Minister for six-year term.

1996   Israel's Grapes of Wrath operation in south Lebanon.

2000   Rafiq Hariri appointed Prime Minister for second term.

            Israel withdraws from south Lebanon on May 4 (except
            for the contested Shebaa Farms area).

2001   September 11 destruction of Twin Towers in New York.

2003   US-led invasion of Iraq; Saddam Hussein toppled.

2004   Rafiq Hariri resigns. Resolution 1559 calling for dis-
            arming of Hizbullah and withdrawal of Syrian troops
            from Lebanon.

2005   14 February – Assassination of Rafiq Hariri.

            March 8 – demonstrations in support of Syria by Hizbullah
            and Amal.

            March 14 – demonstrations in support of the Lebanese
            government by supporters of the 'Cedar Revolution'.

            April 10 – Syria withdraws its troops from Lebanon.

            The UN Security Council sets up the International
            Independent Investigation Commission (IIIC) to investigate
            the murder of Rafiq Hariri.

2006   12 July – Hizbullah capture two Israeli soldiers and
            kill five in cross-border raid; Israel retaliates with aerial
            bombardment, sea blockade and land invasion. The
            thirty-three day 'July War' begins. Forty-three Israeli and
            1,109 Lebanese civilians are killed.

            11 August – The UN Security Council passes Resolution
            1701, providing for the enhancement of UNIFIL by
            the addition of troops from European countries to a
            maximum strength of 15,000. Resolution 1702 provides

for the deployment of up to 15,000 Lebanese army troops to the area south of the Litani river.

14 August – ceasefire declared.

2007   May–September – conflict between the Lebanese army and Fatah al-Islam in Nahr al Bared, a Palestinian refugee camp near Tripoli, in which 460 die.

2008   Confrontation between Hizbullah and Siniora's government over the latter's decision to re-assign the chief of security of Beirut airport and close Hizbullah's telephone network. Hizbullah and Amal militiamen attack Sunni targets in West Beirut.

May – Negotiations in Doha, Qatar result in agreement that Michel Suleiman be the preferred candidate for the presidential election. Suleiman is subsequently elected president.

2009   Barack Obama seeks improved relations with Syria and is followed in this by Saudi Arabia.

March – the UN Special Tribunal for Lebanon opens in The Hague.

June – parliamentary elections are held. March 14 bloc gains 71 seats. March 8 bloc gains 57 seats. Saad Hariri is named by Suleiman as the new prime minister.

November – Following a visit to Damascus, Saad Hariri succeeds in forming a government of national unity.

Thaw in relations between Lebanon and Syria. The two countries exchange ambassadors.

2010   March 14 – Walid Jumblatt makes speech offering to 'forgive and forget', directed at Syria.

MAJOR FIGURES IN THE LEBANESE
POLITICAL ARENA REFERRED TO IN THE TEXT

Yassir Arafat – chairman of the Palestine Liberation Organisation until his death in 2004.

Hafez al Assad – president of Syria from 1971–2000.

Bashar al Assad – Son of Hafez al Assad and president of Syria from 2000 to present.

Michel Aoun – Maronite Christian; former commander of the Lebanese army, nominated prime minister in contravention of the National Pact by Amin Gemmayel in 1988 with support of Iraq; declared himself president in November 1989, opposed the Ta'if Accord and engaged in prolonged battle against the Lebanese Forces and Syria, before fleeing to France in 1990.

Nabbih Berri – Shi'a; lawyer, leader of Amal and Speaker of the Lebanese parliament.

Raymond Edde – Maronite Christian; wartime parliamentary deputy for Jbeil.

Samir Geagea – Maronite Christian; commander of the Lebanese Forces in the late 1980s.

Pierre Gemmayel (senior) – Maronite Christian leader of the Lebanese Phalange party.

Bashir Gemmayel – son of Pierre Gemmayel; elected president in August 1982 but assassinated twenty-two days later.

Amin Gemmayel – son of Pierre Gemmayel; took over presidency after assassination of brother Bashir Gemmayel in 1982. Remained president until 1988.

Pierre Gemmayel (junior, grandson of Pierre Gemmayel senior) – minister in government of Fouad Siniora, assassinated in Beirut in November 2006.

Sa'ad Haddad – Lebanese Christian major appointed by Israelis to lead the South Lebanon Army.

Rafiq Hariri – Sunni Moslem billionaire businessman and prime minister from 1992–1998 and 2000–2004; oversaw the post-war reconstruction of Beirut; assassinated in Beirut on 14 February 2005.

Sa'ad Hariri – son of Rafiq Hariri and appointed prime minister of Lebanon in June 2009.

Elias Hrawi – president of Lebanon 1989–1998.

Kamal Jumblatt – Druze politician and wartime leader of the Lebanese National Movement, assassinated by Syria in 1977.

Walid Jumblatt – son of Kamal Jumblatt and current Druze politician.

Sayyid Hassan Nasrallah – Shi'a cleric, the spiritual leader of Hizbullah.

Fouad Siniora – Sunni Moslem; Prime Minister of Lebanon from July 2005 until June 2009.

Michel Suleiman – Maronite Christian; President of Lebanon from 25 May 2008 to present.

Principal organisations referred to in the text
Amal (The Movement of the Deprived or *Harakat al Mahrumin*)
Hizbullah (The Party of God)
Israeli Defence Force (IDF)
International Independent Investigation Commission (IIIC)
Lebanese Forces (LF)
Lebanese National Movement (LNM)
Palestine Liberation Organisation (PLO)
South Lebanon Army (SLA)
Special Tribunal for Lebanon (STL)
United Nations Interim Force in Lebanon (UNIFIL)

BIBLIOGRAPHY

Non-fiction
The Dream Palace of the Arabs, Fouad Ajami (Pantheon, New York, 1998)
Killing Mr Lebanon, Nicholas Blanford (I.B. Tauris, London, 2009)
The Palestinian Liberation Organisation, Helen Cobban (Cambridge University Press, Cambridge, 1984)
Children of the Siege, Pauline Cutting (Heinemann/Pan, London,1988)
Pity the Nation, Robert Fisk (Oxford University Press, Oxford, 1990)
Lords of the Lebanese Marches: Violence and Narrative in an Arab Society, Michael Gilsenan (I.B. Tauris, London, 1996)
The Gun and the Olive Branch: the Roots of Violence in the Middle East, David Hirst (Faber and Faber, London, 1984)
A History of the Arab Peoples, Albert Hourani (Faber and Faber, London, 1992)
An Evil Cradling, Brian Keenan (Vintage, London, 1993)
Amal and the Shi'a: Struggle for the Soul of Lebanon, Augustus Richard Norton (University of Texas Press, Austin, 1987)
Hezbollah, Augustus Richard Norton (Princeton University Press, Princeton, 2007)
Lebanon, a Shattered Country, Elizabeth Picard (Homes and Meier, New York, 2002)
A House of Many Mansions: the History of Lebanon Reconsidered, Kemal Salibi (I.B. Tauris, London, 1988)
The Modern History of Lebanon, Kemal Salibi (Weidenfeld and Nicholson, London, 1965)
The 33-Day War: Israel's War on Hezbollah in Lebanon and its Aftermath, Gilbert Achcar with Michel Warschawski (Saqi, London, 2007)

Fiction
From Sleep Unbound, Andre Chedid (Serpent's Tail, London, 1987)
The House of Mathilde, Hassan Daoud (Granta, London, 1999)

Borrowed Time, Hassan Daoud (Telegram Books, London, 1999)
The Story of Zahra, Hanan al-Shaykh (Quartet, London, 1991)
Women of Sand and Myrrh, Hanan al-Shaykh (Quartet, London, 1993)

GLOSSARY

Ahlan wa sahlan – welcome

Alhamdulillah – thanks be to God

Briq – long-handled pan for making coffee

Gelabeyyah – full-length dress traditionally worn by Arab women

Habibi – my dear (to a male)

Habibti – my dear (to a female)

Intifada – uprising

Jiddi – grandfather

Ka'ik – seeded bread

Keffiyeh – traditional headscarf worn by Arab men

Menaish bi zaater – flat bread with thyme

Moutabbal – aubergine pate

Muezzin – singer who sings the call to prayer from the minaret of the mosque

Mukhaberaat – secret police

Salaamu aleekum – greetings ('peace to you')

Aleekum issalaam – response ('and to you')

Servees – service taxi

Shu'i – Communist

Tabbouleh – salad made with bulgar, parsley and mint

Zaater – thyme